T0181855

Lecture Notes in Computer Science   13220

More information about this subseries at https://link.springer.com/bookseries/8379

Maciej Koutny · Fabrice Kordon ·
Daniel Moldt (Eds.)

Transactions on
Petri Nets
and Other Models
of Concurrency XVI

 Springer

Editor-in-Chief
Maciej Koutny ⓘ
Newcastle University
Newcastle upon Tyne, UK

Guest Editors
Fabrice Kordon ⓘ
Sorbonne Université
Paris, France

Daniel Moldt
Universität Hamburg
Hamburg, Germany

ISSN 0302-9743 ISSN 1611-3349 (electronic)
Lecture Notes in Computer Science
ISSN 1867-7193 ISSN 1867-7746 (electronic)
Transactions on Petri Nets and Other Models of Concurrency
ISBN 978-3-662-65302-9 ISBN 978-3-662-65303-6 (eBook)
https://doi.org/10.1007/978-3-662-65303-6

This Springer imprint is published by the registered company Springer-Verlag GmbH, DE
part of Springer Nature
The registered company address is: Heidelberger Platz 3, 14197 Berlin, Germany

Preface by Editor-in-Chief

The 16th issue of LNCS Transactions on Petri Nets and Other Models of Concurrency (ToPNoC) contains revised and extended versions of a selection of the best papers from the workshops held at the 41st International Conference on Application and Theory of Petri Nets and Concurrency (Petri Nets 2020, Paris, France, June 23–25, 2020) and the 20th International Conference on Application of Concurrency to System Design (ACSD 2020, Paris, France, June 23–25, 2020).

I would like to thank the two guest editors of this special issue: Fabrice Kordon and Daniel Moldt. Moreover, I would like to thank all authors, reviewers, and organizers of the Petri Nets 2020 and ACSD 2020 satellite workshops, without whom this issue of ToPNoC would not have been possible.

February 2022   Maciej Koutny

LNCS Transactions on Petri Nets and Other Models of Concurrency: Aims and Scope

ToPNoC aims to publish papers from all areas of Petri nets and other models of concurrency ranging from theoretical work to tool support and industrial applications. The foundations of Petri nets were laid by the pioneering work of Carl Adam Petri and his colleagues in the early 1960s. Since then, a huge volume of material has been developed and published in journals and books as well as presented at workshops and conferences.

The annual International Conference on Application and Theory of Petri Nets and Concurrency started in 1980. For more information on the international Petri net community see http://www.informatik.uni-hamburg.de/TGI/PetriNets/.

All issues of ToPNoC are LNCS volumes. Hence, they appear in all main libraries and are also accessible on SpringerLink (electronically). It is possible to subscribe to ToPNoC without subscribing to the rest of LNCS.

ToPNoC contains the following:

- Revised versions of a selection of the best papers from workshops and tutorials concerned with Petri nets and concurrency
- Special issues related to particular subareas (similar to those published in the Advances in Petri Nets series)
- Other papers invited for publication in ToPNoC
- Papers submitted directly to ToPNoC by their authors

Like all other journals, ToPNoC has an Editorial Board, which is responsible for the quality of the journal. The members of the board assist in the reviewing of papers submitted or invited for publication in ToPNoC. Moreover, they may make recommendations concerning collections of papers for special issues. The Editorial Board consists of prominent researchers within the Petri net community and in related fields.

Topics

The topics covered include system design and verification using nets; analysis and synthesis; structure and behavior of nets; relationships between net theory and other approaches; causality/partial order theory of concurrency; net-based semantical, logical, and algebraic calculi; symbolic net representation (graphical or textual); computer tools for nets; experience with using nets, case studies; educational issues related to nets; higher-level net models; timed and stochastic nets; and standardization of nets.

Also included are applications of nets to biological systems; security systems; e-commerce and trading; embedded systems; environmental systems; flexible manufacturing systems; hardware structures; health and medical systems; office automation; operations research; performance evaluation; programming languages; protocols and networks; railway networks; real-time systems; supervisory control; telecommunications; cyber physical systems; and workflow.

For more information about ToPNoC see http://www.springer.com/gp/computer-science/lncs/lncs-transactions/petri-nets-and-other-models-of-concurrency-topnoc-/731240

Submission of Manuscripts

Manuscripts should follow LNCS formatting guidelines, and should be submitted as PDF or zipped PostScript files to ToPNoC@ncl.ac.uk. All queries should be addressed to the same e-mail address.

LNCS Transactions on Petri Nets and Other Models of Concurrency: Editorial Board

Preface by Guest Editors

This volume of ToPNoC contains revised versions of a selection of the best workshop papers presented at satellite events of the 41st International Conference on Application and Theory of Petri Nets and Concurrency (Petri Nets 2020) and the 20th International Conference on Application of Concurrency to System Design (ACSD 2020). These events took place in Paris, France, in June 2020.

As guest editors, we are indebted to the Program Committees of the workshops and in particular to the chairs. Without their enthusiastic efforts, this volume would not have been possible.

The workshop papers considered for this special issue were selected in close cooperation with the workshop chairs. Members of the Program Committees and other colleagues participated in reviewing the new versions of the papers eventually submitted. We received suggestions for papers for this special issue from

- ATAED 2020: Workshop on Algorithms & Theories for the Analysis of Event Data (chairs: Wil van der Aalst, Robin Bergenthum, and Josep Carmona), and
- PNSE 2020: International Workshop on Petri Nets and Software Engineering (chairs: Ekkart Kindler, Michael Köhler-Bußmeier, and Heiko Rölke).

The authors of the suggested papers were invited to improve and extend their results, where possible, on the basis of comments received before and during the workshops. Each resulting revised submission was reviewed by at least two referees. We followed the principle of asking for fresh reviews of the revised papers, also from referees not involved initially in the reviewing of the original workshop contributions. All papers underwent the standard two- or three-stage journal reviewing process, and eventually five papers were accepted after rigorous reviewing and revising.

Structural transformations, by preserving properties of formal models of concurrent systems, ease their verification. The paper 'Property-Preserving Transformations of Elementary Net Systems Based on Morphisms', by Luca Bernardinello, Irina Lomazova, Roman Nesterov, and Lucia Pomello, defines several such transformations focused on local abstractions and refinements. These transformations can be applied on elementary net systems. The original elementary net and the transformed one are related by an α-morphism preserving behavioral properties like deadlocks.

The paper focuses on a rigorous definition of these transformations, as well as an application of these transformation rules to Workflow Net Composition. In this application, ready-to-use solutions to organize correct interactions of components in complex parallel systems are deduced from the transformations.

It is very complex to model semi-structured processes in a meaningful way. Thus, people exploit logs for automatic discovery based on the notion of local process models. However, these techniques rarely find patterns larger than 4–5 events. Thus, too many models are discovered and the same events may be covered many times while others remain unexplained.

In their paper, 'Defining Meaningful Local Process Models', Mitchel Brunings, Dirk Fahland, and Boudewijn van Dongen show how sets of local process models are useful. In particular, a coverage metric is defined to evaluate (sets of) local process models. An application based on the BPIC12 benchmark (defined in 2012 by one of the authors) shows and illustrates how this approach works.

The paper 'Distributed Synthesis of Asynchronously Communicating Distributed Process Models', by Pieter Kwantes and Jetty Kleijn, addresses the challenge of synthesizing distributed process models. Given a language in the form of an event log, process models are created in the form of I-nets. Given processes in the form of E-nets and the common interfaces in the form of channels, a new I-net can be synthesized using an algorithm. The problem that interactions between processes are not included can be addressed by a context-dependent view. The conditions when local behavior that is not revealed from the event logs of the services acting together are specified.

As an application domain, local Enterprise nets are considered as asynchronously communicating local processes, which can be merged into global Industry nets. A formalization of the causal structure of the industrial network is obtained from the derivation of a partial order from the message exchange. It is shown how existing algorithms for the identification of isolated processes can be adapted to constitute higher-level Enterprise nets under certain boundary conditions.

Motivated by application domains that have a large number of tokens in corresponding Petri net models and thus often describe a very large state space, Torsten Liebke and Karsten Wolf pursue an approach that minimizes the initial marking needed for analysis as much as possible, which is described in their paper 'Using Approximation for the Verification of Token-Scaling Models'. By under-approximating the reachable states, model checking of a witness path that also applies to the original state space is enabled. Thus, existential temporal properties (ECTL*) become investigatable, which otherwise cannot be proved. The question of the minimum number of tokens that have to be used is approached by the authors via heuristics. A successful, concrete implementation takes place in the model checker LoLA 2.

Due to the large number of problems in the field of Petri net analysis, numerous verification techniques are used in the verification tools. Since the selection of the right analysis technique is hardly possible due to the respective net models and properties, the tools have to perform an appropriate management, e.g., by a portfolio manager.

Using the LoLA 2 tool as an example, Karsten Wolf shows the architecture of a portfolio manager in his paper 'Portfolio Management in Explicit Model Checking'. Central questions of the design of analysis tools are thus systematically discussed against the background of many years of experience of the practical use of LoLA 2. Resources are managed using a task tree. The internal structure of the task tree represents the logical structure of the portfolio and guides the application of the verification algorithms located in the leaves to optimize the use of resources.

In addition, the paper Practical Distributed Implementation of Very Large Scale Petri Net Simulations by Ashur Rafiev, Jordan Morris, Fei Xia, Alex Yakovlev, Matthew Naylor, Simon Moore, David Thomas, Graeme Bragg, Mark Vousden, and Andrew Brown, submitted directly to ToPNoC, presents a method for simulating large-scale concurrent Petri net models using parallel distributed hardware platforms.

As guest editors, we would like to thank all the authors and referees who have contributed to this issue. The quality of this volume is the result of the high scientific value of their work. Moreover, we would like to acknowledge the excellent cooperation throughout the whole process that has made our work a pleasant task, despite the extremely challenging conditions our communities had to face during the review phase with the COVID-19 pandemic. We are also grateful to the Springer/ToPNoC team for the final production of this issue.

February 2022

Fabrice Kordon
Daniel Moldt

Organization of This Issue

Guest Editors

Fabrice Kordon   Sorbonne Université, France
Daniel Moldt   Universität Hamburg, Germany

Workshop Co-chairs

Wil van der Aalst   RWTH Aachen University, Germany
Robin Bergenthum   FernUniversität in Hagen, Germany
Josep Carmona   Universitat Politècnica de Catalunya, Spain
Ekkart Kindler   Technical University of Denmark, Denmark
Michael   Hamburg University of Applied Sciences, Germany
  Köhler-Bussmeier
Heiko Rölke   University of Applied Sciences Graubünden, Switzerland

Reviewers

Robin Bergenthum   Victor Khomenko
Piotr Chrzastowski-Wachtel   Michał Knapik
Thomas Chatain   Maciej Koutny
Raymond Devillers   Artur Niewiadomski
Claudio Di Ciccio   Wojciech Penczek
Javier Esparza   Jaco van de Pol
Stefan Haar   Jiří Srba

Contents

Property-Preserving Transformations of Elementary Net Systems Based on Morphisms

Luca Bernardinello[2], Irina Lomazova[1], Roman Nesterov[1,2(✉)], and Lucia Pomello[2]

[1] HSE University, 20 Myasnitskaya Ulitsa, 101000 Moscow, Russia
`rnesterov@hse.ru`
[2] Dipartimento di Informatica, Sistemistica e Comunicazione, Università degli Studi di Milano-Bicocca, Viale Sarca 336 - Edificio U14, 20126 Milan, Italy

Abstract. Structural transformations that preserve properties of formal models of concurrent systems make their verification easier. We define structural transformations that allow to abstract and refine elementary net systems. Relations between abstract models and their refinements are formalized using morphisms. Transformations proposed in this paper induce morphisms between elementary net systems as well as preserve their behavioral properties, especially deadlocks. We also show the application of the proposed transformations to the construction of a correct composition of interacting workflow net components.

Keywords: Petri nets · transformations · abstraction · refinement · morphisms

1 Introduction

Petri nets are widely used for modeling concurrent systems as well as for proving their important behavioral properties. Due to the well-known state explosion problem, there are various *structural* techniques developed in Petri net theory. The main advantage of structural techniques is the possibility to verify behavioral properties of Petri nets without computing their reachable markings.

Structural Petri net transformations that preserve classical properties like boundedness, liveness, covering by place invariants make verification of parallel systems easier. On the one hand, starting from a sophisticated model, it is possible to apply *reduction* transformations preserving properties of the initial model and then verify properties using a simplified model. On the other hand, having a simple abstract model, it is possible to apply *refinement* transformations that yield a more detailed model reflecting properties of an initial abstraction.

Petri net transformations have been first described in several works (see, for example, [5,6,14,15,21]), where the authors have defined simple yet powerful local structural reductions and extensions. It has been shown that liveness,

This work is supported by MIUR and the Basic Research Program at HSE University.

M. Koutny et al. (Eds.): ToPNoC XVI, LNCS 13220, pp. 1–23, 2022.
https://doi.org/10.1007/978-3-662-65303-6_1

boundedness (safeness), covering by place invariants, home states and proper termination can be preserved by these transformations.

Free choice Petri nets [11] are also widely adopted to model behavior of parallel systems for their structural constraints on conflicts. The work [9] gives a *complete* set of reduction/synthesis transformations that allows to obtain every live and bounded free choice net. Within the framework of bipolar synchronization schemes [10] strictly related to free choice Petri nets, the authors have also defined a set of local reduction and synthesis rules that yield only well behaved synchronization schemes.

Another series of works [8,18] is devoted to the use of graph transformations in a categorical setting (the double-pushout approach). These transformations are applied to model and analyze behavior of re-configurable systems.

Place [20] and, more generally, resource (sub-marking) [12] bisimulation are also powerful tools to reduce Petri net graphs preserving their observable behavior. These techniques are based on reducing places and resources in Petri nets if they produce bisimilar behavior.

Petri net *morphisms* give a natural yet rigid framework to formalize structural property-preserving relations [7,13,22]). In particular, in [17], morphisms inducing bisimulations have been discussed.

For elementary net systems (EN systems) [3,19] – a basic class of models in net theory – α-morphisms have been introduced in [2]. They help to formalize relations between abstract models and their refinements. Moreover, α-morphisms preserve behavioral properties (reachable markings) as well as reflect them under specific local requirements. However, the direct application of the definition of α-morphisms is rather difficult.

Thus, the main purpose of this paper is to define a set of *local* abstraction/refinement transformations for EN systems. A local transformation acts only on a specific subnet, while the rest of the EN system remains unchanged. We consider EN systems with labeled transitions, where labels specify interactions with the environment. We present transformation rules preserving labeled transitions, while unlabeled transitions are reduced. As a result of applying these transformations, an initial EN system and a transformed EN system are related by an α-morphism, and their reachable markings and, especially, deadlocks are preserved. Interestingly enough, it is also shown that simple Petri net transformations introduced earlier in the literature also yield corresponding α-morphisms.

In addition, we provide two cases of applying transformations defined in our study. Abstraction transformations are used in the context of building a correct composition of interacting workflow nets according to an approach described in [4]. Its correctness is based on abstracting component models with the help of α-morphisms. Refinement transformations are exploited to refine the formal models of abstract interaction patterns [16], which give ready-to-use solutions to organize correct interactions of components in complex parallel systems.

This paper is organized as follows. The following section gives the basic definitions. In Sect. 3, we define local abstraction and refinement transformations for EN systems inducing α-morphisms. Section 4 discusses the application of the proposed transformations to the problem of constructing correct systems with interacting workflow net components, and Sect. 5 concludes the paper.

2 Preliminaries

Here we provide the basic definitions used in the paper.

Let A, B be two sets. A function f from A to B is denoted by $f \colon A \to B$. The set of all finite non-empty sequences over A is denoted by A^+. The set $A^* = A^+ \cup \{\epsilon\}$ is the set of all finite sequences over A, where ϵ is the empty sequence.

A *net* is a triple $N = (P, T, F)$, where P and T are disjoint sets of places and transitions respectively, and $F \subseteq (P \times T) \cup (T \times P)$ is the *flow relation*. Places are depicted by circles, transitions – by boxes, and the flow relation – by arcs.

Let $N = (P, T, F)$ be a net. The *preset* of $x \in P \cup T$ is the set $^\bullet x = \{y \in P \cup T \mid (y, x) \in F\}$. The *postset* of $x \in P \cup T$ is the set $x^\bullet = \{y \in P \cup T \mid (x, y) \in F\}$. The *neighborhood* of $x \in P \cup T$ is the set $^\bullet x^\bullet = {}^\bullet x \cup x^\bullet$. N is *P-simple* iff $\forall p_1, p_2 \in P \colon {}^\bullet p_1 = {}^\bullet p_2$ and $p_1{}^\bullet = p_2{}^\bullet$ implies that $p_1 = p_2$. We consider nets without self-loops, i.e., $\forall t \in T \colon {}^\bullet t \cap t^\bullet = \varnothing$, and without isolated transitions, i.e., $\forall t \in T \colon |{}^\bullet t| \geq 1$ and $|t^\bullet| \geq 1$.

Let $N = (P, T, F)$ be a net, and $Y \subseteq P \cup T$. Then $^\bullet Y = \bigcup_{y \in Y} {}^\bullet y$, $Y^\bullet = \bigcup_{y \in Y} y^\bullet$, and $^\bullet Y^\bullet = {}^\bullet Y \cup Y^\bullet$. $N(Y)$ denotes the subnet of N *generated* by Y, i.e., $N(Y) = (P \cap Y, T \cap Y, F \cap (Y \times Y))$. The set $^\bigcirc N(Y) = \{y \in Y \mid \exists z \in (P \cup T) \setminus Y \colon (z, y) \in F$ or $^\bullet y = \varnothing\}$ is the *input* border, and the set $N(Y)^\bigcirc = \{y \in Y \mid \exists z \in (P \cup T) \setminus Y \colon (y, z) \in F$ or $y^\bullet = \varnothing\}$ is the *output* border of $N(Y)$.

A *marking* in a net $N = (P, T, F)$ is a subset of its places $m \subseteq P$. A marking m has a *contact* if $\exists t \in T \colon {}^\bullet t \subseteq m$ and $t^\bullet \cap m \neq \varnothing$. An *elementary net system* (EN system) is a tuple $N = (P, T, F, m_0)$, where $m_0 \subseteq P$ is the *initial* marking. A marking m is shown by putting black dots inside places belonging to m.

A *state machine* is a connected net $N = (P, T, F)$, s.t. $\forall t \in T \colon |{}^\bullet t| = |t^\bullet| = 1$. The subnet of an EN system $N = (P, T, F, m_0)$ generated by $C \subseteq P$ and $^\bullet C^\bullet$, i.e., $N(C \cup {}^\bullet C^\bullet)$, is a *sequential component* of N iff it is a state machine and it has a single token in its initial marking. An EN system $N = (P, T, F, m_0)$ is *covered* by sequential components if every place in N belongs to at least one sequential component. Then N is called *state machine decomposable* (SMD). For instance, an EN system shown in Fig. 1 has two sequential components generated by $C_1 = \{p_1, p_3, p_4, p_7\}$ and $^\bullet C_1{}^\bullet$ as well as by $C_2 = \{p_2, p_5, p_6, p_7\}$ and $^\bullet C_2{}^\bullet$. Different sequential components in an SMD-EN system can share both places and transitions. When they share a transition, it is natural to say that sequential components *synchronize*.

The *firing rule* defines the behavior of a net system. A *marking* m in an EN system $N = (P, T, F, m_0)$ *enables* a transition $t \in T$, denoted $m[t\rangle$, iff $^\bullet t \subseteq m$ and $t^\bullet \cap m = \varnothing$. When an enabled transition t *fires*, N evolves to a new marking $m' = m \setminus {}^\bullet t \cup t^\bullet$, denoted $m[t\rangle m'$. A sequence $w \in T^*$ is a *firing sequence* of N iff $m_0[t_1\rangle m_1[t_2\rangle \dots m_{n-1}[t_n\rangle m_n$ and $w = t_1 \dots t_n$. Then we write $m_0[w\rangle m_n$. The set of all firing sequences of N is denoted by $FS(N)$.

A *marking* m in an EN system $N = (P, T, F, m_0)$ is *reachable* iff $\exists w \in FS(N) \colon m_0[w\rangle m$. The set of all markings reachable from m is denoted by $[m\rangle$. It can be checked that reachable markings in an SMD-EN system are free from contacts. A reachable marking is a *deadlock* if it does not enable any transition.

A deadlock in an SMD-EN system $N = (P, T, F, m_0)$ can be interpreted as a poor synchronization of its sequential components. Since reachable markings in SMD-EN systems are contact-free, we can consider only those deadlocks, which are caused by the absence of tokens in some input places of transitions. For instance, Fig. 1 shows two deadlocks $\{p_3, p_6\}$ and $\{p_4, p_5\}$ that are reachable in the same SMD-EN system from the initial marking $\{p_1, p_2\}$. These deadlocks result from the independent resolution of the local conflicts between t_1 and t_2 as well as t_3 and t_4 by two sequential components: the left generated by $C_1 = \{p_1, p_3, p_4, p_7\}$ and ${}^\bullet C_1{}^\bullet$ and the right generated by $C_2 = \{p_2, p_5, p_6, p_7\}$ and ${}^\bullet C_2{}^\bullet$. In addition, if these local conflicts are resolved differently, s.t. transition t_5 (t_6) is enabled, then it is possible to reach the other deadlock $\{p_7\}$, which can be interpreted as the proper final state of the SMD-EN system from Fig. 1, since $p_7{}^\bullet = \varnothing$.

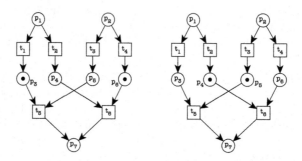

Fig. 1. Two deadlocks after the poor synchronization of sequential components

Abstraction/refinement relations between SMD-EN systems are formalized using α-morphisms introduced in [2]. Below we give the formal definition and briefly discuss the main intuition behind α-morphisms.

Definition 1. *Let $N_i = (P_i, T_i, F_i, m_0^i)$ be an SMD-EN system, $X_i = P_i \cup T_i$ with $i = 1, 2$, where $X_1 \cap X_2 = \varnothing$. An α-morphism from N_1 to N_2 is a total surjective map $\varphi \colon X_1 \to X_2$, also denoted $\varphi \colon N_1 \to N_2$, s.t.:*

1. $\varphi(P_1) = P_2$.
2. $\varphi(m_0^1) = m_0^2$.
3. $\forall t_1 \in T_1$: *if $\varphi(t_1) \in T_2$, then $\varphi({}^\bullet t_1) = {}^\bullet\varphi(t_1)$ and $\varphi(t_1{}^\bullet) = \varphi(t_1){}^\bullet$.*
4. $\forall t_1 \in T_1$: *if $\varphi(t_1) \in P_2$, then $\varphi({}^\bullet t_1{}^\bullet) = \{\varphi(t_1)\}$.*
5. $\forall p_2 \in P_2$:
   (a) $N_1(\varphi^{-1}(p_2))$ *is an acyclic net.*
   (b) $\forall p_1 \in {}^\bigcirc N_1(\varphi^{-1}(p_2))$: $\varphi({}^\bullet p_1) \subseteq {}^\bullet p_2$ *and if ${}^\bullet p_2 \neq \varnothing$, then ${}^\bullet p_1 \neq \varnothing$.*
   (c) $\forall p_1 \in N_1(\varphi^{-1}(p_2))^\bigcirc$: $\varphi(p_1{}^\bullet) = p_2{}^\bullet$.
   (d) $\forall p_1 \in P_1 \cap \varphi^{-1}(p_2)$: $p_1 \notin {}^\bigcirc N_1(\varphi^{-1}(p_2)) \Rightarrow \varphi({}^\bullet p_1) = p_2$ *and* $p_1 \notin N_1(\varphi^{-1}(p_2))^\bigcirc \Rightarrow \varphi(p_1{}^\bullet) = p_2$.
   (e) $\forall p_1 \in P_1 \cap \varphi^{-1}(p_2)$: *there is a sequential component $N' = (P', T', F')$ in N_1, s.t. $p_1 \in P'$, $\varphi^{-1}({}^\bullet p_2{}^\bullet) \subseteq T'$.*

By definition, an α-morphism allows one to substitute a place in an abstract net system N_2 with an acyclic subnet in N_1. The main motivation behind the use of α-morphisms is the ability to ensure that behavioral properties of an abstract model hold in its refinement.

Let $\varphi\colon N_1 \to N_2$ be an α-morphism. Two main properties of α-morphisms, valid without the additional restrictions, are as follows:

1. A subnet $N_1(\varphi^{-1}(p))$ in N_1, which refines a place p in N_2 behaves exactly as p. Firstly, no tokens are left in the places of $N_1(\varphi^{-1}(p))$ after firing a transition in $N_1(\varphi^{-1}(p))^{\bigcirc}$. Secondly, no transitions in $^{\bigcirc}N_1(\varphi^{-1}(p))$ are enabled, when there is a token in the places of $N_1(\varphi^{-1}(p))$.
2. The image of a reachable marking $m \in [m_0^1\rangle$ in N_1 is also a reachable marking in N_2, i.e., $\varphi(m) \in [m_0^2\rangle$. Moreover, $\varphi(m)$ enables the images of transitions enabled by m. In other words, α-morphisms *preserve* reachable markings and transition firings.

The converse of the second property is not always valid, i.e., α-morphisms do not *reflect* reachable markings. As shown in [2], it is necessary to impose additional constraints on the subnets in N_1, which can refine places in N_2.

Figure 2, borrowed from [4], shows an example of α-morphism, where N_1 is a refinement of an abstract SMD-EN system N_2. The subnet $N_1(\varphi^{-1}(p_2))$ in N_1 refines the place p_2 in N_2, and transitions g and h are split into transitions g_1, g_2 and h_1, h_2 in N_1, respectively.

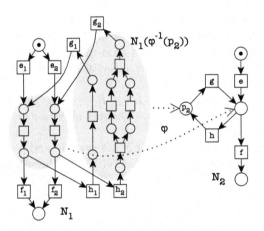

Fig. 2. An α-morphism $\varphi\colon N_1 \to N_2$

3 Structural Transformations of SMD-EN Systems

The direct application of Definition 1 to abstract and refine EN systems may be difficult. In this paper, we consider the use of *structural* transformations of EN systems that induce corresponding α-morphisms. The main purpose of our study is to develop a system of *local* abstraction/refinement transformations of EN systems and to study properties of these transformations.

It is easy to see that an EN system can have several possible abstractions depending on the detail level. To reduce this ambiguity, we add labels to some transitions in EN-systems. Labeled transitions model actions through which an EN system communicates with its environment. Transformations preserve labeled transitions and minimize the number of local transitions corresponding to the internal behavior of an EN system. Specifically, we plan to apply local transformations to construct a correct composition of synchronously and asynchronously interacting workflow nets as described in [4], where labeled transitions in workflow nets model component synchronizations and message exchange.

Let $N = (P, T, F, m_0)$ be an SMD-EN system, and Λ be an alphabet of communication action names. A transition labeling function is a surjective function $h : T \rightarrow \Lambda \cup \{\tau\}$, where $\tau \notin \Lambda$ is the special label of a local action.

We define structural transformation *rules* inducing α-morphisms between initial and transformed EN systems. A transformation rule is a structure $\rho = (L, c_L, R, c_R)$, where:

1. L is the *left* part of a rule that is a subnet in an EN system to be transformed.
2. c_L – flow relation and transition labeling constraints imposed on L.
3. R is the *right* part of a rule that is a subnet replacing L in a net system.
4. c_R – flow relation, marking, transition labeling constraints imposed on R.

L together with c_L define *applicability* constraints of a transformation rule, whereas R and c_R define the transformation itself. We do not give a complete formalization of c_L and c_R, since specific constraints are discussed in the following section. They are necessary to construct an α-morphism between the initial and the transformed EN system. An α-morphism associated with a transformation rule ρ is denoted φ_ρ.

Thus, a transformation rule $\rho = (L, c_L, R, c_R)$ is *applicable* to an SMD-EN system $N = (P, T, F, m_0)$ if there exists a subnet in N isomorphic to L satisfying structural and labeling constraints c_L.

Let $N = (P, T, F, m_0)$ be an SMD-EN net system, and $\rho = (L, c_L, R, c_R)$ be a transformation rule applicable to N. Let $N(X_L)$ be the subnet of N, generated by $X_L \subseteq P \cup T$, s.t. it is isomorphic to L. Then we say that ρ is applicable to the subnet $N(X_L)$ in N. Application of ρ to N includes the following steps:

1. Remove the subnet $N(X_L)$ from N.
2. Add the subnet corresponding to the right part R of ρ to N connecting it with the nodes in the neighborhood ${}^\bullet X_L{}^\bullet$ of the removed subnet.
3. Make necessary changes, i.e., relabel transitions and add tokens to places, in an inserted subnet according to c_R.

The effect of applying ρ to a subnet $N(X_L)$ in N is denoted by $\rho(N, X_L) = (P', T', F', m_0')$ with a new transition labeling function $h' : T' \rightarrow \Lambda \cup \{\tau\}$.

3.1 Abstraction Rules

In this section, we define five simple abstraction rules. They help to abstract SMD-EN systems with labeled transitions. Abstraction rules induce α-morphisms and, correspondingly, preserve reachable markings and deadlocks in EN systems.

For what follows, let $N = (P, T, F, m_0)$ be an SMD-EN system with a transition labeling function $h : T \to \Lambda \cup \{\tau\}$.

A1: Place Simplification

- *applicability constraints*: two places $p_1, p_2 \in P$ in N with the same neighborhood ($^\bullet p_1 = {}^\bullet p_2$ and $p_1{}^\bullet = p_2{}^\bullet$) as shown in Fig. 3(a).
- *transformation*: fusion of p_1 and p_2 into a single place p_{12}, where $^\bullet p_{12} = {}^\bullet p_1 = {}^\bullet p_2$, $p_{12}{}^\bullet = p_1{}^\bullet = p_2{}^\bullet$ and $p_{12} \in m'_0 \Leftrightarrow (p_1 \in m_0$ and $p_2 \in m_0)$.
- *α-morphism* $\varphi_{A1}: N \to N'$, where $N' = \rho_{A1}(N, \{p_1, p_2\})$, maps places p_1 and p_2 in N to the place p_{12} in N'. For other nodes in N, φ_{A1} is the identity mapping between N and N'.

Place simplification is one of the most basic Petri net transformations. It has been discussed earlier, for instance, in [14] (cf. "fusion of parallel places") and in [5] (cf. "simplification of redundant places").

A2: Transition Simplification

- *applicability constraints*: two transitions $t_1, t_2 \in T$ in N with the same neighborhood and label ($^\bullet t_1 = {}^\bullet t_2$, $t_1{}^\bullet = t_2{}^\bullet$ and $h(t_1) = h(t_2)$), see Fig. 3(b)).
- *transformation*: fusion of t_1 and t_2 into a single transition t_{12}, where $^\bullet t_{12} = {}^\bullet t_1 = {}^\bullet t_2$, $t_{12}{}^\bullet = t_1{}^\bullet = t_2{}^\bullet$ and $h'(t_{12}) = h(t_1) = h(t_2)$.
- *α-morphism* $\varphi_{A2}: N \to N'$, where $N' = \rho_{A2}(N, \{t_1, t_2\})$, maps transitions t_1 and t_2 in N to the transition t_{12} in N'. For other nodes in N, φ_{A2} is the identity mapping between N and N'.

Transition simplification (without labeling constraints) is one of the basic Petri net transformations as well. It has been considered, for instance, in [14] (cf. "fusion of parallel transitions").

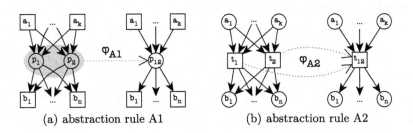

(a) abstraction rule A1　　　　　　(b) abstraction rule A2

Fig. 3. Place and transition simplification

A3: Local Transition Elimination

- *applicability constraints:* a transition $t \in T$ in N, s.t. $h(t) = \tau$ and:
  1. $^\bullet t = \{p_1\}$ and $t^\bullet = \{p_2\}$;
  2. $p_1^\bullet = {}^\bullet p_2 = \{t\}$;
  3. $^\bullet p_1 \neq \varnothing$ or $p_2^\bullet \neq \varnothing$;
  4. $^\bullet p_1 \cap p_2^\bullet = \varnothing$.
- *transformation:* fusion of t, p_1 and p_2 into a single place p_{12}, where $^\bullet p_{12} = {}^\bullet p_1$, $p_{12}^\bullet = p_2^\bullet$ and $p_{12} \in m_0' \Leftrightarrow (p_1 \in m_0$ or $p_2 \in m_0)$.
- *α-morphism* $\varphi_{A3} \colon N \to N'$, where $N' = \rho_{A3}(N, \{p_1, t, p_2\})$, maps t, p_1 and p_2 in N to the place p_{12} in N'. For other nodes in N, φ_{A3} is the identity mapping between N and N'.

Figure 4 shows left and right parts of this rule as well as construction of the α-morphism φ_{A3}. The applicability constraints of ρ_{A3} are aimed to avoid generating isolated places and self-loops in $\rho_{A3}(N, \{p_1, t, p_2\})$. The similar transition transformation "pre-fusion" has been discussed in [5], where it has been expressed as fusion of two transitions connected by a place.

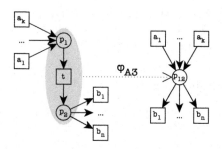

Fig. 4. Abstraction rule A3: local transition elimination

The abstraction rules defined above can be easily generalized: to sets of places and transitions (for ρ_{A1} and ρ_{A2} respectively) or to a "chain" of local transitions (for ρ_{A3}). We propose to apply a simple abstraction rule several times rather than to complicate their applicability constraints.

A4: Postset-Empty Place Simplification

- *applicability constraints:* two places p_1 and p_2 in N, s.t. $p_1^\bullet = p_2^\bullet = \varnothing$ and:
  1. $^\bullet p_1 \cap {}^\bullet p_2 = \varnothing$;
  2. $\forall C \subseteq P$: if $N(C \cup {}^\bullet C^\bullet)$ is a sequential component, then $p_1 \in C \Leftrightarrow p_2 \in C$.
- *transformation:* fusion of p_1 and p_2 into a single place p_{12}, s.t. $^\bullet p_{12} = {}^\bullet p_1 \cup {}^\bullet p_2$, $p_{12}^\bullet = p_1^\bullet = p_2^\bullet$ and $p_{12} \in m_0' \Leftrightarrow (p_1 \in m_0$ or $p_2 \in m_0)$, see Fig. 5.
- *α-morphism* $\varphi_{A4} \colon N \to N'$, where $N' = \rho_{A4}(N, \{p_1, p_2\})$, maps p_1 and p_2 in N to the place p_{12} in N'. For other nodes in N, φ_{A4} is the identity mapping between N and N'.

It is necessary to check that there are no sequential components distinguishing p_1 and p_2 in order to preserve state machine decomposability after transformation. Therefore we also satisfy the requirement 5e of Definition 1.

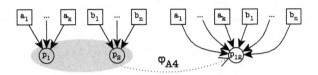

Fig. 5. Abstraction rule A4: Postset-empty place simplification

A5: Preset-Disjoint Transition Simplification

In this abstraction rule ρ_{A5}, we fuse two transitions that have the same postset and disjoint presets as opposed to the abstraction rule ρ_{A2}. Applicability constraints of this rule do not allow us to lose deadlocks present in an initial EN system by abstracting it. The problem of losing deadlocks is the consequence of the fact that α-morphisms do not *reflect* reachable markings without additional restrictions, as discussed in Sect. 2. In the setting of our study, this means that an inverse image of a reachable marking that enables transitions in an abstract model may be a deadlock in an initial EN system.

Let us illustrate the problem of losing deadlocks by the following example based on the EN system shown in Fig. 1. Recall that it has two deadlocks $\{p_3, p_6\}$ and $\{p_4, p_5\}$ reachable from the initial marking $\{p_1, p_2\}$. These deadlocks are caused by the fact that conflicts are resolved independently by two sequential components. Suppose that the two transitions t_5 and t_6 have the same label λ. Then, according to Definition 1, it is possible to fuse p_3 with p_4, p_5 with p_6 and t_5 with t_6 correspondingly (see Fig. 6, where the fusion is indicated by the indices, and the α-morphism φ is provided as well). The image t_{56} of t_5 and t_6 has two places in its preset, and there exists reachable marking $\{p_{34}, p_{56}\}$ enabling t_{56}. However, there exists an inverse image of the marking $\{p_{34}, p_{56}\}$, e.g., the deadlock $\{p_3, p_6\}$ that does not enable an inverse image of t_{56}.

Thus, we impose additional constraints on places in the presets of two transitions to be fused in such a way that if there is a deadlock containing places in the presets of both transitions, then it should not be possible to fuse these transitions. Preset-disjoint transition simplification is defined as follows:

- *applicability constraints:* two transitions t_1 and t_2, s.t. $h(t_1) = h(t_2)$ and:
  1. ${}^\bullet t_1 \cap {}^\bullet t_2 = \varnothing$ and $|{}^\bullet t_1| = |{}^\bullet t_2|$;
  2. $t_1{}^\bullet = t_2{}^\bullet$;
  3. $\forall a \in {}^\bullet t_1 \, \forall b \in {}^\bullet t_2 \, \exists C \subseteq P \colon a, b \in C$ and $N(C \cup {}^\bullet C^\bullet)$ is a sequential component.

- *transformation:* fusion of t_1 and t_2 into a single transition t_{12} with $h'(t_{12}) = h(t_1) = h(t_2)$, $t_{12}{}^\bullet = t_1{}^\bullet = t_2{}^\bullet$ and ${}^\bullet t_{12} = \{(a,b) \mid a \in {}^\bullet t_1, b \in {}^\bullet t_2, g(a) = b\}$, where $g\colon {}^\bullet t_1 \to {}^\bullet t_2$ is a bijection. Input transitions of ${}^\bullet t_1$ and ${}^\bullet t_2$ are preserved, i.e., $\forall (a,b) \in {}^\bullet t_{12}\colon {}^\bullet (a,b) = {}^\bullet a \cup {}^\bullet b$. As for the initial marking m_0' in $\rho_{A5}(N, \{t_1, t_2\})$, we have $\forall (a,b) \in {}^\bullet t_{12}\colon (a,b) \in m_0' \Leftrightarrow (a \in m_0$ or $b \in m_0)$.
- *α-morphism* $\varphi_{A5}\colon N \to N'$, where $N' = \rho_{A5}(N, \{t_1, t_2\})$, maps transitions t_1 and t_2 to the transition t_{12} in N' as well as every pair of places $a \in {}^\bullet t_1$ and $b \in {}^\bullet t_2$, where $g(a) = b$, is mapped to the place $(a,b) \in {}^\bullet t_{12}$. For other nodes in N, φ_{A5} is the identity mapping.

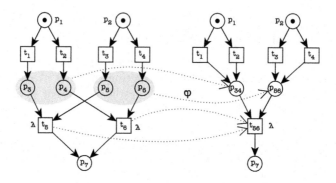

Fig. 6. Deadlocks are not preserved by α-morphisms

In Fig. 7, we provide the left and right parts of the abstraction rule ρ_{A5}, where the pairwise fusion of places is shown only for places a_1 and b_1 with $g(a_1) = b_1$, which are fused into the place $f_1 = (a_1, b_1)$. For other pairs of places, this fusion is performed similarly. The bijection $g\colon {}^\bullet t_1 \to {}^\bullet t_2$ is an integral part of ρ_{A5}, which makes the preset-disjoint transition simplification unambiguous.

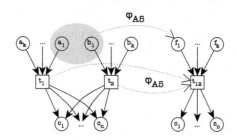

Fig. 7. Abstraction rule A5: Preset-disjoint transition simplification

The third applicability constraint of ρ_{A5} makes sure that every place in ${}^\bullet t_1$ is in conflict with every place in ${}^\bullet t_2$. Then it is easy to check that if there is a reachable marking in N with a token in ${}^\bullet t_1$, then there cannot be a token in ${}^\bullet t_2$ at the same time. The application of this rule involves pairwise place fusion in ${}^\bullet t_1$ and ${}^\bullet t_2$. According to the requirement on sequential components, we define a bijection $g : {}^\bullet t_1 \to {}^\bullet t_2$ and fuse places in ${}^\bullet t_1$ and ${}^\bullet t_2$ corresponding by g.

Let us consider two more detailed examples of applying the abstraction rule ρ_{A5}. There are two SMD-EN systems N_1 and N_2 shown in Fig. 8. Transitions t_1 and t_2 in N_1 as well as transitions e_1 and e_2 in N_2 are candidates to be fused, since they have the same label λ, share the same postset, whereas their presets are disjoint. We have to check whether places in the presets of these transitions are connected by sequential components. The results of this verification for N_1 and N_2 are given in Table 1, where we provide only sets of places corresponding to sequential components.

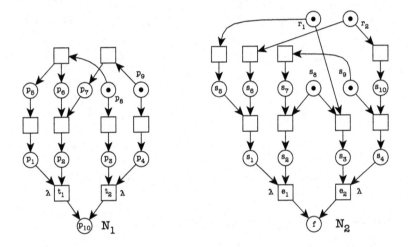

Fig. 8. Two EN systems to check applicability constraints of ρ_{A5}

In N_1, there is no sequential component containing places p_1 and p_4. Indeed, there is the deadlock $\{p_1, p_6, p_4\}$ containing places both from ${}^\bullet t_1$ and ${}^\bullet t_2$. Thus, transitions t_1 and t_2 in N_1 cannot be fused without losing this deadlock.

In N_2, we have found sequential components for all pairs of places from ${}^\bullet e_1$ and ${}^\bullet e_2$. Thus, we can fuse these transition according to the abstraction rule ρ_{A5}. There can be two possible transformations depending on the choice of places to be fused, i.e., either s_1 is fused with s_4 (see Fig. 9(a)) or s_1 is fused with s_3 (see Fig. 9(b)). It is enough to choose a single pair of places to be fused, and other pairs of places are dex termined in the only possible way.

It is worth mentioning that application of rule ρ_{A5} can also be straightforwardly extended to the case when transitions t_1 and t_2 have shared places in their presets. In this context, shared places will be preserved by a transformation.

Table 1. Verification of sequential components in N_1 and N_2 from Fig. 8

Sequential components in N_1		Sequential components in N_2	
p_1 and p_3	$\{p_8, p_5, p_3, p_1, p_{10}\}$	s_1 and s_3	$\{r_1, s_5, s_1, s_3, f\}$
p_1 and p_4	NO	s_1 and s_4	$\{r_2, s_6, s_{10}, s_1, s_4, s_{13}\}$
p_2 and p_3	$\{p_8, p_6, p_2, p_3, p_{10}\}$	s_2 and s_3	$\{s_8, s_2, s_3, f\}$
p_2 and p_4	$\{p_9, p_7, p_2, p_4, p_{10}\}$	s_2 and s_4	$\{s_9, s_7, s_2, s_2, f\}$

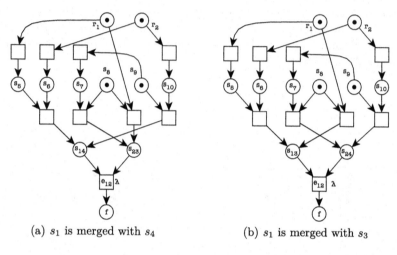

(a) s_1 is merged with s_4 (b) s_1 is merged with s_3

Fig. 9. Two results of applying the rule ρ_{A5} to N_2 from Fig. 8

3.2 Properties of the Abstraction Rules

We next discuss the main properties of the simple abstraction rules. We denote the set of abstraction rules by $AR = \{\rho_{A1}, ..., \rho_{A5}\}$.

By construction, the application of an abstraction rule induces an α-morphism from the initial SMD-EN system towards the transformed one.

Proposition 1. *Let $\rho \in AR$, s.t. ρ is applicable to a subnet $N(X_L)$ in N. Then there is an α-morphism $\varphi_\rho \colon N \to \rho(N, X_L)$.*

Corollary 1. *Let $\rho_1, \rho_2 \in AR$, s.t. ρ_2 is applicable to a subnet in $\rho_1(N, X_L)$ generated by X_L'. Then there is an α-morphism $\varphi_{\rho_2} \circ \varphi_{\rho_1} \colon N \to \rho_2(\rho_1(N, X_L), X_L')$.*

The important property is whether the order of applying abstraction rules matters when at least two abstraction rules are applicable to the same net system. In this case, we distinguish when two abstraction rules (applicable to the same net system) coincide or differ.

Proposition 2. *Let $\rho_1, \rho_2 \in AR$, s.t. ρ_1 is applicable to a subnet $N(X_L^1)$ in N, ρ_2 is applicable to a subnet $N(X_L^2)$ in N and $X_L^1 \neq X_L^2$. Then:*

1. If $\rho_1 = \rho_2$, then the effect of applying ρ_2 to $\rho_1(N, X_L^1)$ is isomorphic to the effect of applying ρ_1 to $\rho_2(N, X_L^2)$.
2. If $\rho_1 \neq \rho_2$ and $X_L^1 \cap X_L^2 = \varnothing$, then $\rho_2(\rho_1(N, X_L^1), X_L^2) = \rho_1(\rho_2(N, X_L^2), X_L^1)$.

The second part of Proposition 2 is easy to check, i.e., the order of applying abstraction rules transforming disjoint subnets is immaterial. However, the first part of this Proposition requires an additional clarification, when $\rho_1 = \rho_2 = \rho_{A5}$. The result of applying the other abstraction rules fully depends on the subnets corresponding to their left parts, which are fixed in Proposition 2.

As discussed above, the bijection g between the input places of two transitions is an integral part of ρ_{A5}. Then we require that for the repeated application of ρ_{A5}, one fix the bijections at the time of checking the applicability constraints. The following example (see Fig. 10) shows a case when ρ_{A5} can be applied twice and explains how to define the correct bijections between input places.

Suppose an SMD-EN system has a subnet shown in Fig. 10(a), which satisfies the applicability constraints of ρ_{A5} for fusing t_1 with t_2, t_2 with t_3, or t_1 with t_3. We need to define two bijections between the input places of any two pairs of transitions, and the bijection for third pair of transitions will be obtained transitively. For instance, let $g_1: \bullet t_1 \to \bullet t_2$ and $g_2: \bullet t_1 \to \bullet t_3$, s.t. $g_1(a_1) = b_1$, $g_1(a_2) = b_2$, $g_2(a_1) = c_2$, and $g_2(a_2) = c_1$. These correspondences between the input places are also shown by dotted lines in Fig. 10(a). Then the third bijection $g_3: \bullet t_2 \to \bullet t_3$ is defined as follows: $g_3(b_2) = c_1$ and $g_3(b_1) = c_2$. Arbitrary definition of the third bijection might break transitivity and, thus, disable the repeated application of the abstraction rule ρ_{A5}. In other words, the number of required bijections corresponds to the number of times ρ_{A5} will be applied.

We next demonstrate that the order of fusing transitions is not important, since the results are isomorphic. Suppose that, firstly, transitions t_1 and t_2 are to be fused. Then they are transformed into a single transition t_{12}, s.t. $\bullet t_{12} = \{(a_1, b_1), (a_2, b_2)\}$ according to g_1. The fusion of t_{12} with t_3 will yield a transition t_{123} with $\bullet t_{123} = \{(a_1, b_1, c_2), (a_2, b_2, c_1)\}$, as shown in Fig. 10(b). Changing the order of the consecutive fusions, we may, for example, obtain a transition t_{231} with $\bullet t_{231} = \{(b_2, c_1, a_2), (b_1, c_2, a_1)\}$ (see Fig. 10(c)), which is isomorphic to the earlier constructed result.

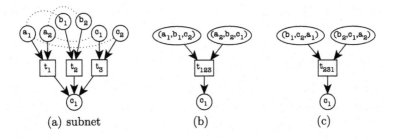

(a) subnet   (b)   (c)

Fig. 10. Repeated application of the abstraction rule ρ_{A5}

Thus, the unambiguity of the repeated application of ρ_{A5} requires that the corresponding bijections between the input places of transition pairs are defined for an initial SMD-EN system.

According to the structural requirements of abstraction rules, we also conclude that if there is a deadlock in an initial net system, then the image of this deadlock is also a deadlock in a transformed net system (see Proposition 3). In proving this statement, we also rely on the fact that α-morphisms *preserve* reachable markings and transition firings, i.e., an image of a reachable marking in a refined EN system is also a reachable marking which, moreover, enables any image of enabled transitions in a refined model.

Proposition 3. *Let $\rho \in AR$, s.t. ρ is applicable to a subnet $N(X_L)$ in N. Let $m \in [m_0\rangle$ be a deadlock in N. Then $\varphi_\rho(m)$ is a deadlock in $\rho(N, X_L)$.*

Proof. Let $N' = \rho(N, X_L)$. If $m^\bullet = \varnothing$, then, by Definition 1, $\varphi_\rho(m)^\bullet = \varnothing$. Thus, $\varphi_\rho(m)$ is a deadlock in N'. If $\exists t \in T : {}^\bullet t \cap m \neq \varnothing$, then the proof is done by contradiction. Suppose that $\varphi_\rho(m)$ is not a deadlock. Then either ${}^\bullet\varphi_\rho(t) = \varphi_\rho(m)$, i.e., a transition t and ${}^\bullet t$ is mapped to the same place, or ${}^\bullet\varphi_\rho(t) \subseteq \varphi_\rho(m)$, i.e., a marking $\varphi_\rho(m)$ enables $\varphi_\rho(t)$ in N'. A transition t cannot be mapped to a place by φ_ρ since $|{}^\bullet t| > 1$, because there are places in ${}^\bullet t$, s.t. ${}^\bullet t \cap m \neq \varnothing$ and there is at least one place $p \in {}^\bullet t$, s.t. $p \notin m$. If a marking $\varphi_\rho(m)$ enables $\varphi_\rho(t)$ in N', then t is fused with another transition t' by ρ, s.t. ${}^\bullet t' \cap m \neq \varnothing$. This fusion is not allowed by the abstraction rule ρ_{A5}, then there is a contradiction.

3.3 Refinement Rules

In this section, we define four simple refinement rules. They allow one to refine a given SMD-EN system. Three out of four proposed refinement rules are the inverse of abstraction rules discussed in the previous section. Refinement rules also induce α-morphisms. The main difference here is that the direction of α-morphisms is the opposite to the direction of a transformation.

For what follows, let $N = (P, T, F, m_0)$ be an SMD-EN system with a transition labeling function $h : T \to \Lambda \cup \{\tau\}$. Recall also that the effect of applying a transformation rule ρ to N is denoted by $\rho(N, X_L) = (P', T', F', m_0')$ with a new transition labeling function $h' : T' \to \Lambda \cup \{\tau\}$, where $X_L \subseteq P \cup T$ and $N(X_L)$ is the subnet in N transformed by ρ.

R1: Place Duplication

- *applicability constraints:* a place p in N.
- *transformation:* split p into two places p_1 and p_2, where ${}^\bullet p_1 = {}^\bullet p_2 = {}^\bullet p$, $p_1{}^\bullet = p_2{}^\bullet = p^\bullet$ and $(p_1 \in m_0'$ and $p_2 \in m_0') \Leftrightarrow p \in m_0$ (see Fig. 11(a)).
- *α-morphism* $\varphi_{R1} : N' \to N$, where $N' = \rho_{R1}(N, \{p\})$, maps places p_1 and p_2 in N' to the place p in N. For other nodes in N', φ_{R1} is the identity mapping between N' and N.

R2: Transition Duplication

- *applicability constraints:* a transition t in N.
- *transformation:* split t into two transitions t_1 and t_2, where $h'(t_1) = h'(t_2) = h(t)$, ${}^{\bullet}t_1 = {}^{\bullet}t_2 = {}^{\bullet}t$ and $t_1{}^{\bullet} = t_2{}^{\bullet} = t^{\bullet}$ (see Fig. 11(b)).
- *α-morphism* $\varphi_{R2} \colon N' \to N$, where $N' = \rho_{R2}(N, \{t\})$, maps transitions t_1 and t_2 in N' to the transition t in N. For other nodes in N', φ_{R2} is the identity mapping between N' and N.

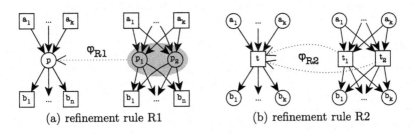

(a) refinement rule R1   (b) refinement rule R2

Fig. 11. Place and transition duplication

R3: Local Transition Introduction

- *applicability constraints:* a place p in N.
- *transformation:* substitution of p with a transition t and two places p_1, p_2 (see Fig. 12), where:
  1. $h'(t) = \tau$;
  2. ${}^{\bullet}t = \{p_1\}$ and $t^{\bullet} = \{p_2\}$;
  3. $p_1{}^{\bullet} = {}^{\bullet}p_2 = \{t\}$;
  4. ${}^{\bullet}p_1 = {}^{\bullet}p$ and $p_2{}^{\bullet} = p^{\bullet}$;
  5. $p \in m_0 \Leftrightarrow ((p_1 \in m_0' \text{ and } p_2 \notin m_0') \text{ or } (p_1 \notin m_0' \text{ and } p_2 \in m_0'))$.
- *α-morphism* $\varphi_{R3} \colon N' \to N$, where $N' = \rho_3(N, \{p\})$, maps t, p_1 and p_2 in N' to the place p in N. For other nodes in N', φ_{R3} is the identity mapping between N' and N.

Refinement rule ρ_{R1} (ρ_{R2}) can be generalized to the case when a place (a transition) in the initial EN system is split into a set of places (transitions). Refinement rule ρ_{R3} can be generalized to the case when a places in the in initial EN system is replaced with a "chain" of local transitions. These extensions are similar to the possible generalizations of abstraction rules ρ_{A1}, ρ_{A2} and ρ_{A3} discussed above.

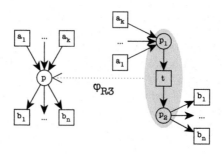

Fig. 12. Refinement rule R3: local transition introduction

R4: Place Split

- *applicability constraints:* a place p in N, s.t. $|{}^\bullet p| > 1$.
- *transformation:* split p into two places p_1 and p_2 (see Fig. 13), where:
  1. ${}^\bullet p_1 \neq \varnothing$ and ${}^\bullet p_2 \neq \varnothing$;
  2. ${}^\bullet p_1 \subset {}^\bullet p$ and ${}^\bullet p_2 \subset {}^\bullet p$;
  3. ${}^\bullet p_1 \cap {}^\bullet p_2 = \varnothing$ and ${}^\bullet p_1 \cup {}^\bullet p_2 = {}^\bullet p$;
  4. $|p_1{}^\bullet| = |p_2{}^\bullet| = |p^\bullet|$, and there is a bijection $f_i \colon p_i{}^\bullet \to p^\bullet$ with $i = 1, 2$, s.t. $\forall x \in p_i{}^\bullet \colon h'(x) = h(f_i(x))$;
  5. $(p_i{}^\bullet)^\bullet = (p^\bullet)^\bullet$ with $i = 1, 2$;
  6. ${}^\bullet(p_i{}^\bullet) \setminus \{p_i\} = {}^\bullet(p^\bullet) \setminus \{p\}$ with $i = 1, 2$;
  7. if $p \in m_0$, then $p_1 \in m_0' \Leftrightarrow p_2 \notin m_0'$.
- *α-morphism* $\varphi_{R4} \colon N' \to N$, where $N' = \rho_{R4}(N, \{p\})$, maps places p_1 and p_2 in N' to to the place p in N and maps each transition $t' \in p_i{}^\bullet$ in N' to a transition $t \in p^\bullet$ in N if $f_i(t') = t$ with $i = 1, 2$. For other nodes in N', φ_{R4} is the identity mapping between N' and N.

While splitting a place p in N, its neighborhood is also split between p_1 and p_2 in $\rho_{R4}(N, \{p\})$. According to constraints 1, 2 and 3, the preset of p is divided into two disjoint, proper and non-empty subsets. According to constraint 4, the postsets of p_1 and p_2 are exactly two copies of the postset of p, s.t. labels of transitions are also preserved. Moreover, by constraints 5 and 6, the input and output places in $p_1{}^\bullet$ and $p_2{}^\bullet$ are the same as the input and output places of $p^\bullet$. These requirements on splitting the neighborhood of p in N are based on the requirements 5b and 5c of Definition 1.

Figure 13 provides the left and right parts of the refinement rule ρ_{R4}, where the corresponding α-morphism maps p_1 and p_2 in the transformed EN system to a place p in the initial EN system. The map from the postsets of p_1 and p_2 to the postset of p is shown only for two pairs of transitions: c_1 is mapped to b_1 since $f_1(c_1) = b_1$; d_1 is also mapped to b_1 since $f_2(d_1) = b_1$, where the bijections f_1 and f_2 are constructed according to constraint 4 of this rule.

3.4 Properties of the Refinement Rules

We continue by discussing the main properties of the proposed refinement rules. Let $RR = \{\rho_{R1}, \dots, \rho_{R4}\}$ be the set of refinement rules.

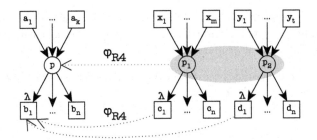

Fig. 13. Refinement rule R4: place split

By construction, the application of a refinement rule induces an α-morphism from a transformed SMD-EN system to an initial SMD-EN system. This also follows from the fact that rules ρ_{R1}, ρ_{R2} and ρ_{R3} are the inverse of the abstraction rules ρ_{A1}, ρ_{A2} and ρ_{A3} respectively.

Proposition 4. *Let $\rho \in RR$, s.t. ρ is applicable to a subnet $N(X_L)$ in N. Then there is an α-morphism $\varphi_\rho \colon \rho(N, X_L) \to N$.*

Corollary 2. *Let $\rho_1, \rho_2 \in RR$, s.t. ρ_2 is applicable to a subnet in $\rho_1(N, X_L)$ generated by X_L'. Then there is an α-morphism $\varphi_{\rho_2} \circ \varphi_{\rho_1} \colon \rho_2(\rho_1(N, X_L), X_L') \to N$.*

Similarly to the abstraction rules, we also observe that application of the refinement rules does not introduce "new" deadlocks to transformed models, i.e., an image of a deadlock in a refined EN system is also a deadlock already present in an initial abstract EN system.

Proposition 5. *Let $\rho \in RR$, s.t. ρ is applicable to a subnet $N(X_L)$ in N. Let $m' \in [m_0'\rangle$ be a deadlock in $\rho(N, X_L)$. Then $\varphi_\rho(m')$ is a deadlock in N.*

Proof. The proof follows from two facts. Firstly, as discussed in Sect. 2, a deadlock m in an SMD-EN system $N = (P, T, F, m_0)$ is such a reachable marking, where for any transition $t \in T$, s.t. ${}^\bullet t \cap m \neq \varnothing$, there is at least one place $p \in {}^\bullet t$, s.t. $p \notin m$. Secondly, the application of the refinement rules, which result in splitting places (thus, generating new inverse images of reachable markings in an initial EN-system N), fully preserves their neighborhoods.

4   Use of Transformations for Workflow Net Composition

Here we show the application of transformations defined in Sect. 3 to a correct composition of interacting workflow nets. Workflow nets have both initial and final markings. We follow an approach to a composition of *generalized workflow nets* (GWF-nets) described in [4]. The correctness of this approach is achieved through the use of α-morphisms. GWF-nets interact by synchronizations and by sending/receiving messages through asynchronous channels. GWF-net interactions are specified using transition labels. Below we recall main definitions.

In our paper, we consider workflow nets covered by sequential components. As mentioned in [1], state machine decomposability is a basic feature that bridges structural and behavioral properties of workflow nets.

Definition 2. *A generalized workflow net (GWF-net) is an SMD-EN system $N = (P, T, F, m_0, m_f)$, where:*

1. $^\bullet m_0 = \varnothing$.
2. $m_f \subseteq P$, *s.t.* $m_f \neq \varnothing$ *and* $m_f{}^\bullet = \varnothing$.
3. $\forall x \in P \cup T \exists s \in m_0 \exists f \in m_f \colon (s, x) \in F^*$ *and* $(x, f) \in F^*$, *where* F^* *is the reflexive transitive closure of* F.

Soundness is the main correctness property of workflow nets.

Definition 3. *A GWF-net $N = (P, T, F, m_0, m_f)$ is sound iff:*

1. $\forall m \in [m_0\rangle \colon m_f \in [m\rangle$.
2. $\forall m \in [m_0\rangle \colon m \supseteq m_f \Rightarrow m = m_f$.
3. $\forall t \in T \exists m \in [m_0\rangle \colon m[t\rangle$.

Two kinds of transition labels for synchronous and asynchronous interactions are assigned to certain transitions in a GWF-net. The composition of two transition-labeled GWF-nets N_1 and N_2 is also a transition-labeled GWF-net denoted by $N_1 \circledast N_2$, and it is fully defined according to transition labels in N_1 and N_2: (a) fusion of transitions with a common synchronous label, (b) addition of a place for an asynchronous channel between two transitions with complement asynchronous labels.

Figure 14 shows an example of adding a channel represented by a labeled place a that is shown by a smaller circle. It connects transition t_1 in N_1 (label $a!$ corresponds to sending a message to channel a) to transition t_2 in N_2 (label $a?$ corresponds to receiving a message from channel a).

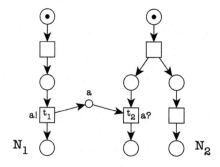

Fig. 14. Addition of a place for an asynchronous channel between two GWF-nets

The main result of [4] on the GWF-net composition correctness is formulated in the following proposition.

Proposition 6 ([4]). *Let R_1, R_2 and A_1, A_2 be four sound transition-labeled GWF-nets, s.t. $\varphi_i\colon R_i \to A_i$ is an α-morphism with $i = 1, 2$. If $A_1 \circledast A_2$ is sound, then $R_1 \circledast R_2$ is sound.*

Thus, the composition of two *detailed* transition-labeled GWF-nets $R_1 \circledast R_2$ is sound if the composition of their *abstractions* $A_1 \circledast A_2$ is sound. Intuitively, $A_1 \circledast A_2$ models an abstract interaction protocol (also referred to as an *interaction pattern*) between detailed transition-labeled GWF-net components. We use transformation rules to define corresponding α-morphisms, as shown further.

4.1   Abstraction of Interacting Workflow Net Components

Here we show the application of the abstraction rules to build abstract representations of interacting transition-labeled GWF-nets. For example, we aim to construct the α-morphism shown in Fig. 2 step by step. Assume that transitions $e_1, e_2, f_1, f_2, g_1, g_2, h_1, h_2$ in N_1 are labeled by names of communication actions from Λ, s.t. $h(e_1) = h(e_2)$, $h(f_1) = h(f_2)$, $h(g_1) = h(g_2)$ and $h(h_1) = h(h_2)$, whereas transitions $y_1, \ldots, y_7$ in N_1 are local, i.e., they are labeled by τ.

Firstly, local transitions $y_1, \ldots, y_5$ can be eliminated using rule ρ_{A3} five times. After collapsing these local transitions, we simplify places p_1 and p_2 (by rule ρ_{A1}) that are generated from eliminating local transitions y_4 and y_5 correspondingly. Figure 15 gives a concise illustration of these transformations.

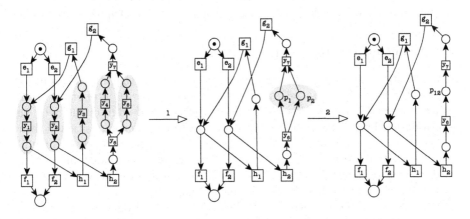

Fig. 15. Abstracting a GWF-net: steps 1 and 2

Now local transitions y_7 and y_8 are also eliminated using rule ρ_{A3} twice (see transformation 3 in Fig. 16). Unfortunately, the fourth transformation shown in Fig. 16 cannot be obtained using the existing simple abstraction rules. We fuse transitions f_1 and f_2, h_1 and h_2, g_1 and g_2 preserving their labels as well as we fuse places p_3 and p_4, p_5 and p_6 in the neighborhood of these transitions. Intuitively, this may be seen as an example of a direct application of Definition 1 by constructing appropriate fusions. We plan to investigate possible local transformations applicable in this case in the future.

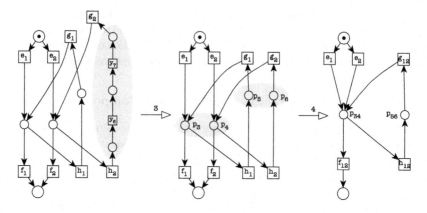

Fig. 16. Abstracting a GWF-net: steps 3 and 4

Finally, we simplify transitions e_1 and e_2 (by rule ρ_{A2}) and obtain the target abstract EN system N_2 previously demonstrated in Fig. 2. To construct the corresponding map between models, we need to compose all α-morphisms induced by applied abstraction rules and by a direct application of Definition 1.

4.2   Refinement of Interaction Patterns

In this section, we apply the refinement rules to solve the inverse problem: the construction of a detailed system model that preserves properties of an initial abstract model. As described above, a protocol of interactions between transition-labeled GWF-net components is represented by a composition of their abstractions. In [16], typical interaction patterns for asynchronously communicating transition-labeled GWF-nets have been discussed. Abstract interaction patterns provide generic solutions that can be used to model and verify component interactions in large-scale distributed systems.

Consider a pattern shown in Fig. 17 (refer to "Send-Receive" interaction pattern in [16]). It models a message exchange between two components: the left sends a message to the right, while the right sends a response back to the left. We aim to construct a possible refinement of this pattern using our rules.

Figure 18 gives a concise illustration for building a possible refinement of the "Send-Receive" interaction pattern. Firstly, we duplicate place p_1 (rule ρ_{R1}) and introduce a local transition instead of place p_2 (rule ρ_{R3}). Secondly, we also introduce local transitions instead of the copies of place p_1, and we duplicate transition t_2 (rule ρ_{R2}). The last transformation shown in Fig. 18 is the split of place p_3 according to the refinement rule ρ_{R4}. Refinement process may be continued until the target detail level is achieved.

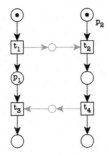

Fig. 17. "Send-Receive" asynchronous interaction pattern

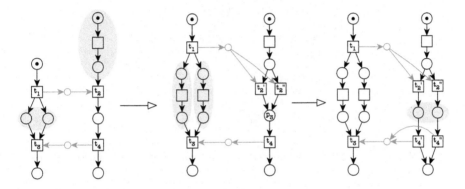

Fig. 18. Refinement of the interaction pattern from Fig. 17

5   Conclusion

In this paper, we have studied the problem of abstracting and refining elementary net systems with the help of α-morphisms. Direct construction of these morphisms is a complicated task. To solve it, we have proposed a set of abstraction/refinement transformation rules. The step-wise application of these transformation rules induces corresponding α-morphisms between initial and transformed models. Some of the transformations (the abstraction rules A1–A3 and their refinement counterparts) have been already discussed in the literature, while the others are new and have been developed in accordance with the definition of α-morphisms. We note that structural applicability constraints of the proposed transformation rules can be efficiently computed. Moreover, locality of abstraction/refinement transformation rules proposed in our study allows us to preserve and reflect not only reachable markings, but also deadlocks. Thus, structural constraints of transformation rules make impossible to lose or introduce deadlocks in models. In addition, we have demonstrated how transformation rules can be applied to compose models of interacting workflow net components.

There are several open theoretical questions that we intend to study in future. It is planned to extend transformations defined in the paper with more liberal yet controlled ways of introducing concurrency rather than by duplicating places only, e.g., it is possible to consider introduction and detection of implicit places.

Consider an α-morphism $\varphi \colon N_1 \to N_2$ shown in Fig. 19, where transitions t_3, t_4 and t_5 in N_1 are local. N_2 cannot be obtained form N_1 (and vice versa) by applying the proposed rules. For instance, to apply the rule ρ_{A5}, the place p_2 has to be duplicated (the rule ρ_{R1}). However, even in this case, after fusing transitions t_1 and t_2 we will not be able to do pairwise simplification of transitions t_3, t_4 and t_5 since they do not have coincident presets and postsets.

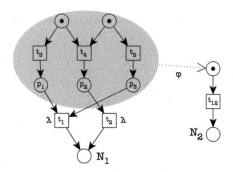

Fig. 19. An α-morphism that cannot be obtained by applying transformations

In this light, it is also rather interesting to study the completeness problem, for instance, to establish whether transformations allow us to generate all possible refinements of a given abstract EN system preserving its properties. Moreover, we also plan to characterize properties of irreducible EN systems.

References

1. van der Aalst, W.M.P.: Workflow verification: finding control-flow errors using petri-net-based techniques. In: van der Aalst, W., Desel, J., Oberweis, A. (eds.) Business Process Management. LNCS, vol. 1806, pp. 161–183. Springer, Heidelberg (2000). https://doi.org/10.1007/3-540-45594-9_11
2. Bernardinello, L., Mangioni, E., Pomello, L.: Local State Refinement and Composition of Elementary Net Systems: An Approach Based on Morphisms. In: Koutny, M., van der Aalst, W.M.P., Yakovlev, A. (eds.) Transactions on Petri Nets and Other Models of Concurrency VIII. LNCS, vol. 8100, pp. 48–70. Springer, Heidelberg (2013). https://doi.org/10.1007/978-3-642-40465-8_3
3. Bernardinello, L., De Cindio, F.: A survey of basic net models and modular net classes. In: Rozenberg, G. (ed.) Advances in Petri Nets 1992. LNCS, vol. 609, pp. 304–351. Springer, Heidelberg (1992). https://doi.org/10.1007/3-540-55610-9_177
4. Bernardinello, L., Lomazova, I., Nesterov, R., Pomello, L.: Soundness-preserving composition of synchronously and asynchronously interacting workflow net components (2020). https://arxiv.org/pdf/2001.08064.pdf

5. Berthelot, G.: Checking properties of nets using transformations. In: Rozenberg, G. (ed.) Advances in Petri Nets 1985. LNCS, vol. 222, pp. 19–40. Springer, Heidelberg (1986). https://doi.org/10.1007/3-540-18086-9
6. Berthelot, G., Roucairol, G.: Reduction of Petri-nets. In: Mazurkiewicz, A. (ed.) Mathematical Foundations of Computer Science 1976. LNCS, vol. 45, pp. 202–209. Springer, Heidelberg (1976). https://doi.org/10.1007/978-1-4612-3086-1
7. Desel, J., Merceron, A.: Vicinity Respecting Homomorphisms for Abstracting System Requirements. In: Jensen, K., Donatelli, S., Koutny, M. (eds.) Transactions on Petri Nets and Other Models of Concurrency IV. LNCS, vol. 6550, pp. 1–20. Springer, Heidelberg (2010). https://doi.org/10.1007/978-3-642-18222-8_1
8. Ehrig, H., Hoffmann, K., Padberg, J.: Transformations of Petri nets. Electr. Notes Theor. Comput. Sci. **148**(1), 151–172 (2006)
9. Esparza, J., Silva, M.: Top-down synthesis of live and bounded free choice nets. In: Rozenberg, G. (ed.) ICATPN 1990. LNCS, vol. 524, pp. 118–139. Springer, Heidelberg (1991). https://doi.org/10.1007/BFb0019972
10. Genrich, H., Thiagarajan, P.: A theory of bipolar synchronisation schemes. Theor. Comput. Sci. **30**(3), 241–318 (1984)
11. Hack, M.: Analysis of Production Schemata by Petri Nets. TR-94. MIT Press, Boston (1972)
12. Lomazova, I.A.: Resource Equivalences in Petri Nets. In: van der Aalst, W., Best, E. (eds.) PETRI NETS 2017. LNCS, vol. 10258, pp. 19–34. Springer, Cham (2017). https://doi.org/10.1007/978-3-319-57861-3_3
13. Mikolajczak, B., Wang, Z.: Conceptual modeling of concurrent systems through stepwise abstraction and refinement using Petri net morphisms. In: Song, I., Liddle, S., Ling, T., Scheuermann, P. (eds.) Conceptual Modeling - ER 2003. LNCS, vol. 2813, pp. 433–445 (2003). https://doi.org/10.1007/b13244
14. Murata, T.: Petri nets: properties, analysis and applications. Proc. IEEE **77**(4), 541–580 (1989)
15. Murata, T., Suzuki, I.: A method for stepwise refinement and abstraction of petri nets. J. Comput. Syst. Sci. **27**(1), 51–76 (1983)
16. Nesterov, R., Lomazova, I.: Asynchronous interaction patterns for mining multi-agent system models from event logs. In: Lomazova, I., Kalenkova, A., Yavorsky, R. (eds.) Proceedings of the MACSPro Workshop 2019. CEUR Workshop Proceedings, vol. 2478, pp. 62–73. CEUR-WS.org (2019)
17. Nielsen, M., Winskel, G.: Petri nets and bisimulations. Theor. Comput. Sci. **153**, 211–244 (1996)
18. Padberg, J., Urbášek, M.: Rule-Based Refinement of Petri Nets: A Survey. In: Ehrig, H., Reisig, W., Rozenberg, G., Weber, H. (eds.) Petri Net Technology for Communication-Based Systems. LNCS, vol. 2472, pp. 161–196. Springer, Heidelberg (2003). https://doi.org/10.1007/978-3-540-40022-6_9
19. Rozenberg, G., Engelfriet, J.: Elementary net systems. In: Reisig, W., Rozenberg, G. (eds.) ACPN 1996. LNCS, vol. 1491, pp. 12–121. Springer, Heidelberg (1998). https://doi.org/10.1007/3-540-65306-6_14
20. Schnoebelen, P., Sidorova, N.: Bisimulation and the reduction of Petri nets. In: Nielsen, M., Simpson, D. (eds.) Application and Theory of Petri Nets 2000. LNCS, vol. 1825, pp. 409–423. Springer, Heidelberg (2000). https://doi.org/10.1007/3-540-44988-4
21. Valette, R.: Analysis of Petri nets by stepwise refinements. J. Comput. Syst. Sci. **18**(1), 35–46 (1979)
22. Winskel, G.: Petri nets, algebras, morphisms, and compositionality. Inf. Comput. **72**(3), 197–238 (1987)

Defining Meaningful Local Process Models

Mitchel Brunings$^{(\boxtimes)}$, Dirk Fahland, and Boudewijn van Dongen

Eindhoven University of Technology, Eindhoven, The Netherlands
{m.d.brunings,d.fahland,b.f.v.dongen}@tue.nl

Abstract. Current process discovery techniques are unable to produce meaningful models for semi-structured processes, as they are either too inaccurate or too complex. In this paper we use the idea of local process models (LPMs) to model fragments of a semi-structured process and explore the potential of sets of LPMs. Automatic LPM discovery finds many small patterns but doesn't find patterns larger than 4–5 events, it produces too many models, and the discovered models describe some events from the log multiple times while leaving others unexplained. We manually construct a set of LPMs for the well-known BPIC12 event log that (1) contains a small number of models that (2) have high accuracy measures such as fitness and precision while (3) they together cover the whole event log and (4) do not cover parts of the log multiple times unnecessarily. We find that existing evaluation techniques for LPMs do not work for sets of LPMs and we propose several measures that help determine the quality of a set of LPMs both as a whole and as individual LPMs. We show that sets of LPMs can indeed be used to model semi-structured processes by not thinking of such processes as monolithic, but rather a collection of smaller processes working together.

Keywords: Process modeling · Local Process Models · Coverage

1 Introduction

Process modelers generally concern themselves with building process models that describe process behavior in a manner that facilitates human understanding of the process for purposes such as analysis of or communication about the process. Whether processes originate from a designed process model or came into existence organically, their behavior may be recorded, and the recorded behavior may be used to discover process models that describe the process.

(Recorded) behavior of a process may be categorized as structured or unstructured or something in between [5,12]: the structuredness of processes falls on a spectrum. In particular, we are interested in modeling *semi-structured behavior*, i.e. modeling behavior that is clearly not structured, but also clearly not unstructured. An example of such behavior could be that of students enrolled in a certain program that follow courses. Students choose different electives and

© Springer-Verlag GmbH Germany, part of Springer Nature 2022
M. Koutny et al. (Eds.): ToPNoC XVI, LNCS 13220, pp. 24–48, 2022.
https://doi.org/10.1007/978-3-662-65303-6_2

may follow their courses in different orders, which is rather unstructured behavior: only constraints of prerequisite courses remain. But the local behavior looks very similar for all students in a particular course: they all get the same classes, homework, and final exam in the same order, which is very structured behavior.

Trying to discover a model from semi-structured behavior using currently existing techniques often yields disappointing results. On structured behavior, techniques such as Inductive Miner [7] and SplitMiner [1] generally work well. But on semi-structured behavior, both produce large, complex models which do not match the desired behavior by allowing runs that cannot happen and disallowing runs that can. On the other end of the spectrum, Declare mining [8] often works well to discover constraints in unstructured behavior, but on semi-structured behavior results in too many constraints, rendering the model incomprehensible.

Of course, there exists a spectrum of process modeling languages and accompanying miners and techniques. For example, visual exploration using the Log Pattern Explorer [9] works well, but is a manual task which does not automatically result in models. Other techniques include DCR graphs [3] and trace clustering [15]. One method in particular is of interest to us: LPMs [14] have been applied to finding patterns in unstructured behavior (like smart home environments). We believe that a set of LPMs that work together to describe a process may be a very powerful tool. In other words: We look at a different part of the solution space of models. Not start-to-end, not Declare, not LPMs, but sets of LPMs. Inside this space we do find solutions. Once we're there, we ask questions about what is a good set of LPMs, how to measure their quality, and how to discover sets of LPMs.

The main contributions of this paper are that we show that sets of LPMs are useful to model semi-structured processes, and we introduce a coverage metric and visualize this for (sets of) LPMs. A lesser contribution of this paper is the set of LPMs in Fig. 7 that describes the whole process flow of BPIC12 [17] accurately and in a fully understandable manner.

The rest of this paper is structured as follows: In Sect. 2, we look at a specific log that shows semi-structured behavior. We show that the process cannot be captured in a monolithic model, and that LPMs are not sufficient to explain the whole process. In Sect. 3, we model the process manually, and see that splitting the process over a set of LPMs works well for understandability. We also explain how a set of LPMs together describes the whole process and formulate some requirements for meaningful sets of LPMs. In Sect. 4, we explain why the existing quality metrics for LPMs don't work for sets of LPMs. We then propose measures for both individual LPMs and for complete sets of LPMs. In Sect. 5, we draw our conclusions and lay out several avenues of further research.

2   Process Model Discovery on Semi-structured Behavior

In this section, we discuss how literature differentiates between structured and unstructured behavior recorded in an event log in terms of a spectrum in

Sect. 2.1. We identify semi-structured behavior as a middle-ground between these two ends and propose a formalization of semi-structured behavior in terms of local process models in Sect. 2.2. We then discuss an example of a semi-structured event log in Sect. 2.3 and how existing start-to-end process discovery algorithms cannot discover satisfactory models in Sect. 2.4. We summarize the idea of local process models as proposed by Tax et al. [14] in Sect. 2.5 and discuss how local process model discovery algorithms also cannot discover satisfactory models in Sect. 2.6.

2.1 Structured, Unstructured, and Semi-structured Behavior

When we think about a real-world process in the context of process modeling, it is usually in terms of its behavior: the possible executions of that process. For a real-world process P, the set of all possible executions of P is what we call its language $lang(P) \subseteq A^*$, where A is the set of individual (atomic) activities happening in the process and a sequence $\sigma \in lang(P)$ is an execution (or *trace*) of P. The goal of process modeling is to obtain a process model M of P such that the language of M equals the language of P: $lang(M) = lang(P)$. The language of a model depends on the modeling language, for example for a Petri net [13] the language is the set of all valid firing sequences, and for a Declare [8] model the language is the set of all sequences that satisfy all constraints. We usually record the behavior of a real-world process P in a log $L \subseteq lang(P)$ which is a subset of the language of that process. Given a log from a process, we cannot know if the process itself is structured; we can only reason about the log. Therefore, for the rest of this paper, we will talk about logs. Our task is to describe the behavioral information in the log, because that is what we have.

The structuredness of logs forms a spectrum ranging from *structured* to *unstructured* [5,12] as illustrated in Fig. 1.

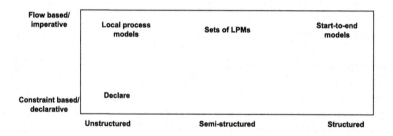

Fig. 1. A 2D view on the spectrum of process modeling languages showing structuredness as a spectrum.

We call a log L *structured* if there exists an imperative [5] model M that has no label duplication and consists of only basic constructs such as sequence, choice, parallelism, and loops (Free-choice Workflow nets [6], for example) such that $lang(M) = L$. Given a log from a structured process, discovery techniques such as the Inductive Miner [7] and SplitMiner [1] typically work well.

We call L *unstructured* when we can only find relations between individual activities or pairs of activity types that can be expressed in logical constraints, such as Declare constraints [8]. For example: frequency (how often an activity can appear), coexistence (either both or neither of a pair of activities happen), precedence (when we see the first activity of the pair, the second must have happened before), etc.

Structured and unstructured logs are the extremes of this spectrum. There still exists a whole range of logs in between that we call *semi-structured logs*. This is when we cannot provide an understandable model M such that $lang(M) = L$, but we can find reoccurring patterns in the log that involve more than just pairs of activity types.

Recall the example from Sect. 1 where students all follow different sets of courses in the same program, which is behavior that is not structured, but the local behavior of all students in a specific course is structured.

2.2 Formalizing Semi-structured Behavior

Such patterns of reoccurring behaviors can be modeled in terms of *oclets* [4], i.e., conflict-free Petri net fragments with enabling preconditions, or *local process models* [14], i.e., short workflow models including choices and loops but without enabling conditions. Such models consist of a collection of smaller process models that only aim to model the pattern and ignore everything else. Because local process models don't model the whole log, but only such patterns, their semantics in relation to the whole log L is not easy to define. Existing works on local process models [14] do not provide an actual semantics; oclets [4] are defined over partially ordered runs of Petri nets, which makes them inapplicable to a more general setting of a log describing just sequences of activity executions.

In the following, we propose a new way to formalize how (a set of) local models can relate to an event log. Our idea is to collect all instances of the same (or somewhat similar) pattern of behavior in a *local log*. In other words, a local log contains those subsequences of behavior from the full log L that are somewhat similar to each other. We understand these subsequences as the executions of a local process model. A local process model should then describe all the executions or instances in the local log. What exactly constitutes similar behavior, i.e., which instances belong to the same local log, is subject to domain knowledge. We therefore introduce the notion of an *oracle* for this task.

Let L be an event log, let $\sigma \in L$ be a trace. We write $\iota \subseteq \sigma$ if $\iota \in A^*$ is a subsequence of σ.

Let M be a process model. We call ι an *instance* of M if $\iota \in lang(M)$, i.e., the subsequence in σ is an execution of M.

To find the instances of a model M within a trace σ, we use an oracle O which is a function: $O : A^* \times \mathcal{M} \to \mathcal{P}(A^*)$, where $\mathcal{M}$ is the set of (local) models. O takes as input an execution sequence σ and a model M, and returns as output all the instances $\iota_1, \iota_2, ...$ of M in σ.

The local log of a process P with log $L \subseteq lang(P)$ for local process model M using oracle O is defined by the instances of M in L as $local_O(L, M) = \bigcup_{\sigma \in L} O(\sigma, M) = \{\iota | \exists \sigma \in L : \iota \in O(\sigma, M)\}$.

From these definitions we see that a local process model can *cover* some, but not necessarily all events. We define if an event $e \in \sigma \in L$ is covered by model M as follows: $covered_O(e, L, M) = \exists \iota \in local_O(L, M) : e \in \iota$.

While we introduced these definitions with the notion of a local process model in mind, they generally apply also to structured and unstructured behavior. For a structured process with log L and process model M, the oracle evaluates as follows: $O(\sigma \in L, M) = \{\sigma\}$. That is, the instances of the model are simply the complete traces of the log.

For an unstructured process with log L and Declare rules $\{rule(a, b),$ $rule(c), ...\}$, the oracle evaluates as follows: $O(\sigma \in L, rule(x, y)) = \{\sigma \upharpoonright_{\{x,y\}}\}$, or with a single activity: $O(\sigma \in L, rule(x)) = \{\sigma \upharpoonright_{\{x\}}\}$. That is, the instances of each rule are the complete traces of the log projected on the activity or pair of activities involved in the rule.

According to this framework, structured, semi-structured, and unstructured processes differ in the length or size of the instances returned by the oracle O, where structured processes are described in terms of the entire trace, unstructured processes only in terms of single activities or pairs of activities, and semi-structured processes in terms of larger parts of behavior. In the following, we illustrate the difference between structured and semi-structured behavior and the shortcomings of existing definitions of local process models on an example.

2.3   Concrete Example of Semi-structured Logs

As a concrete example of a semi-structured log, we take the log from the Business Process Intelligence Challenge from 2012 [17] (L_{BPIC12}). L_{BPIC12} is a well-known log that comes from a loan application process in a bank. Each application goes through several phases of checks and follow-ups. If a check or follow-up was not successful, it may need to be repeated. An application can also be cancelled or declined at any point. While the checks and follow-ups (i.e. local behavior) follow very regular patterns, there are many possible variations in process flow for the applications as a whole (global behavior). In the rest of this section, we show that this log is neither structured nor unstructured.

L_{BPIC12} consists of 262200 events in 13087 traces. There are 36 event classes and 3353 trace variants. In Table 1 we count the event classes observed in L_{BPIC12}. This table also serves as a legend for the shorthand (in parentheses) that we use for the event classes in this log. Table 2 contains translations for the Dutch labels in Table 1.

Once we had gotten very familiar with L_{BPIC12}, we found that all parallelism only occurred with events with identical timestamps, making their relative order in the trace unreliable. Upon investigating events of the same types occurring together, we noticed that some did have unique timestamps, and of those with unique timestamps, we noticed that they always occurred in the same order.

Table 1. Event occurrence matrix for L_{BPIC12} (with shorthand notation in parentheses).

concept:name		SCHEDULE (0)	START (1)	COMPLETE (2)
		lifecycle:transition		
A_ACCEPTED	(A_ACC)	–	–	5113
A_ACTIVATED	(A_ACT)	–	–	2246
A_APPROVED	(A_APP)	–	–	2246
A_CANCELLED	(A_CAN)	–	–	2807
A_DECLINED	(A_DEC)	–	–	7635
A_FINALIZED	(A_FIN)	–	–	5015
A_PARTLYSUBMITTED	(A_PAR)	–	–	13087
A_PREACCEPTED	(A_PRE)	–	–	7367
A_REGISTERED	(A_REG)	–	–	2246
A_SUBMITTED	(A_SUB)	–	–	13087
O_ACCEPTED	(O_ACC)	–	–	2243
O_CANCELLED	(O_CAN)	–	–	3655
O_CREATED	(O_CRE)	–	–	7030
O_DECLINED	(O_DEC)	–	–	802
O_SELECTED	(O_SEL)	–	–	7030
O_SENT	(O_SEN)	–	–	7030
O_SENT_BACK	(O_SBA)	–	–	3454
W_Afhandelen leads	(W_Afh)	4771	5897	5898
W_Beoordelen fraude	(W_Beo)	124	270	270
W_Completeren aanvraag	(W_Com)	7371	23512	23967
W_Nabellen incomplete dossiers	(W_Nid)	2383	11400	11407
W_Nabellen offertes	(W_Nof)	6634	22406	22976
W_Valideren aanvraag	(W_Val)	5023	7891	7895
W_Wijzigen contractgegevens	(W_Wij)	12	–	–

Table 2. English translations of the Dutch labels from Table 1.

Dutch	English
Afhandelen leads	Handling leads
Beoordelen fraude	Assess fraud
Completeren aanvraag	Complete application
Nabellen incomplete dossiers	Calling incomplete files
Nabellen offertes	Calling quotes
Valideren aanvraag	Validate application
Wijzigen contractgegevens	Change contract details

Therefore, we sorted all events with the same timestamp according to the order we found among those same event types with unique timestamps.

2.4   Discovering Start-to-End Process Models from Semi-structured Logs

Applying the Inductive Miner - infrequent [7] (at 20% threshold) on L_{BPIC12} results in the model shown in Fig. 2. The Inductive Miner produces a complex Petri net that is also inaccurate: it allows behavior that we know does not exist in the log. For instance, it allows W_Beo+1 and W_Beo+2 to occur or be skipped any number of times independently of each other, while we know that every W_Beo+1 is (eventually) followed by W_Beo+2. Several other patterns that are known from L_{BPIC12} have been missed in a similar fashion.

Applying the SplitMiner (using standard settings) on L_{BPIC12} results in the model shown in Fig. 3[1]. The SplitMiner also produces a complex Petri net that is also inaccurate: it disallows behavior that we know exists. For instance, this model claims that W_Beo+0, W_Beo+1, W_Beo+2 terminates a case, though we know the process may continue afterwards. Several other patterns that are known from L_{BPIC12} have been missed in a similar fashion.

These examples of state-of-the-art process discovery tools for start-to-end processes show that they are unable to deal with the structure of L_{BPIC12}. They result in models that may perform well on quality measures such as fitness or precision, but these models are rather large and complex, with Fig. 2 containing tau-skips for almost all transitions, and Fig. 3 containing many loops and several jumps between paths. We want models that are accurate (i.e. have high fitness and precision scores), as inaccurate models do not describe the process we are trying to understand, but we also want models that are simple, because incomprehensible models will not help our understanding of the processes they describe. The models in Fig. 2 and Fig. 3 show that start-to-end model discovery techniques are not able to discover models from semi-structured logs that are both accurate and simple.

2.5   Local Process Models

Tax et al. [14] also show that existing process model discovery techniques are unable to deal with event logs that contain a lot of repetition within traces. They introduce *local process models* (LPMs) to describe patterns that are smaller than the full observed behavior, but can still capture more behavior than simple sequences, such as concurrency and choice.

As an example, they provide the event log shown in Fig. 4a. The authors describe this log as events from a fictional sales department, where each trace describes the activities of a particular sales person on a particular day. A sales person may work on multiple cases in a day, and multiple sales persons may be working on the same case. However, despite this chaotic behavior, a frequent pattern still emerges: When a sales person performs activity 'A', they often perform both activities 'B' and 'C' shortly after that on the same day.

---

[1] Note that the SplitMiner [1] doesn't explicitly consider life cycle events, therefore we include the life cycle data in the event name using the "Bring Lifecycle to Event Name" plugin in ProM 6.9.

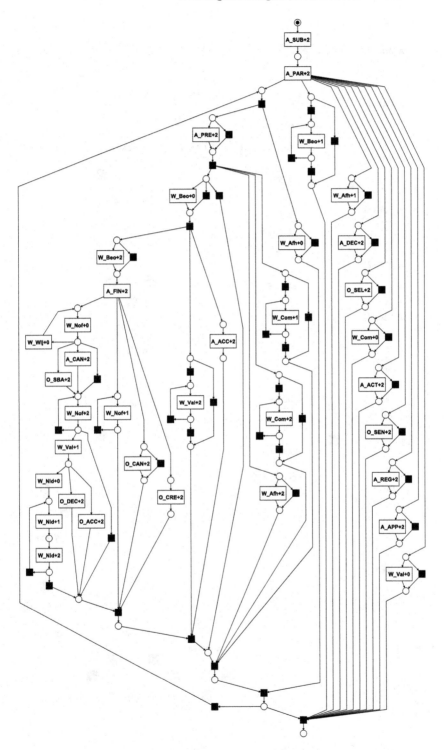

Fig. 2. The resulting Petri net of IMf [7] on L_{BPIC12}

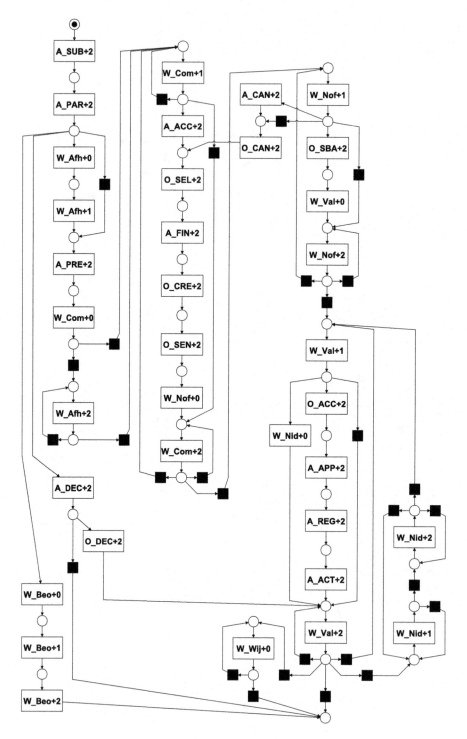

Fig. 3. The resulting Petri net of SplitMiner [1] on L_{BPIC12}.

Applying the Inductive Miner - infrequent [7] (at 20% threshold) on this example log produces the model shown in Fig. 4b, which allows nearly all behavior. The authors show that there is a model that describes the frequent pattern from Fig. 4a in Fig. 4c. In this model we see that 13 times out of 21 total occurrences of 'A', it is followed by a 'B' and a 'C' in any order. Indeed, applying the oracle of Sect. 2.2 to the log of Fig. 4a and the model of Fig. 4c yields the same instances as identified by the authors of [14], highlighted in this log.

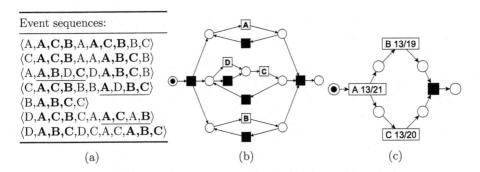

Event sequences:

⟨A,**A,C,B**,A,**A,C,B**,B,C⟩
⟨C,**A,C,B**,A,A,**A,B,C**,B⟩
⟨**A,A,B**,D,**C**,D,**A,B,C**,B⟩
⟨C,**A,C,B**,B,B,<u>**A**,D,**B,C**</u>⟩
⟨B,**A,B,C**,C⟩
⟨D,**A,C,B**,C,A,<u>**A,C**,A,**B**</u>⟩
⟨D,**A,B,C**,D,C,A,C,**A,B,C**⟩

(a)   (b)   (c)

Fig. 4. (a) A log of event sequences with **highlighted** instances of a frequent pattern. Gapped instances are <u>underlined</u>. Source: [14]. (b) The resulting Petri net of IMf [7] on the event sequences shown in Fig. 4a. (c) An LPM showing the frequent behavior pattern from Fig. 4a. Source: [14].

Tax et al. managed to discover an LPM that describes a pattern that could not be discovered or displayed before. This suggests that LPMs are worth exploring as an alternative to traditional start-to-end model discovery and as an improvement on sequential pattern mining.

2.6   Discovering LPMs from Semi-structured Logs

Applying "Search for Local Process Models" on L_{BPIC12} with all the default settings yields 100 LPMs divided into 39 groups[2]. Each LPM has 2 to 4 labeled transitions and all LPMs together describe events of 22 event classes out of the 36 event classes that appear in the log. In Fig. 5 we show a visualization of which event classes occur in which group(s) of LPMs. Each black 'pixel' represents a particular event class (y-axis) being present in a particular group (x-axis). From this visualization, we can quickly see that many LPM groups cover different combinations of the same few event classes.

---

[2] Note that the "Search for Local Process Models" plugin in ProM 6.9 only looks at the event names, therefore we include the life cycle data in the event name using the "Bring Lifecycle to Event Name" plugin.

Fig. 5. Event class occurrence for the 39 groups of LPMs.

We manually inspected these 39 groups of LPMs and found several interesting issues with them. For example: in Fig. 6, the two LPMs on the right show significant overlap (highlighted), where they both cover all 3655 occurrences of O_CAN+2 in L_{BPIC12}, and 3655 out of 7030 occurrences of O_SEL+2, which implies an overlap of at least 280 occurrences.

Fig. 6. A selection of LPMs discovered from L_{BPIC12} (same labels highlighted).

We conclude that the discovered LPMs are not meaningful for three reasons: (1) We get too many of them. (2) They leave large parts of the log uncovered: the 14 missing event classes alone already represent 96311 out of the 262200 events in L_{BPIC12}. (3) They cover some events multiple times: these events are described by multiple transitions in multiple different LPMs. We show in Sect. 4 as we evaluate "coverage" of events that this is indeed the case.

3   The Potential of Local Process Models

In Sect. 2 we introduced L_{BPIC12} and saw that there are no good start-to-end process models for this particular log. In this section, we show a manually created set of LPMs to describe the behavior from this log. We then discuss why our set of LPMs is preferable over the models we saw in Sect. 2.6 both in terms of accuracy and understandability.

3.1   Local Process Models that Could Be

In this section we show that a meaningful set of LPMs can be derived from L_{BPIC12} through log inspection and manual modeling, i.e. by using a human oracle. In contrast to [2], we did not focus on a single resource here, but we considered all resources. This caused us to end up with a few more and slightly larger LPMs. These LPMs are larger than those by Tax et al., but there are fewer and with less overlap. We then discuss how this set of LPMs can be interpreted in a meaningful manner.

We observed that nearly all A_... and O_... events occur between pairs of W_...+1 (start) and W_...+2 (complete) events and that these start and complete event pairs never overlap. We split the traces into trace fragments consisting of these pairs of W_...+1 and W_...+2 and the events between them. Our intention is that these trace fragments become the instances that make up a local log. This means that we have already defined the output of the oracle, we just don't have the models yet. We grouped these trace fragments (i.e. instances) into local logs according to their W_... events, e.g. all instances starting with W_Afh+1 and ending with W_Afh+2 are grouped into L_{Afh}. We collected the instances of events before the first W_...+1 event in an extra local log L_{start}, as these events are never between W_... events. We then analyzed the local logs L_{start}, L_{Afh}, L_{Beo}, L_{Com}, L_{Nid}, L_{Nof}, and L_{Val} one by one and observed the following:

- Each instance in a local log has the same start event;
- For most local logs each instance has the same end event;
- For most local logs the penultimate event of each instance determines the outcome: end of case, or a specific next LPM, except for L_{start}, where all final events are unique and are associated with their own outcome.

With these observations in mind, we created the Petri nets shown in Fig. 7. This small set is fitting and precise. It is easy to explain each model in the context of the log and the models are fairly disjoint.

We used these observations to create a few 'guidelines' that we followed while constructing our LPMs:

- Only use a single initial place - this will make it clear what can happen when the model is activated.
- Use different final places for different outcomes - this will make it clear what can happen once the model is done.
- Allow label duplication, especially between different branches - this will avoid the illusion of branches merging and splitting again.

We did not model loops in our LPMs, but they do exist in L_{BPIC12}. These loops exist on a higher level than we modeled, as they encompass whole LPMs. For example: there are traces in L_{BPIC12} that have many instances of M_{Afh} (Fig. 7b) in a row. We did not encounter any parallelism in L_{BPIC12}.

Looking at an individual LPM in Fig. 7, we can tell whether a final place is transitional or terminal by looking at the activities just before it. Terminal situations occur when an application is declined or canceled (A_DEC/A_CAN). A situation is transitional when we see W_...+0 (schedule) before the end, signaling which LPM is coming next. When no activities occur between W_...+1 and W_...+2, it seems to indicate an attempt was made to execute the LPM, but

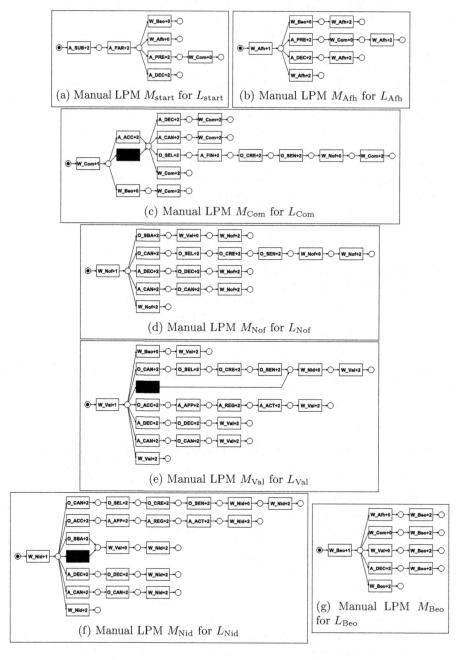

(a) Manual LPM M_{start} for L_{start}

(b) Manual LPM M_{Afh} for L_{Afh}

(c) Manual LPM M_{Com} for L_{Com}

(d) Manual LPM M_{Nof} for L_{Nof}

(e) Manual LPM M_{Val} for L_{Val}

(f) Manual LPM M_{Nid} for L_{Nid}

(g) Manual LPM M_{Beo} for L_{Beo}

Fig. 7. Manually constructed set of LPMs for L_{BPIC12}.

it was unsuccessful and needs to be tried again. We visualize this cooperation between LPMs in Sect. 4.3.

We now compare our LPMs to the LPMs obtained in Sect. 2.6. Each of our LPMs represents a local log, just like the LPMs in Sect. 2.6, but in contrast to those LPMs, our 7 LPMs are significantly larger, as we have found much larger patterns. Most top LPMs (best of their group) from Sect. 2.6 that were found with the plugin by Tax et al. appear as parts of our larger LPMs, for example, the LPM on the left in Fig. 6 occurs in M_{Val} (Fig. 7e) as its first and last activity. We also see that in our set of LPMs all event classes except W_Wij+0 occur as a transition at least once, and several event classes occur in more than one LPM. Not only do our LPMs each represent larger local logs, but we also only need 7 LPMs to describe nearly all of L_{BPIC12}. We explain this quality criterion we call *coverage* in Sect. 3.3.

3.2 Structure of LPMs

Before we go into our thoughts on what makes a good LPM, let us clarify that even though one end of an LPM in our set can 'trigger' another LPM, we provide no formal semantics for this in this paper.

Because of our manual work, we made a lot of decisions on how to model LPMs. The guidelines that we followed can be generalized: By using a single initial place and multiple final places each with a distinct and specific meaning, we gain the ability to link the different final places of one LPM to specific initial places of other LPMs. By using label duplication, we may end up with larger LPMs, but we avoid more complex structures and potential confusion between different paths through an LPM.

From these guidelines we conclude that any decision point or parallel split must be modeled explicitly in an LPM. If and where such a split should join remains free. A process can have multiple and even asynchronous end points.

Loops, on the other hand, don't have to be explicit in an LPM. We can loop over a complete LPM by linking one of its final places to its own initial place. This does not, however, prevent us from modeling smaller loops inside LPMs. Having multiple end states suggests that LPMs terminate, but it's possible to construct a set of LPMs that continue looping without possible termination.

The mix of splits and joins inside and outside of LPMs and the initialization through final and initial places makes soundness complicated. We do not discuss that further in this paper. It suffices to say that our set in Fig. 7 is sound.

A notable difference between our LPMs and usual start-to-end models considered in process discovery is that we have label duplication and multiple final places. Because of label duplication we can disentangle complex structure in favor of simpler structures. Deviating from workflow structure allows us to have separate final places representing different final situations. Some of these final situations are terminal (i.e. the full case stops here) while other situations are transitional (i.e. the LPM stops here, but the case still continues in another instance of some LPM, perhaps even the same LPM).

We can also draw some similarities: at the end of a start-to-end model, all decisions are done and a single terminal final place in one of the LPMs is reached, but in the middle of such a start-to-end model, we may still have choices or parallelism that are yet to be concluded. It is an interesting question if (and how) a set of LPMs can be combined into a single, sound start-to-end process model. However, this question is beyond the scope of this paper. Instead, we look at coverage as a quality metric for a set of LPMs in relation to an event log.

3.3   Coverage

We want a set of LPMs to cover as much of the log as possible with minimal redundancy. To this end, we introduce the terms *coverage* and *duplicate coverage*. In Sect. 2.2 we defined $covered_O(e, L, M)$ to determine events covered by an LPM. We now define coverage on an individual LPM as the fraction of events from the log that are actually covered by the given LPM:

$$coverage_O(L, M) = \frac{\#\{e | e \in \sigma \wedge \sigma \in L \wedge covered_O(e, L, M)\}}{\#\{e | e \in \sigma \wedge \sigma \in L\}}.$$

This differs from the coverage metric in [14] which measures the fraction of events from the log that *might* be covered by the LPM because the LPM has a transition with a matching label.

We define coverage for a set of LPMs as follows:

$$coverage_O(L, LPMs) = \frac{\#\{e | e \in \sigma \wedge \sigma \in L \wedge \exists M \in LPMs : covered_O(e, L, M)\}}{\#\{e | e \in \sigma \wedge \sigma \in L\}}.$$

We consider an event covered if there is at least one LPM in the set that covers it. The coverage is then computed by counting all covered events and dividing by the total number of events in the log. The result is the fraction of the observed behavior that is covered by the set of LPMs.

Because of the way we split L_{BPIC12} up into local logs and then made an LPM for each local log, all instances of these local logs are associated with a specific LPM. If our models are 100% fitting, this means all instances are covered. As typical in practice, our models do not account for every small deviation. Therefore, some events cannot be replayed. To accurately measure coverage, we calculate the alignment of instances from the local log on the LPM and then take the number of synchronous moves in the alignment and divide by the total number of events in the log.

To calculate the coverage of our set of LPMs from Fig. 7 we can simply sum up the coverage for all individual LPMs and see that our LPMs together cover 259501 out of 262200 events recorded in the log (99.0%). The sum is valid because we did not duplicate any event when we split the log.

To define duplicate coverage of a set of LPMs, we first define when an event is duplicate covered as follows:

$$duplicateCovered_O(e, L, LPMs)$$
$$= \exists M, M' \in LPMs : M \neq M' \land covered_O(e, L, M) \land covered_O(e, L, M').$$

Now we define duplicate coverage:

$$duplicateCoverage_O(L, LPMs)$$
$$= \frac{\#\{e|e \in \sigma \land \sigma \in L \land duplicateCovered_O(e, L, LPMs)\}}{\#\{e|e \in \sigma \land \sigma \in L\}}.$$

We count the number of events that are covered by more than one LPM and divide by the total number of events in the log. The result is the fraction of the observed behavior that is covered multiple times by the set of LPMs. There are many reasons why one might want to avoid or include duplicate coverage. For example: If we have a set of LPMs based on the roles of actors in a process and a log of that process includes events that are executed by multiple actors of different roles, then we expect to see duplicate coverage of these events.

With our set of LPMs (Fig. 7) we do not want duplicate coverage because each LPM describes a different part of the process without overlap. This means any duplicate coverage is redundant for us. By keeping this number low, we keep redundancy in our set of LPMs low.

Because we did not duplicate any event in splitting the log, we know that our manually constructed set of LPMs doesn't cover any event more than once.

3.4   Trivial Oracles

As shown in Sect. 2.2, not all oracles are very complex. We saw an oracle that returned the traces projected on one or two event classes, or that returned the complete traces. These oracles correspond with how we interpret declare models and start-to-end models respectively.

There's another trivial oracle: one that returns individual events as instances. This oracle also corresponds with a flower model. But if we consider a set of LPMs, this oracle corresponds with a set of LPMs that each consist of only a single transition, one for each event class. Such LPMs give us no useful information on how events are related to each other. Not all is done with coverage and duplicate coverage. The combination of a trivial oracle, the flower model, and coverage and duplicate coverage shows this. Instead, we want meaningful LPMs. Declare LPMs (high duplicate coverage) are meaningful if you want a declarative model.

3.5   Requirements for Meaningful Sets of LPMs

The aim of this paper is not to introduce a new LPM discovery technique, but to share our vision on what a set of LPMs should look like. We generalize the theories of start-to-end modeling. To more formally define our vision, we define the following requirements for meaningful sets of LPMs:

R1 The set of LPMs should consist of individual LPMs that are accurate, i.e. have high fitness and precision scores, because we want to describe the observed behavior and nothing else;

R2 The set of LPMs should maximize coverage, because we want to describe all observed behavior;

R3 The set of LPMs should minimize redundancy, in our case this means limiting duplicate coverage, but there are other scenarios where duplicate coverage could be desirable;

R4 The set of LPMs should be limited in size, because with too many models it will be hard to comprehend the set as a whole;

R5 It must be clear how LPMs relate to each other: for example in our LPMs, start and end places overlap, while in declare models, it's the conjunction of all rules that must hold.

When we check our manually constructed set of LPMs against these requirements, we see that all requirements are satisfied. R4 is satisfied as we only have 7 LPMs, R2 is satisfied because only 2699 out of 262200 events (1.03%) are not covered, and R3 is satisfied because no event is explained more than once. For R1 we show in Sect. 4 how to calculate accuracy measures for LPMs, and that these scores are indeed good for our set of LPMs.

In Sect. 4, we suggest quality measurement techniques based on existing measures in literature that measure the degree to which these requirements are met.

4 Evaluating Quality of LPMs

Tax et al. [14] suggest a list of quality criteria (support, confidence, language fit, determinism, and coverage) to measure the quality of individual LPMs. In Sect. 4.1, we explain these measures and use them to evaluate the LPMs discovered by Tax et al. and the LPMs we constructed manually on the BPIC12 data set [17]. Comparing these results, we observe that several measures cannot adequately describe the quality of a *set* of LPMs. We then propose several new measures that we believe help us to better describe the quality of a set of LPMs. We therefore propose new measures for individual LPMs in Sect. 4.2 and measures for sets of LPMs in Sect. 4.3.

4.1 Quality Metrics Designed by Tax et al.

First, we provide a short description of each quality criterion developed by Tax et al. For the exact definition, we refer to [14].

The support of an LPM measures how often the pattern described by the LPM occurs (a.k.a. *frequency*) on a scale from 0 to 1.

The confidence of an LPM measures the likelihood that an event whose class appears as one of the transitions in the LPM is part of a pattern that this LPM describes on a scale from 0 to 1.

The language fit of an LPM is the ratio of the behavior that is allowed by the LPM that is observed in the log.

The determinism of an LPM measures how well the LPM can predict the next event of a fitting trace on a scale from 0 to 1.

The coverage of an LPM is the ratio of events in the log of types that occur in the LPM. (Note that this is not the same as the coverage measure we define in Sect. 3.3.)

The score on an LPM is a weighted average of its support, confidence, language fit, determinism, and coverage.

We computed the above measures on two sets of LPMs on the BPIC12 data set: on the LPMs discovered by Tax et al. (see Sect. 2.6), and on the manually constructed LPMs (see Sect. 3.1). We use the "Rescore Local Process Model ranking to Log" plugin in ProM 6.9 to calculate these measures[3]. In Table 3 and Table 4 we show the scores on these measures for both the top discovered LPM of each group from Sect. 2.6 and the manual LPMs from Sect. 3.1. Note that instead of reporting the support, this plugin reports the frequency of LPMs.

Comparing these results, we see that the manual LPMs in Table 4 have lower scores than the discovered LPMs in Table 3 because the manual LPMs have lower confidence and determinism. The manual LPMs have lower confidence because they contain activities which can only be used to replay (i.e., cover) a fraction of the events of all occurrences of this activity in the log. For instance, A_DEC+2 occurs in each LPM in Fig. 7. This is by design, as the same activities may occur in different phases of the process, and thus occur in different LPMs. The manual LPMs have lower determinism, as we constructed larger LPMs with more choice than those discovered in Sect. 2.6.

Most manual LPMs have higher frequency and coverage than the discovered LPMs, but some manual LPMs (e.g., 2 and 7) have lower frequency and coverage.

We now discuss how well these measures allow us to decide whether an LPM should be included in the set of LPMs so that this set is *meaningful* as defined in Sect. 3.5. We observe that the manual LPMs have lower confidence and determinism (and in some cases also frequency) by design. If we used low confidence and determinism as criterion to exclude LPMs from the results, most manual LPMs would not be in the result set. In comparison, most discovered LPMs (Table 3) show high confidence and determinism which would require us to include most of these LPMs. In turn, language fit and coverage as defined above do not seem to strongly distinguish models in both sets to decide whether to include or exclude them for a meaningful set of LPMs. In the rest of this section, we explore measures that better evaluate sets of LPMs in line with being *meaningful*.

---

[3] We had to merge the end places of the manual LPMs for the plugin to work, as it only considers a single final marking.

Table 3. The scores attained by the discovered LPMs from Section 2.6.

group	score	frequency	confidence	determinism	language fit	coverage
1	0.879	7889	0.999	1.000	1.000	0.060
2	0.879	7030	1.000	1.000	1.000	0.054
3	0.879	4771	1.000	1.000	1.000	0.041
4	0.877	2246	1.000	1.000	1.000	0.017
5	0.877	2243	0.999	1.000	1.000	0.017
6	0.877	2243	0.999	1.000	1.000	0.017
7	0.877	2243	0.999	1.000	1.000	0.017
8	0.877	2243	0.999	1.000	1.000	0.026
9	0.875	5015	0.990	1.000	1.000	0.046
10	0.875	5015	0.990	1.000	1.000	0.045
11	0.868	5015	0.974	1.000	1.000	0.072
12	0.843	5875	0.910	1.000	1.000	0.114
13	0.843	5875	0.910	1.000	1.000	0.114
14	0.755	2246	0.857	0.784	1.000	0.039
15	0.752	3655	0.684	1.000	1.000	0.041
16	0.752	3655	0.684	1.000	1.000	0.041
17	0.751	6605	0.930	0.667	1.000	0.054
18	0.751	6605	0.930	0.667	1.000	0.054
19	0.745	5875	0.884	0.852	0.571	0.141
20	0.728	7889	0.870	0.667	1.000	0.069
21	0.726	3655	0.619	1.000	1.000	0.068
22	0.720	2190	0.607	1.000	1.000	0.063
23	0.715	3454	0.592	1.000	1.000	0.067
24	0.702	5015	0.697	0.815	1.000	0.134
25	0.697	5015	0.685	0.815	1.000	0.136
26	0.691	1230	0.540	1.000	1.000	0.035
27	0.680	5015	0.643	0.815	1.000	0.142
28	0.678	6694	0.519	0.969	1.000	0.128
29	0.678	6694	0.519	0.969	1.000	0.128
30	0.677	1625	0.503	1.000	1.000	0.025
31	0.675	2049	0.496	1.000	1.000	0.047
32	0.672	6605	0.775	0.719	0.667	0.081
33	0.668	5015	0.474	1.000	1.000	0.161
34	0.662	3255	0.591	0.826	1.000	0.105
35	0.659	4958	0.700	0.667	1.000	0.051
36	0.659	4958	0.700	0.667	1.000	0.051
37	0.650	6075	0.446	0.975	1.000	0.128
38	0.650	6075	0.446	0.975	1.000	0.128
39	0.650	8568	0.629	0.729	1.000	0.154

Table 4. The scores attained by the manual LPMs from Section 3.1.

LPM	score	frequency	confidence	determinism	language fit	coverage
1	0.612	13087	0.671	0.543	1.000	0.204
2	0.346	5897	0.029	0.519	1.000	0.131
3	0.331	23511	0.002	0.495	1.000	0.366
4	0.313	22405	0.023	0.407	1.000	0.368
5	0.322	7833	0.022	0.445	1.000	0.241
6	0.287	11385	0.032	0.313	1.000	0.300
7	0.285	270	0.001	0.379	1.000	0.097

4.2   New Quality Measures for Individual LPMs

In the previous subsection we explained why the existing measures for LPMs are not measuring what we want. In this subsection, we explore some measures that we believe are better.

A model should not leave large parts of the log unexplained. For traditional start-to-end models, there exist fitness measures that try to measure how much of a log is explained by a model. In this paper, we use the replay method explained in [16]. However, replaying L_{BPIC12} on the LPMs in this paper yields very low fitness scores for every LPM, as LPMs do not represent the whole log by design. Instead, we limit our replays to the respective local log for each LPM.

As we have split the log up by the W_...+1 and W_...+2 events to construct our manual LPMs, it makes sense to split the log the same way for their evaluation. Because we want to evaluate the automatically discovered LPMs using the same techniques, we need a way to find a local log from a log based on a given LPM. In other words, we need to implement an oracle for this task. To that end, we use the following method: Instances should not include events for which there is no matching activity in the LPM, as these are clearly not events that the LPM is describing, so we filter out any such events. An LPM describes behavior that starts with its first activity, so we make sure all of our instances start with such an event. For similar reasons, and using similar methods, we stop instances when we encounter final events. Should we encounter a start event before we encountered a final event, we simply finish the previous instance at that point, and start a new one. The resulting set of instances can then be used as a local log, which should have as many traces as there are occurrences of the first activity in the original log. This local log can then be replayed on the LPM, and the resulting alignment yields the fitness.

A model should not allow much more behavior than what is observed. For traditional start-to-end models, there exist precision measures that try to measure how much unobserved behavior is allowed by a model. In this paper, we use the escaping-edge based method explained in [11]. We calculate precision for an LPM using the same local log and resulting alignment as we use for calculating fitness.

Applying these fitness and precision measuring techniques on the same sets of LPMs as used in Sect. 4.1 yields the results shown in Table 5a and 5b. These tables also include the coverage measured as described in Sect. 3.3.

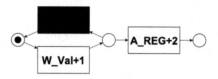

Fig. 8. Top discovered LPM from group 14 for L_{BPIC12}.

We realize that this log splitting technique (or oracle) doesn't work well for all automatically discovered LPMs. For example, the LPM shown in Fig. 8 starts with any number of its initial activity, while our oracle would consider each occurrence of this initial activity to be the start of a new instance. However, we had to make limiting choices to operationalize it for this paper, and this method works fine for the LPMs which have clear initial and final activities, which is still a majority. We could investigate other oracles, but that is out of scope for this paper.

With these results, we conclude that the manual LPMs satisfy R1 from Sect. 3.5. We also see that some of the discovered LPMs have low fitness and/or precision, meaning they don't satisfy R1.

4.3   Quality Measures for Sets of LPMs

For R4 it is easy to see that we have far fewer manual LPMs than automatically discovered LPMs. Clearly neither set consists of a single LPM, but our manual LPMs do better on this requirement than the automatically discovered LPMs.

To determine how well a set of LPMs satisfies R2 and R3, we project the coverage of the individual LPMs back on the original log. To do so, we check for each event by which LPMs it is covered and we record if it is covered at least once and if it is covered more than once. Satisfaction of R2 is measured by the fraction of events in the log that is covered at least once. Satisfaction of R3 is measured by the fraction of events in the log that is covered more than once.

Calculating coverage and duplicate coverage for the LPMs discovered in Sect. 2.6 yields a total coverage of 0.633 and a duplicate coverage of 0.441. This means that these 39 models explain less than two-thirds of the log, and they explain over half of the events that they do explain more than once. In contrast, the LPMs constructed in Sect. 3.1 have a total coverage of 0.990 with a duplicate coverage of precisely 0. Our manual LPMs explain nearly the entire log, without explaining any event more than once.

We can also visualize the coverage of LPMs, as we show in Fig. 9 for the LPMs from Sect. 3.1. This fragment only shows the most frequent trace variants,

Table 5. The scores attained by the LPMs from:

(a) Section 2.6.

(b) Section 3.1.

group	fitness	precision	coverage
1	1.000	1.000	0.060
2	1.000	1.000	0.054
3	1.000	1.000	0.041
4	1.000	1.000	0.017
5	1.000	1.000	0.017
6	1.000	1.000	0.017
7	1.000	1.000	0.017
8	1.000	1.000	0.026
9	0.994	1.000	0.046
10	0.994	1.000	0.045
11	0.981	1.000	0.070
12	0.945	1.000	0.114
13	0.945	1.000	0.114
14	0.762	0.667	0.039
15	0.840	1.000	0.041
16	0.840	1.000	0.041
17	0.966	1.000	0.052
18	0.966	1.000	0.052
19	0.967	0.930	0.141
20	0.948	1.000	0.060
21	0.904	1.000	0.068
22	0.812	0.998	0.063
23	0.898	1.000	0.067
24	0.608	0.750	0.128
25	0.608	0.750	0.128
26	0.710	1.000	0.023
27	0.607	0.750	0.128
28	0.932	1.000	0.114
29	0.932	1.000	0.114
30	0.860	1.000	0.017
31	0.983	1.000	0.025
32	0.887	0.899	0.066
33	0.529	1.000	0.147
34	0.715	0.667	0.098
35	0.902	1.000	0.046
36	0.898	1.000	0.046
37	0.887	1.000	0.115
38	0.894	1.000	0.105
39	0.980	1.000	0.026

model	fitness	precision	coverage
1	1.000	1.000	0.168
2	1.000	1.000	0.073
3	1.000	1.000	0.301
4	1.000	1.000	0.234
5	1.000	1.000	0.108
6	1.000	1.000	0.103
7	1.000	1.000	0.003

as the full visualization would span multiple pages. Each column represents an LPM from the set, except for the right-most column which represents the total (selected) set. The table at the top shows the LPM numbers and a check box to select which LPMs to include in the total. The table also shows absolute (number of events) and relative (share of events) coverage. Below that is the actual visualization. Trace variants are in order of frequency and separated by a small gap. Events are shown as thin horizontal lines, with the color corresponding to the legend at the bottom. In this figure we can easily see that each LPM is responsible for its own part of the behavior in L_{BPIC12}: LPM 1 is responsible for the initial phase of the process. LPM 1 then terminates the process or hands off to either LPM 2 or LPM 3. LPM 2 terminates or hands off to LPM 3. LPM 3 to 4. Et cetera.

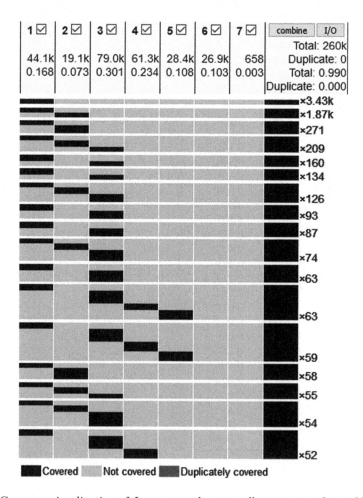

Fig. 9. Coverage visualization of L_{BPIC12} on the manually constructed set of LPMs as shown in Fig. 7.

5   Conclusion

On semi-structured behavior, state-of-the-art start-to-end process model discovery techniques yield models that are too complex and unable to match the language of the process. New LPM discovery techniques yield too many models that repeatedly describe the same small fractions of behavior, and are not able to explain all observed behavior. However, it is possible to use sets of larger LPMs that do not have these problems. Therefore, the following requirements need to be met: (1) the individual LPMs should be accurate, (2) the set of LPMs together should maximize coverage, (3) the set of LPMs should minimize redundancy, (4) there should not be too many LPMs in the set, and (5) the LPMs in the set should be related to each other.

It is possible to create a set of LPMs for L_{BPIC12} that satisfies these requirements, but they do not score well on the existing quality measures for LPMs. This indicates that these quality measures do not measure the qualities that our requirements demand. Adapting existing fitness and precision measurement techniques of start-to-end models for use on LPMs yields results that better describe the accuracy of individual LPMs. Accurately determining which events are described by which LPM shows both how well a set of models covers a log, and how much of that log is covered multiple times. These new techniques help distinguish good sets of LPMs from bad.

A major limitation of this paper is that it has only been shown to work on the BPIC12 data set, and has not been tested on other data sets. However, the goal of this paper was to show a new way of thinking about LPMs: not as models of small pieces of an unstructured process, but rather as models of larger chunks of behavior in a semi-structured process.

Our goal in the end is to be able to automatically discover meaningful sets of LPMs, but before we can do that, there are other steps that need to be taken. We need to explore how sets of LPMs work together, and how we can model and visualize this. This will require looking at many different kinds of semi-structured processes to properly understand their differences and similarities. Once we have a formal semantics for sets of LPMs, we can start developing quality criteria to allow us to evaluate the quality of sets of LPMs for comparison between different sets as well as for conformance checking. These quality criteria should be developed in tandem with a set of modeling guidelines, much like 7PMG [10] for start-to-end imperative models, but for sets of LPMs. Once we have quality criteria and guidelines, we can properly formulate what we want from automatic discovery techniques.

References

1. Augusto, A., Conforti, R., Dumas, M., La Rosa, M.: Split miner: discovering accurate and simple business process models from event logs. In: 2017 IEEE International Conference on Data Mining (ICDM), pp. 1–10. IEEE (2017)

2. Brunings, M., Fahland, D., van Dongen, B.F.: Defining meaningful local process models. In: van der Aalst, W.M.P., Bergenthum, R., Carmona, J. (eds.) Proceedings of the International Workshop on Algorithms and Theories for the Analysis of Event Data 2020 Satellite event of the 41st International Conference on Application and Theory of Petri Nets and Concurrency Petri Nets 2020, virtual workshop, 24 June 2020, volume 2625 of CEUR Workshop Proceedings, pp. 6–19. CEUR-WS.org (2020)

3. Debois, S., Hildebrandt, T.T., Laursen, PH., Ulrik, K.R.: Declarative process mining for DCR graphs. In: Proceedings of the SAC 2017 (2017)

4. Fahland, D.: Oclets – scenario-based modeling with petri nets. In: Franceschinis, G., Wolf, K. (eds.) PETRI NETS 2009. LNCS, vol. 5606, pp. 223–242. Springer, Heidelberg (2009). https://doi.org/10.1007/978-3-642-02424-5_14

5. Fahland, D., et al.: Declarative versus imperative process modeling languages: the issue of understandability. In: Halpin, T., et al. (eds.) BPMDS/EMMSAD -2009. LNBIP, vol. 29, pp. 353–366. Springer, Heidelberg (2009). https://doi.org/10.1007/978-3-642-01862-6_29

6. Favre, C., Fahland, D., Völzer, H.: The relationship between workflow graphs and free-choice workflow nets. Inf. Syst. **47**, 197–219 (2015)

7. Leemans, S.J.J., Fahland, D., van der Aalst, W.M.P.: Discovering block-structured process models from event logs containing infrequent behaviour. In: Lohmann, N., Song, M., Wohed, P. (eds.) BPM 2013. LNBIP, vol. 171, pp. 66–78. Springer, Cham (2014). https://doi.org/10.1007/978-3-319-06257-0_6

8. Leno, V., Dumas, M., Maggi, F.M., La Rosa, M., Polyvyanyy, A.: Automated discovery of declarative process models with correlated data conditions. Inf. Syst. **89**, 101482 (2020)

9. Lu, X., et al.: Semi-supervised log pattern detection and exploration using event concurrence and contextual information. In: Panetto, H., et al. (eds.) OTM 2017, Part I. LNCS, vol. 10573, pp. 154–174. Springer, Cham (2017). https://doi.org/10.1007/978-3-319-69462-7_11

10. Mendling, J., Reijers, H.A., van der Aalst, W.M.P.: Seven process modeling guidelines (7PMG). Inf. Softw. Technol. **52**(2), 127–136 (2010)

11. Munoz-Gama, J., et al.: Conformance Checking and Diagnosis in Process Mining. LNBIP, Springer, Cham (2016). https://doi.org/10.1007/978-3-319-49451-7

12. Pesic, M., Schonenberg, H., van der Aalst, W.: Declarative workflow. In: Hofstede, A., Adams, M., Russell, N. (eds.) Modern Business Process Automation. Springer, Heidelberg (2010). https://doi.org/10.1007/978-3-642-03121-

13. Reisig, W.: Understanding Petri Nets - Modeling Techniques, Analysis Methods. Springer, Case Studies. Springer, Heidelberg (2013). https://doi.org/10.1007/978-3-642-33278-4

14. Tax, N., Sidorova, N., Haakma, R., van der Aalst, W.M.P.: Mining local process models. J. Innov. Digit. Ecosyst. **3**(2), 183–196 (2016)

15. Tom, T., Ternis, S.F., Fettke, P., Loos, P.: A comparative analysis of process instance cluster techniques. Wirtschaftsinformatik **2015**, 423–437 (2015)

16. van der Aalst, W.M.P., Adriansyah, A., van Dongen, B.F.: Replaying history on process models for conformance checking and performance analysis. Wiley Interdisc. Rev. Data Min. Knowl. Discov. **2**(2), 182–192 (2012)

17. van Dongen, B.F.: BPI Challenge 2012 (2012)

Distributed Synthesis of Asynchronously Communicating Distributed Process Models

Pieter Kwantes$^{(\boxtimes)}$ and Jetty Kleijn

LIACS, Leiden University, P.O. Box 9512, 2300 RA Leiden, The Netherlands
{p.m.kwantes,h.c.m.kleijn}@liacs.leidenuniv.nl

Abstract. We investigate to what extent existing algorithms for the discovery of component models from event logs can be leveraged to a system of asynchronously communicating components. Here, Enterprise nets model local processes, while Industry nets are compositions of Enterprise nets which interact through asynchronous message passing. We investigate the relation between the behaviour of an Industry net and that of its constituting Enterprise nets and we formalise the (causal) structure of global (Industry net) behaviour in terms of a partial order derived from the message passing. Next, we specify how (existing) algorithms for the discovery of isolated processes, can be adapted to enable the discovery of Enterprise nets, and we demonstrate how to combine these Enterprise nets into an Industry net. Using the results on the structure of the global behaviour, we relate the behaviour of the Industry net thus synthesised to the behaviour of the Enterprise nets and show how fitness of the Enterprise nets (the event log provided as input is included in the behaviour of the discovered net) is preserved as fitness of the Industry net. Moreover, we discuss possible underfitting of the global model (the model exhibits more behaviour than observed in the event log) and show how it can be explained in terms of concurrency between the component models and a completeness property of the event log.

Keywords: Enterprise net · Industry net · process discovery · distributed process · asynchronous communication · partial order

1 Introduction

Industry nets have been introduced in [21] as a framework to model global communication between enterprises where the design of their internal operations is left to the local level. In this set-up, operations at the enterprise level are represented by Enterprise nets (Petri nets with input, output, and internal transitions) and Industry nets are compositions of Enterprise nets that interact by exchanging messages through channels. In [21], a method is proposed to establish global compliance of an Industry net with a reference model by local checks

© Springer-Verlag GmbH Germany, part of Springer Nature 2022
M. Koutny et al. (Eds.): ToPNoC XVI, LNCS 13220, pp. 49–72, 2022.
https://doi.org/10.1007/978-3-662-65303-6_3

(of Enterprise nets) only. In this paper, we focus on the synthesis of an Industry net from the (observed) combined behaviour of a collection of collaborating enterprises.

Business process modelling and process mining are nowadays very active research areas and there are many approaches both to process discovery and conformance checking (see, eg., [6,8,12]). Here, we take advantage of this in the sense that we consider the synthesis of *distributed* processes (in the form of Industry nets) from component processes, while assuming the existence of an algorithm for the discovery of component processes (in the form of Enterprise nets).

To be precise, we assume an algorithm that discovers from an event log (a set of action sequences) a Petri net such that fitness of the discovered Petri net (the event log provided as input is included in the behaviour of the discovered net) is guaranteed. Moreover, we show how from this Petri net an Enterprise net with the same behaviour can be derived. Then, given an event log representing (observed) global behaviour of a distributed process, we first identify the behaviours of its components. Next, we show how an Industry net can be constructed by combining the Enterprise nets discovered from the respective local behaviours, such that fitness is preserved.

In order to be able to relate the given global behaviour to the behaviour of the synthesised Industry net, we first investigate, after the preliminary Sect. 2, in Sects. 3, 4, and 5, the structure of the behaviour of an Industry net in terms of the behaviours of its component Enterprise nets. In Sect. 6, working under the assumption that an algorithm for the discovery of Petri net models from isolated component behaviours is available, we explain how to derive Enterprise nets from these Petri net models. Then we show how these Enterprise nets can be used for the synthesis of Industry nets. Based on the results from the earlier sections, we then argue how fitness of the local models delivered by the original algorithm guarantees the fitness of the distributed model. Moreover, we discuss underfitting of the model (the model exhibits more behaviour than observed in the event log). In the final Sect. 7, we give an overview, compare our set-up with some approaches from the literature and briefly discuss possible future work.

This paper is a revised and extended version of the workshop paper [20]. Proofs and examples have been added. Also a notion of completeness of an event log is added as well as several results on the relationship between completeness and properties of the I-net synthesised from the event log.

2 Preliminaries

$\mathbb{N} = \{0, 1, 2, \ldots\}$ is the set of natural numbers including 0. For $n \in \mathbb{N}$, we set $[n] = \{1, 2, 3, \ldots, n\}$ and if $n = 0$, then $[n] = \emptyset$. The *restriction* of a function $f : A \to B$ to a set $C \subseteq A$, is the function $f|_C : C \to B$, defined by $f|_C(b) = f(b)$ for all $b \in C$. Given a partial order $R \subseteq A \times A$, we refer to a total order $R' \subseteq A \times A$ such that $R \subseteq R'$, as a *linearisation of R*.

An *alphabet* is a finite, non-empty, set of *symbols*. Let Σ be an alphabet. A *word* over Σ is a sequence $w = a_1 \cdots a_n$, with $n \geq 0$ and $a_i \in \Sigma$, for all $i \in [n]$;

we refer to n as the *length* of w, denoted by $|w|$. If $n = 0$ then w is the *empty word* denoted by λ. The set of all words over Σ is denoted as Σ^*. Any subset of Σ^* is a *language* (over Σ). It is often convenient to consider a word $w = a_1 \cdots a_n$ with $a_i \in \Sigma$ for all $i \in [n]$, as a function $w : [n] \to \Sigma$, defined by $w(i) = a_i$ for all $i \in [n]$. The *alphabet* of w is $\mathtt{alph}(w) = \{w(i) \mid i \in [[w]]\}$. Hence $\mathtt{alph}(\lambda) = \emptyset$. For a language L, $\mathtt{Alph}(L) = \bigcup\{\mathtt{alph}(w) \mid w \in L\}$ is the set of all symbols that occur in a word of L.

If a word w is a concatenation of words v_1 and v_2, i.e., $w = v_1 v_2$, then v_1 is said to be a *prefix* of w. The set of all prefixes of w is denoted by $\mathtt{pref}(w)$. The set of all prefixes of a language L is $\mathtt{Pref}(L) = \bigcup\{\mathtt{pref}(w) \mid w \in L\}$.

The number of *occurrences of* $a \in \Sigma$ in $w \in \Sigma^*$ is defined as $\#_a(w) = |\{i \mid w(i) = a\}|$ and *the set of occurrences in* w is $\mathtt{occ}(w) = \{(a,i) \mid a \in \mathtt{alph}(w) \wedge 1 \le i \le \#_a(w)\}$. In addition, we allocate a position with each occurrence in w through the function $\mathtt{pos}_w : \mathtt{occ}(w) \to [[w]]$ as follows: for all $(a,i) \in \mathtt{occ}(w)$, $\mathtt{pos}_w((a,i)) = k$ if $w(k) = a$ and $\#_a(w(1) \cdots w(k)) = i$. Consider eg., $w = abbab$. Then $\mathtt{alph}(w) = \{a,b\}$ and $\mathtt{occ}(w) = \{(a,1),(a,2),(b,1),(b,2),(b,3)\}$. Moreover, $\mathtt{pos}_w((a,1)) = 1$, $\mathtt{pos}_w((a,2)) = 4$, $\mathtt{pos}_w((b,1)) = 2$, $\mathtt{pos}_w((b,2)) = 3$ and $\mathtt{pos}_w((b,3)) = 5$.

For a subset Δ of Σ, the projection of Σ^* on Δ^* is $\mathtt{proj}_{\Sigma,\Delta} : \Sigma^* \to \Delta^*$, defined by $\mathtt{proj}_{\Sigma,\Delta}(a) = a$ if $a \in \Delta$, $\mathtt{proj}_{\Sigma,\Delta}(a) = \lambda$ if $a \in (\Sigma \setminus \Delta) \cup \{\lambda\}$, and $\mathtt{proj}_{\Sigma,\Delta}(wa) = \mathtt{proj}_{\Sigma,\Delta}(w)\mathtt{proj}_{\Sigma,\Delta}(a)$ whenever $w \in \Sigma^*$ and $a \in \Sigma$. We omit the subscript Σ if it is clear from the context and thus write $\mathtt{proj}_\Delta(w)$ instead of $\mathtt{proj}_{\Sigma,\Delta}(w)$. The notation is extended to languages $L \subseteq \Sigma^*$ by $\mathtt{proj}_\Delta(L) = \{\mathtt{proj}_\Delta(w) \mid w \in L\}$. As an example, let $L = \{abbab, abcbdab, cbbbad\}$. Then $\mathtt{proj}_{\{a\}}(L) = \{a, aa\}$, $\mathtt{proj}_{\{a,b\}}(L) = \{abbab, bbba\}$, and $\mathtt{proj}_{\{c,d\}}(L) = \{cd\}$.

Petri Nets. A Petri net is a triple $N = (P,T,F)$, where P is a finite set of *places*, T is a finite non-empty set of *transitions* such that $P \cap T = \emptyset$, and $F \subseteq (P \times T) \cup (T \times P)$ is a set of arcs.

Let $N = (P,T,F)$ be a Petri net. If $N' = (P',T',F')$ is a Petri net such that $P \cup T$ and $P' \cup T'$ have no elements in common, then N and N' are *disjoint*. Let $x \in P \cup T$. Then ${}^\bullet x = \{y \mid (y,x) \in F\}$ and $x^\bullet = \{y \mid (x,y) \in F\}$ are the *preset* and the *postset*, respectively, of x (in N). A *marking* μ of N is a function $\mu : P \to \mathbb{N}$. Let $t \in T$ and μ a marking of N. Then t is *enabled* at μ if $\mu(p) > 0$ for all $p \in {}^\bullet t$. If t is enabled at μ, it may *occur*, and thus lead to a new marking μ' of N, denoted $\mu \xrightarrow{t}_N \mu'$, with $\mu'(p) = \mu(p) - 1$ if $p \in {}^\bullet t \setminus t^\bullet$; $\mu'(p) = \mu(p) + 1$ if $p \in t^\bullet \setminus {}^\bullet t$; and $\mu'(p) = \mu(p)$ otherwise. We extend the notation $\mu \xrightarrow{t}_N \mu'$ to sequences $w \in T^*$ as follows[1]: $\mu \xrightarrow{\lambda}_N \mu$ for all μ; and $\mu \xrightarrow{wt}_N \mu'$ for markings μ, μ' of N, $w \in T^*$ and $t \in T$, whenever there is a marking μ'' such that $\mu \xrightarrow{w}_N \mu''$ and $\mu'' \xrightarrow{t}_N \mu'$. If $\mu \xrightarrow{w}_N \mu'$, for some $w \in T^*$, then w is a *firing sequence (in N)* from μ to μ' and μ' is said to be *reachable from* μ (in N). If N is clear from the context, we may omit the subscript N and write $\xrightarrow{w}$ rather than $\xrightarrow{w}_N$. We write $\mathcal{L}(N,\mu)$ for $\{w \in T^* \mid \mu \xrightarrow{w}_N \mu'$ for some marking $\mu'\}$. A place $p \in P$ is a *source*

---

[1] We thus view T as an alphabet.

place of N if $^\bullet p = \emptyset$. The marking μ of N such that, for all $p \in P$, $\mu(p) = 1$ if p is a source place and $\mu(p) = 0$ otherwise, is the *default initial marking* of N. If μ is the default initial marking of N, we also write $\mathcal{L}(N)$ to denote $\mathcal{L}(N, \mu)$ and refer to it as the behaviour or *language* of N. Note that $\mathcal{L}(N)$ is *prefix-closed*, i.e., $w \in \mathcal{L}(N)$ implies $v \in \mathcal{L}(N)$ for all prefixes v of w.

Enterprise Nets and Industry Nets. We recall the definitions of Enterprise and Industry nets from [21]. Enterprise nets (or E-nets, for short) are Petri nets equipped for asynchronous communication with other E-nets; they have transitions designated to receive input and transitions designated to produce output. An interaction between E-nets is realised by an occurrence of an output transition of one E-net and an occurrence of an input transition of another E-net that is connected to the output transition by a dedicated intermediate place and that has a matching *message type*.

Throughout this paper, we assume a fixed set $\mathcal{M}$ of message types.

Definition 1. *An Enterprise net is a tuple $\mathcal{E} = (P, \langle T_{int}, T_{inp}, T_{out} \rangle, F, M)$ such that $T_{int}, T_{inp},$ and T_{out} are mutually disjoint sets; T_{int} is the set of internal transitions of $\mathcal{E}$, T_{inp} its set of input transitions, and T_{out} its set of output transitions; furthermore, the underlying Petri net of $\mathcal{E}$, $und(\mathcal{E}) = (P, T_{int} \cup T_{inp} \cup T_{out}, F)$, is a Petri net with exactly one source place; finally $M : T_{inp} \cup T_{out} \to \mathcal{M}$ is the communication function of $\mathcal{E}$.* $\square$

Given an Enterprise net $\mathcal{E}$, $\mathcal{L}(\mathcal{E}) = \mathcal{L}(und(\mathcal{E}))$ is *the language of $\mathcal{E}$*.

Composing E-nets yields an Industry-net (or I-net, for short) with multiple source places. The E-nets involved are pairwise disjoint, i.e., their underlying Petri nets are disjoint. When combining them into an I-net, output and input transitions are matched via their message types.

Definition 2. *Let $n \geq 2$. Let $V = \{\mathcal{E}_i \mid i \in [n]\}$ be a set of pairwise disjoint E-nets with $\mathcal{E}_i = (P_i, \langle T_{i,int}, T_{i,inp}, T_{i,out} \rangle, F_i, M_i)$ for each $i \in [n]$.*
A matching over V is a bijection $\varphi : \bigcup_{i \in [n]} T_{i,out} \to \bigcup_{j \in [n]} T_{j,inp}$ such that whenever $t \in T_{i,out}$ and $\varphi(t) \in T_{j,inp}$, for some i, j, then $i \neq j$ and $M_i(t) = M_j(\varphi(t))$. $\square$

A set V of mutually disjoint E-nets is said to be *composable* if there exists a matching over V. To construct an I-net from a composable set V and a matching φ over V, matching output and input transitions of the E-nets in V are connected through (new) channel places using channel arcs.

Definition 3. *Let $n \geq 2$. Let $V = \{\mathcal{E}_i : i \in [n]\}$ be a composable set of E-nets with $\mathcal{E}_i = (P_i, \langle T_{i,int}, T_{i,inp}, T_{i,out} \rangle, F_i, M_i)$ and $T_i = T_{i,int} \cup T_{i,inp} \cup T_{i,out}$ for all $i \in [n]$. Let φ be a matching over V.*
Then $P(V, \varphi) = \{[t, \varphi(t)] \mid t \in T_{i,out}, i \in [n]\}$ is the set of channel places of V and φ, and $F(V, \varphi) = \{(t, [t, \varphi(t)]) \mid t \in T_{i,out}, i \in [n]\} \cup \{([t, \varphi(t)], \varphi(t)) \mid t \in T_{i,out}, i \in [n]\}$ is the set of channel arcs of V and φ. The sets $P(V, \varphi)$, $F(V, \varphi)$, and P_i, T_i, F_i, where $i \in [n]$, are all pairwise disjoint.

The Industry net over (V, φ) *is the Petri net* $\mathcal{I}(V, \varphi) = (P, T, F)$ *with* $P = \bigcup_{i \in [n]} P_i \cup P(V, \varphi)$, $T = \bigcup_{i \in [n]} T_i$, *and* $F = \bigcup_{i \in [n]} F_i \cup F(V, \varphi)$.   □

Example 1. Consider two enterprises, an Investment Firm and an Exchange modelled by the E-nets $\mathcal{E}_1$ and $\mathcal{E}_2$ in Figs. 1(a) and 1(b), respectively. The Investment Firm sends order messages to the Exchange (modelled by output transition **so** with message type m_o). The Exchange, upon receiving a message (via input transition **ro** with message type m_o), subsequently sends an order confirmation message to the Investment Firm (output transition **sc** with message type m_c). This message can be received by the Investment Firm through input transition **rc** with message type m_c. Then $\mathcal{I}(V, \varphi)$, the I-net in Fig. 1(c), with $V = \{\mathcal{E}_1, \mathcal{E}_2\}$ and φ defined by $\varphi(\mathbf{so}) = \mathbf{ro}$ and $\varphi(\mathbf{sc}) = \mathbf{rc}$, models the collaboration between the Investment Firm and the Exchange. Note that this V allows for only one matching.   □

Related models. E-nets can be considered as a generalisation of *workflow nets*. Workflow nets (see [7]) are Petri nets with a single source place. They, moreover, have a single sink place (i.e., a place p with $p^\bullet = \emptyset$) and a default final marking that assigns a single token to the sink place. Additional requirements are that all places and transitions are on a path from source to sink and that the final marking is an always reachable marking. These (so-called soundness) criteria are not a priori imposed on E-nets. All possible firing sequences reflect possible behaviour and the language of an E-net is always prefix-closed. E-nets, moreover, explicitly capture the potential interaction with other enterprises by a bilateral, asynchronous exchange of messages of a specified type (for applications, see eg., [13,18,24,28]). With the term "industry" used to loosely refer to a sector of enterprises, Industry nets model collaborating Enterprise nets. Overall, the ideas underlying the concepts of E-nets and I-nets belong to a well-established branch of research concerned with composing systems modelled as Petri nets, into larger correctly functioning (concurrent) systems [14,15,26,27]. An overview of how this line of research is concerned with combining compatible business processes (or services) in Service Oriented Architectures' can be found in [3].

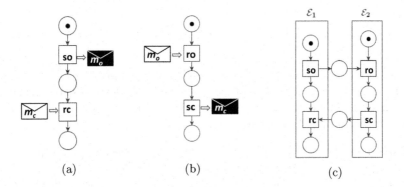

Fig. 1. (a) E-net $\mathcal{E}_1$. (b) E-net $\mathcal{E}_2$. (c) The I-net

Open Petri nets, introduced in [9], are proposed in [16] as a formalization of workflows with a capability to interact with other workflows through *open places*. The composition of open Petri nets is characterised as a pushout in the corresponding category, suitable to model both interaction through open places and synchronization of transitions. Decomposing Petri nets into *functional Petri nets* to speed up analysis is described in [30,31]. Compositions of *open workflow nets*, a model similar to functional Petri nets, are considered in [1,23,29]. Functional Petri nets have disjoint sets of input places and output places and composition is based on identifying corresponding elements. In [15], I/O-Petri nets which are similar to I-nets, are considered. These nets have transitions as interface elements that have input and output labels and communicate via places. The advantage of this approach, as argued in [15], is that it leads to a better separation of concerns: eg., the designer of a local system does not have to consider how it will be used; this is a concern for the designer of the global system. Composition of Petri nets by sharing places in [9,16,23] or by connecting transitions through channel places as in [15] and our approach, models *asynchronous communication* between the component nets.

3   E-net Languages and I-net Languages

Let the composable system V, specified as in Definition 3, and the matching φ over V be fixed for this section and Sects. 4 and 5.

Clearly, the construction of $\mathcal{I}(V, \varphi)$ does not affect the internal structure of the E-nets in V and the set of source places of $\mathcal{I}(V, \varphi)$ consists of all source places of the $\mathcal{E}_i$. Moreover, removing channel places from $\mathcal{I}(V, \varphi)$ does not restrict the behaviour of its E-nets. In other words, if $\mu \xrightarrow{w} \mu'$ in $\mathcal{I}(V, \varphi)$, then $\mu|_{P_i} \xrightarrow{proj_{T_i}(w)} \mu'|_{P_i}$ in $\mathcal{E}_i$. Consequently, the firing sequences in $\mathcal{L}(\mathcal{I}(V, \varphi))$ are combinations of firing sequences of the Enterprise nets. Actually, as formulated in the next lemma, this statement can be strengthened to include all prefixes of firing sequences in $\mathcal{L}(\mathcal{I}(V, \varphi))$, because $\mathtt{proj}_{T_i}(v) \in \mathtt{pref}(\mathtt{proj}_{T_i}(w))$, for all $v, w \in T^*$ such that $v \in \mathtt{pref}(w)$, and $\mathcal{L}(\mathcal{I}(V, \varphi))$ and $\mathcal{L}(\mathcal{E}_i)$, $i \in [n]$, are prefix-closed.

Lemma 1. *If $w \in \mathcal{L}(\mathcal{I}(V, \varphi))$, then $\mathtt{proj}_{T_i}(v) \in \mathcal{L}(\mathcal{E}_i)$ for all $v \in \mathtt{pref}(w)$ and all $i \in [n]$.* □

However, the composition of E-nets into an I-net adds channel places to the presets of input transitions. The property defined next describes how the number of occurrences of input transitions depends on the number of occurrences of corresponding output transitions.

Definition 4. *Let $w \in T^*$. Then w has the* prefix property *with respect to φ if $\#_a(v) \geq \#_{\varphi(a)}(v)$ for all $v \in \mathtt{pref}(w)$ and all $a \in T_{out}$.*
A language $L \subseteq T^*$ has the prefix property with respect to φ if all $w \in L$ have this property. □

In other words, w has the prefix property with respect to φ if $\#_b(v) \leq \#_{\varphi^{-1}(b)}(v)$ for all prefixes v of w and all $b \in T_{inp}$. Clearly, if w has the prefix property with respect to φ, then all its prefixes have this property as well.

Henceforth, we will omit the reference to φ as it is fixed.

Since channel places are not source places and consequently not marked by the default initial marking, it follows that the firing sequences of $\mathcal{I}(V, \varphi)$ have the prefix property.

Lemma 2. *If $w \in \mathcal{L}(\mathcal{I}(V, \varphi))$, then w has the prefix property.*   □

Conversely, any sequence $w \in T^*$ that can be (locally) executed by all E-nets and that satisfies the prefix property, belongs to $\mathcal{L}(\mathcal{I}(V, \varphi))$.

Lemma 3. *Let $w \in T^*$ be such that $\mathrm{proj}_{T_i}(w) \in \mathcal{L}(\mathcal{E}_i)$ for all $i \in [n]$. If w has the prefix property, then $w \in \mathcal{L}(\mathcal{I}(V, \varphi))$.*

Proof. If $w = \lambda$ then $w \in \mathcal{L}(\mathcal{I}(V, \varphi))$. Assume now that $w = xa$ with $|x| \geq 0$ and $a \in T_k$ for some $k \in [n]$, and that w has the prefix property. Then x being a prefix of w, has the prefix property as well. Moreover, by Lemma 1, $\mathrm{proj}_{T_i}(x) \in \mathcal{L}(\mathcal{E}_i)$, for all $i \in [n]$. Hence, we may assume by an inductive argument that $x \in \mathcal{L}(\mathcal{I}(V, \varphi))$. Consequently, there exist a marking μ' of $\mathcal{I}(V, \varphi)$ such that $\mu \xrightarrow{x} \mu'$ in $\mathcal{I}(V, \varphi)$, where μ is the default initial marking of $\mathcal{I}(V, \varphi)$. This implies that $\mu|_{P_k} \xrightarrow{\mathrm{proj}_{T_k}(x)} \mu'|_{P_k}$ in $\mathcal{E}_k$ with $\mu|_{P_k}$ the default initial marking of $\mathcal{E}_k$. By assumption $\mathrm{proj}_{T_k}(w) = \mathrm{proj}_{T_k}(xa) = \mathrm{proj}_{T_k}(x)a \in \mathcal{L}(\mathcal{E}_k)$ and so a is enabled at $\mu'|_{P_k}$ in $\mathcal{E}_k$. We distinguish two cases:

(i) If $a \notin T_{inp}$, it directly follows that a is enabled at μ' thus $w \in \mathcal{L}(\mathcal{I}(V, \varphi))$.
(ii) If $a \in T_{inp}$, then it has a corresponding output transition $t = \varphi^{-1}(a)$ in some $\mathcal{E}_i$ and a channel place $[t, a] \notin P_k$ such that $(t, [t, a]), ([t, a], a) \in F$. Note that a is otherwise only connnected to places in P_k. Since w has the prefix property, $\#_a(w) \leq \#_t(w)$. So $\#_a(x) < \#_t(x)$. Hence $\mu'([t, a]) > 0$, and a is enabled at μ'. Consequently, also in this case, $w \in \mathcal{L}(\mathcal{I}(V, \varphi))$.   □

Example 2. (Ex. 1 ctd.) We have $T_1 = \{\mathbf{so}, \mathbf{rc}\}$, $T_2 = \{\mathbf{ro}, \mathbf{sc}\}$ (with T_1 and T_2 the transitions of $\mathcal{E}_1$ and $\mathcal{E}_2$ from Example 1 respectively), and $T = \{\mathbf{so}, \mathbf{rc}, \mathbf{ro}, \mathbf{sc}\}$. Consider $w = \langle \mathbf{so}, \mathbf{ro}, \mathbf{sc}, \mathbf{rc} \rangle$.[2] Now $\mathrm{proj}_{T_1}(w) = \langle \mathbf{so}, \mathbf{rc} \rangle \in \mathcal{L}(\mathcal{E}_1)$ and $\mathrm{proj}_{T_2}(w) = \langle \mathbf{ro}, \mathbf{sc} \rangle \in \mathcal{L}(\mathcal{E}_1)$. Clearly, w has the prefix property. Thus $w \in \mathcal{L}(\mathcal{I}(V, \varphi))$ by Lemma 3. For $w' = \langle \mathbf{so}, \mathbf{ro}, \mathbf{rc}, \mathbf{sc} \rangle$, we have $\mathrm{proj}_{T_1}(w') = \mathrm{proj}_{T_1}(w)$ and $\mathrm{proj}_{T_2}(w') = \mathrm{proj}_{T_2}(w)$. However, w' does not have the prefix property: in $u = \langle \mathbf{so}, \mathbf{ro}, \mathbf{rc} \rangle$, a prefix of w', we have $\#_{\mathbf{rc}}(u) = 1$, but $\#_{\mathbf{sc}}(u) = 0$. Indeed, $w' \notin \mathcal{L}(\mathcal{I}(V, \varphi))$.   □

The next theorem is an immediate consequence of Lemmas 1, 2, and 3.

---

[2] The elements of the alphabet T are symbols consisting of two letters. We denote in this and similar examples, any sequence $a_1 \cdots a_n$ with $a_i \in T$ for each $i \in [n]$ by $\langle a_1, \cdots, a_n \rangle$.

Theorem 1. *Let $L \subseteq T^*$. Then $L \subseteq \mathcal{L}(\mathcal{I}(V, \varphi))$ if and only if L has the prefix property and $\mathrm{proj}_{T_i}(L) \subseteq \mathcal{L}(\mathcal{E}_i)$ for all $i \in [n]$.* □

In case there exists a language L that has the prefix property and is such that $\mathrm{proj}_{T_i}(L) = \mathcal{L}(\mathcal{E}_i)$ for all $i \in [n]$, the behaviour of the I-net encompasses the full unrestricted behaviour of each E-net. This is captured in Theorem 2.

Theorem 2. *Let $L \subseteq T^*$ be a language with the prefix property and let $\mathrm{proj}_{T_i}(L) = \mathcal{L}(\mathcal{E}_i)$ for all $i \in [n]$. Then $\mathrm{proj}_{T_i}(\mathcal{L}(\mathcal{I}(V, \varphi))) = \mathcal{L}(\mathcal{E}_i)$ for all $i \in [n]$.*

Proof. $L \subseteq \mathcal{L}(\mathcal{I}(V, \varphi))$ follows from Theorem 1. Hence, for all $i \in [n]$, $\mathrm{proj}_{T_i}(L) \subseteq \mathrm{proj}_{T_i}(\mathcal{L}(\mathcal{I}(V, \varphi)))$. By Lemma 1, $\mathrm{proj}_{T_i}(\mathcal{L}(\mathcal{I}(V, \varphi))) \subseteq \mathcal{L}(\mathcal{E}_i)$ for all $i \in [n]$. By assumption $\mathrm{proj}_{T_i}(L) = \mathcal{L}(\mathcal{E}_i)$ for all $i \in [n]$. Thus $\mathcal{L}(\mathcal{E}_i) \subseteq \mathrm{proj}_{T_i}(\mathcal{L}(\mathcal{I}(V, \varphi))) \subseteq \mathcal{L}(\mathcal{E}_i)$ for all $i \in [n]$ and the statement follows. □

It should however be noted, that the conditions on L in Theorem 2 do not imply that $L = \mathcal{L}(\mathcal{I}(V, \varphi))$. By Theorem 1, $L \subseteq \mathcal{L}(\mathcal{I}(V, \varphi))$, and as illustrated in the following example, this inclusion may be strict even in case L satisfies the conditions from Theorem 2.

Example 3. Consider a collaboration between three enterprises, an Investment Firm, an Exchange and a *Central Securities Depository* (modelled by E-nets $\mathcal{E}_1$, $\mathcal{E}_2$ and $\mathcal{E}_3$ respectively, with transitions $T_1 = \{\mathbf{so}, \mathbf{rc}, \mathbf{rs}\}$, $T_2 = \{\mathbf{ro}, \mathbf{sc}, \mathbf{si}\}$ and $T_3 = \{\mathbf{ri}, \mathbf{ss}\}$) represented by the I-net in Fig. 2. The interaction between the Investment Firm and the Exchange is the same as in Example 2. After sending a confirmation (output transition $\mathbf{sc}$) to the Investment Firm, the Exchange can send (output transition $\mathbf{si}$) a settlement instruction to the Central Securities Depository to transfer ordered securities to the Investment Firm. The Central Securities Depository - after receiving (input transition $\mathbf{ri}$ matching $\mathbf{si}$) the settlement instruction - sends (output transition $\mathbf{ss}$) a confirmation of settlement to the Investment Firm (that receives the message via input transition $\mathbf{rs}$). Let $w = \langle \mathbf{so}, \mathbf{ro}, \mathbf{sc}, \mathbf{rc}, \mathbf{si}, \mathbf{ri}, \mathbf{ss}, \mathbf{rs} \rangle$ and let $L = \mathrm{pref}(\{w\})$.

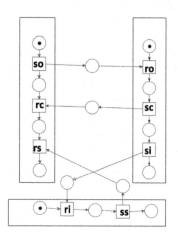

Fig. 2. The extended I-net

Clearly $proj_{T_i}(L) = \mathcal{L}(\mathcal{E}_i)$ for each $i \in [3]$. Also, L has the prefix property (w.r.t. φ displayed in Fig. 2). Hence L satisfies the conditions in Theorem 2, and, indeed, $proj_{T_i}(\mathcal{L}(\mathcal{I}(\{\mathcal{E}_1, \mathcal{E}_2, \mathcal{E}_3\}, \varphi))) = proj_{T_i}(L)$ for each $i \in [3]$. Now, consider the sequence $v = \langle \mathbf{so}, \mathbf{ro}, \mathbf{sc}, \mathbf{si}, \mathbf{rc}, \mathbf{ri}, \mathbf{ss}, \mathbf{rs} \rangle$, obtained by exchanging the occurrences of $\mathbf{rc}$ and $\mathbf{si}$ in w. It is easy to see that v is also in the language of the I-net in Fig. 2. Hence this I-net exhibits behaviour not included in L.   □

4   Structuring Words with the Prefix Property

In this section, we identify a property of I-net languages that explains why the conditions of Theorem 2 imposed on L are not sufficient to guarantee that $L = \mathcal{L}(\mathcal{I}(V, \varphi))$. First, we demonstrate how the occurrences in words with the prefix property, can be seen as partially ordered sets. The occurrences $\mathbf{rc}$ and $\mathbf{si}$ in the word w from Example 3, can be exchanged (to obtain v) because they are unrelated in this partial order (i.e., they are from different components and not connected by an input/output relation with each other, see Example 6 below). We will show that any word obtained from a word in $\mathcal{L}(\mathcal{I}(V, \varphi))$, by exchanging unrelated occurrences, is included in $\mathcal{L}(\mathcal{I}(V, \varphi))$. To define the partial order, we introduce the notion of an assignment function. Whereas the prefix property is based on a simple comparison of numbers of occurrences, assignment functions, as defined next, relate each occurrence of an input transition to a corresponding occurrence of an output transition.

Definition 5. *An* assignment function *with respect to φ for a word $w \in T^*$ is an injective function $\theta : (\mathrm{occ}(w) \cap (T_{inp} \times \mathbb{N})) \to (\mathrm{occ}(w) \cap (T_{out} \times \mathbb{N}))$ such that for every occurrence $(b, j) \in \mathrm{occ}(w)$ with $b \in T_{inp}$, $\theta(b, j) = (a, i)$ implies that $a = \varphi^{-1}(b)$ and i is such that $\mathrm{pos}_w(a, i) < \mathrm{pos}_w(b, j)$.*   □

Again, since φ is fixed, we will omit the reference to φ.

Example 4. Assume $T = \{a, b\}$ and $\varphi(a) = b$. Let $w = aabb$. Then w has two assignment functions: θ defined by $\theta(b, 1) = (a, 1)$ and $\theta(b, 2) = (a, 2)$; and θ' defined by $\theta'(b, 1) = (a, 2)$ and $\theta'(b, 2) = (a, 1)$.   □

The notion of an assignment function is closely related to the prefix property, as captured in Theorem 3.

Theorem 3. *Let $w \in T^*$. Then w has the prefix property if and only if there exists an assignment function for w.*

Proof. Let θ be an assignment function for w. Since θ is injective, we have that for every input transition b and every $1 \le j \le \#_b(w)$, the j-th occurrence (b, j) of b in w is preceded by at least j occurrences of output transition $\varphi^{-1}(b)$. In other words $\#_b(u) \le \#_{\varphi^{-1}(b)}(u)$ for every prefix u of w as desired.

Next, assume that w has the prefix property and consider the function θ with domain $\mathrm{occ}(w) \cap (T_{inp} \times \mathbb{N})$ defined by $\theta(b, j) = (\varphi^{-1}(b), j)$ for all $(b, j) \in \mathrm{occ}(w) \cap (T_{inp} \times \mathbb{N})$. As we argue next, θ is an assignment function for w.

Let $(b, j) \in occ(w)$ with $b \in T_{inp}$. Hence there exists a prefix xb of w such that $\#_b(xb) = j$. Since w has the prefix property, $\#_b(xb) \leq \#_{\varphi^{-1}(b)}(xb)$, thus $\#_{\varphi^{-1}(b)}(xb) \geq j$ and therefore $\mathrm{pos}_w(\varphi^{-1}(b), j) < \mathrm{pos}_w(b, j)$ as required. $\qquad\square$

Theorem 3 implies that every word with the prefix property has an assignment function. As Example 4 shows, in general, each such word can have more than one assignment function. We will now show how each assignment function θ for a word w determines a partial order on $occ(w)$. First the relation $\leq_{w,\theta}$ is defined.

Definition 6. *Let $w \in T^*$ and let θ be an assignment function for w. Let $(a, i), (b, j) \in occ(w)$, with $a \in T_k$ and $b \in T_l$ for some $k, l \in [n]$.*
    Then $(a, i) \leq_{w,\theta} (b, j)$ if

(1) $k = l$ and $\mathrm{pos}_w(a, i) \leq \mathrm{pos}_w(b, j)$ or
(2) $k \neq l$ and $b \in T_{inp}$ and $\theta(b, j) = (a, i)$. $\qquad\square$

By condition (1), $\leq_{w,\theta}$ respects the ordering of occurrences of transitions in w that originate from the same E-net; by (2), it fixes the order between an occurrence of an input transition and its assigned output transition occurrence. As usual, $\leq_{w,\theta}^+$ denotes the transitive closure of $\leq_{w,\theta}$. The following lemma states that $\leq_{w,\theta}^+$ moreover respects the relative position of all occurrences in w.

Lemma 4. *Let $w \in T^*$ and let θ be an assignment function for w. Then $x \leq_{w,\theta}^+ y$ implies $\mathrm{pos}_w(x) \leq \mathrm{pos}_w(y)$, for all $x, y \in occ(w)$.*

Proof. Let $x, y \in occ(w)$ and assume $x \leq_{w,\theta}^+ y$ holds. So, there exist occurrences $o_1, \ldots, o_m$ in $occ(w)$, with $m \leq |w|$, such that $o_1 = x$, $o_m = y$ and $o_i \leq_{w,\theta} o_{i+1}$, for all $i \in [m-1]$. Hence, using Definition 6 and Definition 5, it follows that $\mathrm{pos}_w(o_i) \leq \mathrm{pos}_w(o_{i+1})$, for all $i \in [m-1]$. Since $\leq$ is a total order on the positions of w, we have $\mathrm{pos}_w(x) \leq \mathrm{pos}_w(y)$. $\qquad\square$

Using this observation, we can now prove that indeed $\leq_{w,\theta}^+$ is a partial order on the occurrences of w.

Lemma 5. *Let $w \in T^*$ and let θ be an assignment function for w. Then $\leq_{w,\theta}^+$ is a partial order on $occ(w)$.*

Proof. From condition (1) in Definition 6 it follows that $\leq_{w,\theta}^+$ is reflexive, while transitivity is immediate. Let $x \leq_{w,\theta}^+ y$ and $y \leq_{w,\theta}^+ x$ for some $x, y \in occ(w)$. By Lemma 4, $\mathrm{pos}_w(x) = \mathrm{pos}_w(y)$ and so $x = y$. Hence $\leq_{w,\theta}^+$ is anti-symmetric. $\qquad\square$

By Lemmas 4 and 5, given an assignment function θ for w, the partial order $\leq_{w,\theta}^+$ is a subset of the total order induced by pos_w. The linearisations of $\leq_{w,\theta}^+$, where w is a word and θ an assignment function for w, are those words that can be obtained from w by (repeatedly) interchanging the positions of occurrences not related by $\leq_{w,\theta}^+$.

Definition 7. *Let $w \in T^*$ and let θ be an assignment function for w. Then* $\text{lin}_\theta(w) = \{v \in T^* \mid \text{occ}(v) = \text{occ}(w) \text{ and for all } x, y \in \text{occ}(v), x \leq^+_{w,\theta} y \text{ implies } \text{pos}_v(x) \leq \text{pos}_v(y)\}$ *is the set of θ-linearisations of w.* ☐

The next example shows that if v is a θ-linearisation of w than w is also a θ-linearisation of v.

Example 5. (Ex. 4 ctd.) Let $v = abab$. Then $\text{occ}(v) = \text{occ}(w)$ and $\text{lin}_\theta(w) = \{v, w\}$. Clearly, θ is an assignment function for v and $\text{lin}_\theta(v) = \text{lin}_\theta(w)$. Note that $\text{lin}_{\theta'}(w) = \{w\}$ and θ' is not an assignment function for v. ☐

We now turn to the proof of the main result of this section by which for every firing sequence w of an I-net and each of the assignment functions θ of w, also all its θ-linearisations are firing sequences of the I-net. We first list some basic properties of linearisations.

Lemma 6. *Let w and θ be as in Definition 7 and let $v \in \text{lin}_\theta(w)$. Then the following statements hold:*

(1) $w \in \text{lin}_\theta(w)$;
(2) $\text{proj}_{T_i}(v) = \text{proj}_{T_i}(w)$ for all $i \in [n]$;
(3) θ is an assignment function for v and $\leq_{v,\theta} = \leq_{w,\theta}$;
(4) $\text{lin}_\theta(v) = \text{lin}_\theta(w)$;
(5) v has the prefix property.

Proof. (1) follows directly from Definition 7 and Lemma 4.

(2) is proved by contradiction. Assume (2) to be false and let $k \in [n]$ be such that $\text{proj}_{T_k}(v) \neq \text{proj}_{T_k}(w)$. Since $\text{occ}(v) = \text{occ}(w)$ by Definition 7, this implies that there are $x, y, z \in T^*$ and $a, b \in T_k$, such that $\text{proj}_{T_k}(v) = xay$ and $\text{proj}_{T_k}(w) = xbz$ with $a \neq b$. Moreover, $\text{occ}(v) = \text{occ}(w)$ implies that $\text{occ}(\text{proj}_{T_k}(v)) = \text{occ}(\text{proj}_{T_k}(w))$, i.e., $\text{occ}(xay) = \text{occ}(xbz)$. Let now $\#_a(xa) = i$ and $\#_b(xb) = j$. Then $\text{pos}_{xay}((b, j)) > |xa|$ and $\text{pos}_{xbz}((a, i)) > |xb|$. Thus $\text{pos}_v(a, i) < \text{pos}_v(b, j)$ and $\text{pos}_w(b, j) < \text{pos}_w(a, i)$. The latter inequality combined with condition (1) from Definition 6 shows that $(b, j) \leq^+_{w,\theta} (a, i)$. Hence the first inequality implies that $v \notin \text{lin}_\theta(w)$ by Definition 7, a contradiction. Consequently, (2) must be true.

(3) Let $(b, j) \in \text{occ}(v) = \text{occ}(w)$ with $b \in T_{inp}$ and let $\theta(b, j) = (a, i)$. Since θ is an assignment function for w, it follows from condition (2) from Definition 6 that $(a, i) \leq_{w,\theta} (b, j)$. With $v \in \text{lin}_\theta(w)$ this implies that $\text{pos}_v(a, i) \leq \text{pos}_v(b, j)$. Hence θ is an assignment function for v.
Next we investigate $\leq_{v,\theta}$ (which is defined because θ is an assignment function for v). Let $x, y \in \text{occ}(v) = \text{occ}(w)$ with $x = (a, i)$ and $y = (b, j)$ where $a \in T_k$ and $b \in T_l$ with $k, l \in [n]$.
Firstly, assume $x \leq_{w,\theta} y$. Then $\text{pos}_v(x) \leq \text{pos}_v(y)$, because $v \in \text{lin}_\theta(w)$. In case $k = l$, $x \leq_{v,\theta} y$ by condition (1) of Definition 6. If $k \neq l$, then $x \leq_{w,\theta} y$ must be a consequence of $\theta(b, j) = (a, i)$ (condition (2) of Definition 6) and hence also $x \leq_{v,\theta} y$.
Secondly, assume $x \leq_{v,\theta} y$. In case $k = l$, $\text{pos}_v(x) \leq \text{pos}_v(y)$ by condition

(1) of Definition 6. We claim that also $\mathbf{pos}_w(x) \leq \mathbf{pos}_w(y)$: if not, then $\mathbf{pos}_w(y) < \mathbf{pos}_w(x)$ which would imply $x \neq y$ and $y \leq_{w,\theta} x$ by condition (1) of Definition 6 and hence $\mathbf{pos}_v(y) < \mathbf{pos}_v(x)$, because $v \in lin_\theta(w)$, a contradiction. From $\mathbf{pos}_w(x) \leq \mathbf{pos}_w(y)$ and condition (1) of Definition 6, it follows that $x \leq_{w,\theta} y$. Finally, let $k \neq l$. Then $x = \theta(y)$ follows from $x \leq_{v,\theta} y$ and condition (2) of Definition 6. This implies that also $x \leq_{w,\theta} y$.

(4) Follows from the definitions of $lin_\theta(w)$ and $lin_\theta(v)$ since $occ(v) = occ(w)$ and $\leq_{v,\theta} = \leq_{w,\theta}$ by (3).

(5) follows from (3) and Theorem 3.   □

Combining Lemma 6 with Lemma 3 shows that whenever a word with the prefix property can be locally executed by all component E-nets, then, for all its assignment functions θ, each of its θ-linearisations can be executed globally by the I-net.

Theorem 4. *Let $w \in T^*$ be such that $\mathbf{proj}_{T_i}(w) \in \mathcal{L}(\mathcal{E}_i)$ for all $i \in [n]$. If θ is an assignment function for w, then $lin_\theta(w) \subseteq \mathcal{L}(\mathcal{I}(V, \varphi))$.*

Proof. Assume θ is an assignment function for w. Let $v \in lin_\theta(w)$. From Lemma 6(2) it follows that $\mathbf{proj}_{T_i}(v) = \mathbf{proj}_{T_i}(w)$ for all $i \in [n]$ and from Lemma 6(5) that v has the prefix property. Using Lemma 3, we can then conclude that $v \in \mathcal{L}(\mathcal{I}(V, \varphi))$.   □

Example 6. (Ex. 3 ctd.) Consider the word w from Example 3. Define θ by $\theta(\mathbf{ro}, 1) = (\mathbf{so}, 1)$, $\theta(\mathbf{rc}, 1) = (\mathbf{sc}, 1)$, $\theta(\mathbf{ri}, 1) = (\mathbf{si}, 1)$, and $\theta(\mathbf{rs}, 1) = (\mathbf{ss}, 1)$. This θ is an (the only) assignment function for w (w.r.t. φ). Then v, obtained from w by exchanging $(\mathbf{si}, 1)$ and $(\mathbf{rc}, 1)$. These occurrences are not ordered by $\leq_{w,\theta}^+$. Hence $v \in lin_\theta(w)$ and v is, like w, in the language of the I-net.   □

5   Assignment Functions of Type FIFO

By Theorem 4, every assignment function θ for a word w (with the prefix property) that can be locally executed by all component E-nets, determines a set of words $lin_\theta(w)$ that can be executed by the I-net. In this section, we demonstrate that considering one particular type of assignment function is sufficient to describe all possible linearisations.

Intuitively, in terms of the I-net, one could say that each assignment function describes for each occurrence of an input transition, which token to take from its channel place (namely the token deposited by the assigned occurrence of the output transition). Based on this point of view, the following two types of assignment functions represent natural policies to deal with the messages (tokens) in the channel places.

Definition 8. *Let $w \in T^*$ and let θ be an assignment function for w. Then*

(1) θ is of type FIFO with respect to φ if $\theta(b,j) = (\varphi^{-1}(b),j)$ for every $(b,j) \in$ occ(w) such that $b \in T_{inp}$;

(2) θ is of type LIFO with respect to φ if for every $(b,j) \in$ occ(w) such that $b \in T_{inp}$ and $\theta(b,j) = (a,i)$ where $a = \varphi^{-1}(b)$, there exist $x,y,z \in T^*$ such that $w = xaybz$ with $i = \#_a(xa)$, $j = \#_b(xayb)$, and $\#_a(y) = \#_b(y)$. □

Again, since φ is fixed, we will omit the reference to φ.

When scrutinising the proof of Theorem 3, one sees that the function θ constructed there is of type FIFO. Hence we have the following corollary.

Corollary 1. *Every word with the prefix property has an assignment function of type FIFO.* □

Actually, the argument in the proof of Theorem 3 could also have been based on the construction of an assignment function of type LIFO. In other words, every word with the prefix property has an assignment function of type LIFO. Finally, it is easily seen that each w with the prefix property has exactly one assignment function of type FIFO; also its assignment function of type LIFO is unique (the proof of which we leave to the reader).

Example 7. (Ex. 4 and Ex. 5 ctd.) Assignment function θ of w is of type FIFO and θ' is of type LIFO. For v, however, θ is an assignment function both of type FIFO and of type LIFO. □

We now investigate the assignment functions of type FIFO. It will be shown that the assignment function of type FIFO of a word w defines the least restrictive ordering on occ(w) in the sense that its set of linearisations is maximal (w.r.t. set inclusion) among all sets of θ-linearisations of w.

In the sequel, θ_w^{fifo} denotes the assignment function of type FIFO of any word $w \in T^*$ with the prefix property. In addition, if $L \subseteq T^*$ is a language with the prefix property, then $\text{lin}_{\text{FIFO}}(L) = \bigcup \{\text{lin}_{\theta_w^{\text{fifo}}}(w) \mid w \in L\}$ consists of all *FIFO-linearisations of L.*

Lemma 7. *Let $v,w \in T^*$ be such that v and w have the prefix property and* occ$(v) =$ occ(w). *Then* $\theta_v^{\text{fifo}} = \theta_w^{\text{fifo}}$.

Proof. By Corollary 1, θ_v^{fifo} and θ_w^{fifo} exist. Let $(b,j) \in occ(v)$, with $b \in T_{inp}$ for some $j \geq 1$. Then $\theta_v^{\text{fifo}}(b,j) = (\varphi^{-1}(b),j) = \theta_w^{\text{fifo}}$ as required. □

A similar result does not hold for assignment functions of type LIFO (cf. Example 7).

The set of linearisations determined by an assignment function of type FIFO can be characterised as follows.

Lemma 8. *Let $w \in T^*$ have the prefix property. Then* $\text{lin}_{\theta_w^{\text{fifo}}}(w) = \{v \in T^* \mid v$ *has the prefix property and* $\text{proj}_{T_i}(v) = \text{proj}_{T_i}(w)$ *for all $i \in [n]\}$.*

Proof. The inclusion from left to right follows immediately from Lemma 6(2) and Lemma 6(5).

To prove the converse inclusion, consider a word $v \in T^*$ such that v has the prefix property and $\text{proj}_{T_i}(v) = \text{proj}_{T_i}(w)$ for all $i \in [n]$. Hence $\text{occ}(v) = \text{occ}(w)$. Let now $(a, i), (b, j) \in \text{occ}(v)$ be such that $(a, i) \leq^+_{w, \theta^{\text{fifo}}_w} (b, j)$. We prove that $\text{pos}_v(a, i) \leq \text{pos}_v(b, j)$ from which it then follows that $v \in \text{lin}_{\theta^{\text{fifo}}_w}(w)$ by Definition 7.

Since $(a, i) \leq^+_{w, \theta^{\text{fifo}}_w} (b, j)$, we have $\text{pos}_w(a, i) \leq \text{pos}_w(b, j)$ by Lemma 4. If $a, b \in T_k$ for some $k \in [n]$, then also $\text{pos}_v(a, i) \leq \text{pos}_v(b, j)$ because $\text{proj}_{T_k}(v) = \text{proj}_{T_k}(w)$.

If $a \in T_k$ and $b \in T_l$, for some $k \neq l$, we first consider the case that $(a, i) \leq_{w, \theta^{\text{fifo}}_w} (b, j)$. This implies that $\theta^{\text{fifo}}_w(b, j) = (a, i)$ and hence $i = j$. Since v has the prefix property, $\text{pos}_v(a, j) \leq \text{pos}_v(b, j)$. Otherwise there exist occurrences $o_1, \ldots, o_m$ in $\text{occ}(w)$, with $m \leq |w|$, such that $o_1 = (a, i)$, $o_m = (b, j)$, and $o_i \leq_{w, \theta} o_{i+1}$, for all $i \in [m-1]$. With a reasoning similar to the above, we obtain $\text{pos}_v(o_i) \leq \text{pos}_v(o_{i+1})$, for all $i \in [m-1]$ and so $\text{pos}_v(a, i) \leq \text{pos}_v(b, j)$. □

Example 8. (Ex 2. Ctd.) The Investment Firm and Exchange from Example 2 are now extended with the possibility to repeatedly send and receive orders and their sets of transitions extended to $T'_1 = \{\textbf{so}, \textbf{rc}, \textbf{ii1}, \textbf{ii2}\}$ and $T'_2 = \{\textbf{ro}, \textbf{sc}, \textbf{ei1}, \textbf{ei2}\}$. The composition of the thus extended E-nets leads to the I-net in Fig. 3.

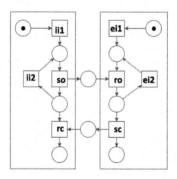

Fig. 3. I-net with option to repeat orders

Consider words $v = \langle \textbf{ei1}, \textbf{ii1}, \textbf{so}, \textbf{ii2}, \textbf{ro}, \textbf{ei2}, \textbf{so}, \textbf{ii2}, \textbf{ro}, \textbf{ei2}, \textbf{so}, \textbf{ro}, \textbf{sc}, \textbf{rc} \rangle$ and $w = \langle \textbf{ei1}, \textbf{ii1}, \textbf{so}, \textbf{ii2}, \textbf{so}, \textbf{ii2}, \textbf{so}, \textbf{ro}, \textbf{ei2}, \textbf{ro}, \textbf{ei2}, \textbf{ro}, \textbf{sc}, \textbf{rc} \rangle$. Both v and w have the prefix property and $\text{proj}_{T'_i}(v) = \text{proj}_{T'_i}(w)$ for $i \in \{1, 2\}$. Let θ be the assignment function for w of type FIFO. From Lemma 8, we know that $v \in \text{lin}_\theta(w)$. The assignment function θ' of w of type LIFO however has $\theta'(\textbf{ro}, 1) = (\textbf{so}, 3)$ and so $v \in \text{lin}_{\theta'}(w)$ does not hold. □

For a language L that has the prefix property, we denote by $\text{lin}(L)$ the language consisting of all words that can be obtained as a θ-linearisation of any word $w \in L$ for whatever assignment function θ for w. Thus $\mathrm{lin}(L) = \bigcup\{\mathrm{lin}_\theta(w) \mid w \in L$ and θ an assignment function for $w\}$.

Lemma 8 shows that indeed and as announced, the assignment functions of type FIFO are the most "generous" in the sense that they determine a maximal (w.r.t. set inclusion) set of linearisations. This observation is formalised in the following statement which is an extension of Theorem 4.

Theorem 5. *Let $L \subseteq T^*$ be a language with the prefix property such that $\mathrm{proj}_{T_i}(L) \subseteq \mathcal{L}(\mathcal{E}_i)$ for all $i \in [n]$. Then $L \subseteq \mathrm{lin}(L) = \mathrm{lin}_{\mathrm{FIFO}}(L) \subseteq \mathcal{L}(\mathcal{I}(V,\varphi))$.*

Proof. The two inclusions are immediate: $\mathrm{lin}_{\mathrm{FIFO}}(L) \subseteq \mathcal{L}(\mathcal{I}(V,\varphi))$ follows from Theorem 4 and $L \subseteq \mathrm{lin}(L)$ from Lemma 6(1). By definition $\mathrm{lin}_{\mathrm{FIFO}}(L) \subseteq \mathrm{lin}(L)$. So we only have to prove that $\mathrm{lin}(L) \subseteq \mathrm{lin}_{\mathrm{FIFO}}(L)$.

Let $v \in \mathrm{lin}(L)$. Hence there exists a $w \in L$ and an assignment function θ for w such that $v \in \mathrm{lin}_\theta(w)$. From Lemma 6(2) and (5), we know that $\mathrm{proj}_{T_i}(v) = \mathrm{proj}_{T_i}(w)$ and that v has the prefix property. Hence $v \in \mathrm{lin}_{\theta_w^{\mathrm{fifo}}}(w)$ by Lemma 8 (note that θ_w^{fifo} exists by Corollary 1). Consequently, $v \in \mathrm{lin}_{\mathrm{FIFO}}(L)$. $\square$

An immediate consequence of Theorem 5 is the closure of the languages of I-nets under exchanging unordered occurrences of transitions.

Corollary 2. $\mathrm{lin}(\mathcal{L}(\mathcal{I}(V,\varphi))) = \mathrm{lin}_{\mathrm{FIFO}}(\mathcal{L}(\mathcal{I}(V,\varphi))) = \mathcal{L}(\mathcal{I}(V,\varphi))$. $\square$

The inclusion $\mathrm{lin}_{\mathrm{FIFO}}(L) \subseteq \mathcal{L}(\mathcal{I}(V,\varphi))$ in Theorem 5 may be strict even if all inclusions $\mathrm{proj}_{T_i}(L) \subseteq \mathcal{L}(\mathcal{E}_i)$ for all $i \in [n]$, are equalities (see Example 9 below). In fact, as we demonstrate next, it may be the case that not all words in $\mathcal{L}(\mathcal{I}(V,\varphi))$ are represented in L. This is expressed by means of the following notion.

Definition 9. *Let $L \subseteq T^*$ be a language with the prefix property. Then L is complete with respect to $\mathcal{I}(V,\varphi))$ if for all $w \in \mathcal{L}(\mathcal{I}(V,\varphi))$ there exists a $w' \in L$ such that $\mathrm{proj}_{T_i}(w) = \mathrm{proj}_{T_i}(w')$ for all $i \in [n]$.* $\square$

By Theorem 5 we know that for a language L with the prefix property, that is locally executable by the component E-nets of $\mathcal{I}(V,\varphi)$, the FIFO-linearisation of L is included in the language of $\mathcal{I}(V,\varphi)$. The next theorem adds to this result by showing that this inclusion is an equality in case L is complete with respect to $\mathcal{I}(V,\varphi)$.

Theorem 6. *Let $L \subseteq T^*$ be a language with the prefix property such that $\mathrm{proj}_{T_i}(L) \subseteq \mathcal{L}(\mathcal{E}_i)$ for all $i \in [n]$. If $L \subseteq T^*$ is complete with respect to $\mathcal{I}(V,\varphi)$, then $\mathrm{lin}_{\mathrm{FIFO}}(L) = \mathcal{L}(\mathcal{I}(V,\varphi))$.*

Proof. Assume L is complete and let $w \in \mathcal{L}(\mathcal{I}(V,\varphi))$. Let $w' \in L$ be such that $\mathrm{proj}_{T_i}(w) = \mathrm{proj}_{T_i}(w')$ for all $i \in [n]$. Since L is complete, such w' exists. Moreover, w' has the prefix property. So, by Corollary 1, $\theta_{w'}^{\mathrm{fifo}}$ exists. Since $w \in \mathcal{L}(\mathcal{I}(V,\varphi))$, w has the prefix property by Lemma 2. Now we can apply Lemma 8 to conclude that $w \in \mathrm{lin}_{\theta_{w'}^{\mathrm{fifo}}}(w')$, i.e., $w \in \mathrm{lin}_{\mathrm{FIFO}}(L)$. We conclude that $\mathcal{L}(\mathcal{I}(V,\varphi)) \subseteq \mathrm{lin}_{\mathrm{FIFO}}(L)$. By Theorem 5, $\mathrm{lin}_{\mathrm{FIFO}}(L) \subseteq \mathcal{L}(\mathcal{I}(V,\varphi))$. Hence equality follows. $\square$

Example 9. (Ex 2. Ctd.) The E-nets $\mathcal{E}_1''$ and $\mathcal{E}_2''$ in Figs. 4(a) and 4(b), with transitions $T_1'' = \{\mathbf{so}, \mathbf{rc}, \mathbf{ii}\}$ and $T_2'' = \{\mathbf{so}, \mathbf{rc}, \mathbf{ei}\}$, are extensions of the E-nets in Fig. 1(a) and Fig. 1(b). Each has an extra internal action (**ii** and **ie**, respectively). The I-net in Fig. 3(c) is the composition of $\mathcal{E}_1''$ and $\mathcal{E}_2''$. Let $v = \langle \mathbf{so}, \mathbf{ro}, \mathbf{sc}, \mathbf{rc} \rangle$, $w = \langle \mathbf{so}, \mathbf{ro}, \mathbf{ie}, \mathbf{ii} \rangle$ and let $L = \mathtt{Pref}(\{v, w\})$. Then $\mathtt{proj}_{T_1''}(L) = \mathtt{Pref}(\{\langle \mathbf{so}, \mathbf{ii} \rangle, \langle \mathbf{so}, \mathbf{rc} \rangle\}) = \mathcal{L}(\mathcal{E}_1'')$ and $\mathtt{proj}_{T_2''}(L) = \mathtt{Pref}(\{\langle \mathbf{ro}, \mathbf{ie} \rangle, \langle \mathbf{ro}, \mathbf{sc} \rangle\}) = \mathcal{L}(\mathcal{E}_2'')$. Furthermore, we have $\mathtt{lin}_{\mathtt{FIFO}}(L) = \mathtt{Pref}(\{v, w, x\})$ where $x = \langle \mathbf{so}, \mathbf{ro}, \mathbf{ii}, \mathbf{ie} \rangle$.

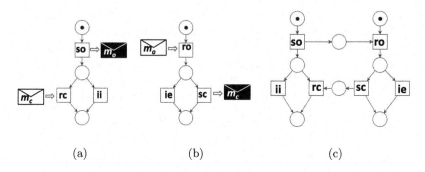

(a)   (b)   (c)

Fig. 4. (a) E-net $\mathcal{E}_1''$ (b) E-net $\mathcal{E}_2''$ (c) Their I-net

$\mathcal{L}(\mathcal{I}(V, \varphi)) = \mathtt{Pref}(\{v, w, x, y, z\})$ where $y = \langle \mathbf{so}, \mathbf{ro}, \mathbf{sc}, \mathbf{ii} \rangle$, and $z = \langle \mathbf{so}, \mathbf{ro}, \mathbf{ii}, \mathbf{sc} \rangle$. Hence $\mathtt{lin}_{\mathtt{FIFO}}(L) \subseteq \mathcal{L}(\mathcal{I}(V, \varphi))$. Even though $\mathtt{proj}_{T_1''}(L) = \mathcal{L}(\mathcal{E}_1'')$ and $\mathtt{proj}_{T_2''}(L) = \mathcal{L}(\mathcal{E}_2'')$, this inclusion is strict. L is not complete with respect to $\mathcal{I}(V, \varphi)$ because y does not have a representation in L. Neither v nor w (nor their prefixes) are such that their projection on T_1'' would yield $\mathtt{proj}_{T_1''}(y)$ and their projection on T_2'' would yield $\mathtt{proj}_{T_2''}(y)$: $\mathtt{proj}_{T_1''}(y) = \langle \mathbf{so}, \mathbf{ii} \rangle \neq \langle \mathbf{so}, \mathbf{rc} \rangle = \mathtt{proj}_{T_1''}(v)$ and, similarly, $\mathtt{proj}_{T_2''}(y) = \langle \mathbf{ro}, \mathbf{sc} \rangle \neq \langle \mathbf{ro}, \mathbf{ie} \rangle = \mathtt{proj}_{T_2'}(w)$. In contrast, $L' = L \cup \mathtt{pref}(y)$ is complete and we have $\mathtt{lin}_{\mathtt{FIFO}}(L') = \mathcal{L}(\mathcal{I}(V, \varphi))$. Note that $z \in \mathtt{lin}_{\mathtt{FIFO}}(L')$ as $\mathtt{proj}_{T_1''}(y) = \mathtt{proj}_{T_1''}(z)$ and $\mathtt{proj}_{T_2''}(y) = \mathtt{proj}_{T_2''}(z)$. $\square$

Recall that $\mathcal{L}(\mathcal{I}(V, \varphi))$ has the prefix property. Hence combining Lemma 6(2) – by which $\mathtt{proj}_{T_i}(L) = \mathtt{proj}_{T_i}(\mathtt{lin}_{\mathtt{FIFO}}(L))$ whenever language L has the prefix property – with Theorem 6 leads to the observation that L and $\mathcal{L}(\mathcal{I}(V, \varphi))$ are in full agreement on their recordings of the components' behaviours.

Corollary 3. *Let $L \subseteq T^*$ be a language with the prefix property such that $\mathtt{proj}_{T_i}(L) \subseteq \mathcal{L}(\mathcal{E}_i)$ for all $i \in [n]$. If $L \subseteq T^*$ is complete with respect to $\mathcal{I}(V, \varphi)$, then $\mathtt{proj}_{T_i}(L) = \mathtt{proj}_{T_i}(\mathcal{L}(\mathcal{I}(V, \varphi)))$ for all $i \in [n]$.* $\square$

As illustrated next in Example 10, Corollary 3 does not imply that $\mathtt{proj}_{T_i}(L) = \mathcal{L}(\mathcal{E}_i)$ for all $i \in [n]$.

Example 10. Consider the I-net $\mathcal{I}(V, \varphi)$ in Fig. 5(c) composed of E-nets $\mathcal{E}_1$ in Fig. 5(a) and $\mathcal{E}_2$ in Fig. 5(b). Thus $\mathcal{L}(\mathcal{I}(V, \varphi)) = \text{Pref}(\{abc, bac\})$.

Consider now $L = \text{Pref}(\{abc\})$ which is complete with respect to $\mathcal{I}(V, \varphi)$. Moreover, L has the prefix property and $\text{proj}_{\{a\}}(\mathcal{L}(\mathcal{I}(V, \varphi))) = \text{proj}_{\{a\}}(L) = \text{Pref}(\{a\}) = \mathcal{L}(\mathcal{E}_1)$ as well as $\text{proj}_{\{b,c\}}(\mathcal{L}(\mathcal{I}(V, \varphi))) = \text{proj}_{\{b,c\}}(L) = \text{Pref}(\{bc\}) \subseteq \mathcal{L}(\mathcal{E}_2)$. However, $\text{proj}_{\{b,c\}}(L) = \mathcal{L}(\mathcal{E}_2)$ does not hold. □

6   Synthesising I-nets

We are now ready to address our initial question. Assume that we have an algorithm to discover Petri net models of isolated (i.e. not interacting) component processes from a description of their behaviour (in the form of action sequences). Then, when given an event log (a language), representing the observed behaviour of a given number of distinct collaborating processes, construct an I-net that generates this observed behaviour. A formal definition of the assumed process discovery algorithm, based on [6], is given next.

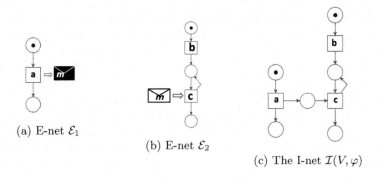

(a) E-net $\mathcal{E}_1$

(b) E-net $\mathcal{E}_2$

(c) The I-net $\mathcal{I}(V, \varphi)$

Fig. 5. (a) E-net $\mathcal{E}_1$ (b) E-net $\mathcal{E}_2$ (c) The I-net $\mathcal{I}(V, \varphi)$

Definition 10. *Let $\mathbb{L}$ be a family of languages. A* process discovery algorithm $\mathcal{A}$ *for $\mathbb{L}$ is an algorithm that computes for all $L \in \mathbb{L}$, a Petri net $\mathcal{A}(L) = (P, T, F)$ with a single source place such that $T = \text{Alph}(L)$ and $L \subseteq \mathcal{L}(\mathcal{A}(L))$.* □

Note that we require that the Petri nets discovered have a single source place (as E-nets have). Actually, such algorithms exist [6]. The Inductive Miner [22], a tool for discovering a workflow net implementing the communicating (input/output) behaviour, is one example. The similarity between E-nets and workflow nets makes it possible to leverage the large amount of research into the automated discovery of workflow nets, for the purpose of automated discovery of E-nets. A comprehensive overview of existing algorithms including an evaluation of their performance can be found in [8]. To leverage such an algorithm to a system of asynchronously communicating nets, one needs to describe the distribution of actions over components in combination with their role as internal, input, or output action. This leads to the concept of a distributed communicating alphabet defined next.

Definition 11. *Let $n \geq 1$. An n-dimensional distributed communicating alphabet (or n-DCA, for short) is a tuple*
$$DA = (\langle \Sigma_1, \ldots, \Sigma_n \rangle, \langle \Sigma_{int}, \Sigma_{inp}, \Sigma_{out} \rangle, mt, cp) \text{ such that}$$

- $\Sigma_1, \ldots, \Sigma_n$ *are non-empty, pairwise disjoint alphabets;*
- $\Sigma_{int}, \Sigma_{inp}, \Sigma_{out}$ *are pairwise disjoint alphabets consisting of* internal actions, input actions *and* output actions, *respectively;*
- $\bigcup_{i \in [n]} \Sigma_i = \Sigma_{int} \cup \Sigma_{inp} \cup \Sigma_{out}$;
- $mt : \Sigma_{inp} \cup \Sigma_{out} \to \mathcal{M}$ *is a function that assigns message types to the input and output actions;*
- $cp : \Sigma_{inp} \cup \Sigma_{out} \to \Sigma_{inp} \cup \Sigma_{out}$ *is a (complementing) bijection, which is not defined ($cp = \emptyset$) if $n = 1$, and otherwise ($n \geq 2$), for all $a \in \Sigma_{inp} \cup \Sigma_{out}$: if $a \in \Sigma_{inp}$, then $cp(a) \in \Sigma_{out}$ and if $a \in \Sigma_{out}$, then $cp(a) \in \Sigma_{inp}$; if $a \in \Sigma_i$ for some $i \in [n]$, then $cp(a) \in \Sigma_j$ where $j \in [n]$ is such that $i \neq j$; $mt(cp(a)) = mt(a)$; and $cp(cp(a)) = a$.* □

The alphabet $\bigcup_{i \in [n]} \Sigma_i = \Sigma_{int} \cup \Sigma_{inp} \cup \Sigma_{out}$ in Definition 11, also referred to as the *underlying alphabet of the n-DCA DA*, is intended to represent the actions available to n interacting enterprises. DA describes both their distribution across the enterprises and their interaction capacities. A 1-*DCA* consists of a single enterprise. When specifying a 1-*DCA*, we can omit its complementing bijection cp as it is not defined (and not needed). For $i \in [n]$, we refer to the 1-*DCA* $DA_i = (\langle \Sigma_i \rangle, [\Sigma_{i,int}, \Sigma_{i,inp}, \Sigma_{i,out} \rangle, mt_i)$ as the *i-th component of DA*.

For the rest of this section we assume a fixed family of languages $\mathbb{L}$ and a fixed process discovery algorithm $\mathcal{A}$ for $\mathbb{L}$. Moreover, we assume that we know the desired distribution of $\texttt{Alph}(L)$ over internal, input and output actions. The following definition describes how the discovery of E-nets depends on these assumptions.

Definition 12. *The E-net discovery algorithm derived from $\mathcal{A}$, is the algorithm $\mathcal{A}_E$ that computes, for all pairs (L, DA) such that $L \in \mathbb{L}$ with $\mathcal{A}(L) = (P, T, F)$, and $DA = (\langle T \rangle, \langle T_{int}, T_{inp}, T_{out} \rangle, mt)$ is a 1-DCA with $\texttt{Alph}(L) = T$ as its underlying alphabet, the E-net $\mathcal{A}_E(L, DA) = (P, \langle T_{int}, T_{inp}, T_{out} \rangle, F, mt)$.* □

Thus $\mathcal{A}_E(L, DA)$ adds the information from DA, about the distribution of actions, to the transitions of $\mathcal{A}(L)$. Clearly, $\mathcal{A}_E(L, DA)$ is an E-net.[3] Henceforth we fix an $\mathcal{A}_E$, as specified in Definition 12. The following lemma shows that the behaviour of $\mathcal{A}_E(L)$ is the same as that of $\mathcal{A}(L)$.

Lemma 9. *Let $L \in \mathbb{L}$ and DA a 1-DCA with $\texttt{Alph}(L)$ as its underlying alphabet. Then $\mathcal{L}(\mathcal{A}(L)) = \mathcal{L}(\mathcal{A}_E(L, DA))$.*

Proof. The statement follows directly from Definition 12.

---

[3] In case $\mathcal{A}$ is an algorithm for the discovery of workflow nets, like the Inductive Miner [22], $\mathcal{A}_E(L, DA)$ would have the structure of a workflow net.

Now we move to the discovery of I-nets on the basis of $\mathcal{A}$.

Definition 13. *The I-net discovery algorithm derived from $\mathcal{A}$, is the algorithm $\mathcal{A}_I$ that computes, for all pairs $(L, \mathcal{DA})$ such that*

- *$\mathcal{DA} = (\langle \Sigma_1, \ldots, \Sigma_n \rangle, \langle \Sigma_{int}, \Sigma_{inp}, \Sigma_{out} \rangle, mt, cp)$ is an n-DCA for an $n \geq 2$,*
- *$\mathrm{Alph}(L) = \bigcup_{i \in [n]} \Sigma_i$, the underlying alphabet of $\mathcal{DA}$, and*
- *$\mathrm{proj}_{\Sigma_i}(L) \in \mathbb{L}$ for all $i \in [n]$,*
  the I-net $\mathcal{A}_I(L, \mathcal{DA}) = \mathcal{I}(V, \varphi)$ with $V = \{\mathcal{A}_E(\mathrm{proj}_{\Sigma_i}(L), \mathcal{DA}_i) \mid i \in [n]\}$ and $\varphi(a) = cp(a)$ for all $a \in \Sigma_{out}$. □

Note that $\mathcal{A}_I(L, \mathcal{DA}) = \mathcal{I}(V, \varphi)$ in Definition 13 is indeed an I-net, since, by Definition 12, for all $i \in [n]$, $\mathcal{A}_E(\mathrm{proj}_{\Sigma_i}(L), \mathcal{DA}_i)$ is an E-net with set of transitions Σ_i; the Σ_i are mutually disjoint; and the properties of cp described in Definition 11 guarantee that φ is a matching for V.

By Definitions 10 and 13, we can transfer Theorem 5 and Theorem 6 to the setting of discovering an I-net from a given language L.

Corollary 4. *Let L be a language with the prefix property and $\mathcal{DA}$ an n-DCA, both as specified in Definition 13. Then,*

(1) $\mathrm{lin}_{\mathrm{FIFO}}(L) \subseteq \mathcal{L}(\mathcal{A}_I(L, \mathcal{DA}))$;
(2) $\mathrm{lin}_{\mathrm{FIFO}}(L) = \mathcal{L}(\mathcal{A}_I(L, \mathcal{DA}))$ if L is complete with respect to $\mathcal{A}_I(L, \mathcal{DA})$. □

Thus, given a language L with the prefix property representing an event log of a system of n enterprises, and an n-dimensional distributed communicating alphabet, we can construct an I-net in the way described in Definition 13. This I-net has all words in L in its language together with all their linearisations (obtained by exchanging occurrences of independent actions). In fact, it is sufficient to consider only their FIFO-linearisations. Even then, though, there may in general be more firing sequences than what can be deduced from the description L of the observed behaviour. On the other hand, by Corollary 4(2), in case L is complete with respect to the I-net, i.e., each firing sequence of the constructed I-net has a representation in L, then the additional behaviour exhibited by the I-net, not observed in L (underfitting), can be fully explained by the concurrency between the E-nets.

Example 11. (Ex. 8 ctd.) Let w and v be as in Example 8 and let $L = \{w\}$. Let $\mathcal{DA} = (\langle \Sigma_1, \Sigma_2 \rangle, \langle \Sigma_{int}, \Sigma_{inp}, \Sigma_{out} \rangle, mt, cp)$ be the 2-*DCA*, with components $\mathcal{DA}_1$ and $\mathcal{DA}_2$, as given in Fig. 6, representing the actions available to the collaboration between the Investment firm and the Exchange from Example 8. Let $\mathcal{A}_E$ and $\mathcal{A}_I$ be the E-net and I-net discovery algorithms, respectively, derived from process discovery algorithm $\mathcal{A}$. Furthermore, assume that the E-nets discovered from L, $\mathcal{A}_E(\mathrm{proj}_{\Sigma_1}(L))$ and $\mathcal{A}_E(\mathrm{proj}_{\Sigma_2}(L))$, are as depicted in Figs. 7(a) and (b), respectively. Then $\mathcal{A}_I(L, \mathcal{DA})$ is the I-net in Fig. 3. By Corollary 4(1), we have $L \subseteq \mathrm{lin}_{\mathrm{FIFO}}(L) \subseteq \mathcal{L}(\mathcal{A}_I(L, \mathcal{DA}))$. Hence, also $v \in \mathcal{L}(\mathcal{A}_I(L, \mathcal{DA}))$ since $v \in \mathrm{lin}_{\mathrm{FIFO}}(w)$ as outlined in Example 8. □

The next example serves as an illustration of Corollary 4(2).

	Σ_{int}	Σ_{inp}	Σ_{out}
Σ_1	ii1,ii2	rc	so
Σ_2	ei1,ei2	ro	sc

mt(so)=m_o	cp(so)=ro
mt(ro)=m_o	cp(ro)=so
mt(sc)=m_c	cp(sc)=rc
mt(rc)=m_c	cp(rc)=sc

Fig. 6. The 2-DCA $\mathcal{DA}$

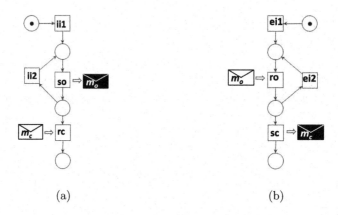

(a)   (b)

Fig. 7. (a) E-net $\mathcal{A}_E(proj_{\Sigma_1}(L))$ (b) E-net $\mathcal{A}_E(proj_{\Sigma_2}(L))$

Example 12. (Ex. 3 ctd.) Let $\mathcal{A}_E$ and $\mathcal{A}_\mathcal{I}$ be the E-net and I-net discovery algorithms respectively, derived from the process discovery algorithm $\mathcal{A}$. Let $w = \langle \mathbf{so}, \mathbf{ro}, \mathbf{sc}, \mathbf{rc}, \mathbf{si}, \mathbf{ri}, \mathbf{ss}, \mathbf{rs} \rangle$ as in Example 3 and let $L = \{w\}$. The 3-*DCA* $\mathcal{DA} = (\langle \Sigma_1, \Sigma_2, \Sigma_3 \rangle, \langle \Sigma_{int}, \Sigma_{inp}, \Sigma_{out} \rangle, mt, cp)$ is specified in Fig. 8.

It represents the actions for the collaboration between the Investment firm, the Exchange and the Central Securities Depository from Example 3 Let $\mathcal{DA}_1$, $\mathcal{DA}_2$, $\mathcal{DA}_3$ denote the first, second, and third component, resp., of $\mathcal{DA}$. Assume that $\mathcal{A}_E(proj_{\Sigma_1}(L), \mathcal{DA}_1)$, $\mathcal{A}_E(proj_{\Sigma_2}(L), \mathcal{DA}_2)$, and $\mathcal{A}_E(proj_{\Sigma_3}(L), \mathcal{DA}_3)$ are the E-nets depicted in Figs. 9(a), (b), (c) resp. Then $\mathcal{A}_\mathcal{I}(L, \mathcal{DA})$ is the I-net in Fig. 2.

	Σ_{int}	Σ_{inp}	Σ_{out}
Σ_1		rc,rs	so
Σ_2		ro	sc,si
Σ_3		ri	ss

mt(so)=m_o	cp(so)=ro
mt(ro)=m_o	cp(ro)=so
mt(sc)=m_c	cp(sc)=rc
mt(rc)=m_c	cp(rc)=sc
mt(ss)=m_s	cp(ss)=rs
mt(rs)=m_s	cp(rs)=ss
mt(si)=m_i	cp(si)=ri
mt(ri)=m_i	cp(ri)=si

Fig. 8. The 3-DCA $\mathcal{DA}$

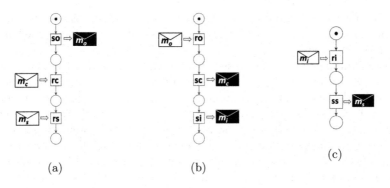

Fig. 9. (a) $\mathcal{A}_E(proj_{\Sigma_1}(L), \mathcal{D}\mathcal{A}_1)$ (b) $\mathcal{A}_E(proj_{\Sigma_2}(L), \mathcal{D}\mathcal{A}_2)$ (c) $\mathcal{A}_E(proj_{\Sigma_3}(L), \mathcal{D}\mathcal{A}_3)$

Now, let $v = \langle \mathbf{so}, \mathbf{ro}, \mathbf{sc}, \mathbf{si}, \mathbf{rc}, \mathbf{ri}, \ \mathbf{ss}, \mathbf{rs} \rangle$ as in Example 3, $x = \langle \mathbf{so}, \mathbf{ro},$ $\mathbf{sc}, \mathbf{si}, \mathbf{ri}, \ \mathbf{rc}, \mathbf{ss}, \mathbf{rs} \rangle$ and $y = \langle \mathbf{so}, \mathbf{ro}, \mathbf{sc}, \mathbf{si}, \mathbf{ri}, \mathbf{ss}, \mathbf{rc}, \mathbf{rs} \rangle$. Then $\mathcal{L}(\mathcal{A}_\mathcal{I}(L, \mathcal{D}\mathcal{A})) =$ $\mathtt{Pref}(\{w, v, x, y\})$. Note here that $\mathtt{lin}_{\mathrm{FIFO}}(\{w\}) = \{w, v, x, y\}$.

Next, we observe that L is complete with respect to $\mathtt{Pref}(\{w, v, x, y\})$ as $proj_{\Sigma_i}(v) = proj_{\Sigma_i}(x) = proj_{\Sigma_i}(y) = proj_{\Sigma_i}(w) \in proj_{\Sigma_i}(L)$ for each $i \in \{1, 2, 3\}$ and similar for their prefixes. Furthermore, we know from Example 3 that L has the prefix property. And indeed $\mathcal{L}(\mathcal{A}_\mathcal{I}(L, \mathcal{D}\mathcal{A})) = \mathtt{lin}_{\mathrm{FIFO}}(L)$.   □

7 Discussion

In this paper we have considered the problem of the synthesis of a distributed process model (in the form of an I-net) from an event log (given in the form of a language). Also the number of participating processes (modelled as E-nets) is known as are their channels (in the form of matching input and output actions). We have shown how, given an algorithm for the discovery of Petri net models from event logs of isolated processes, the discovered models can be used for the synthesis of a new I-net. Moreover, by Theorems 1 and 5, fitness of the resulting I-net is guaranteed if and only if fitness of the component nets is guaranteed and the event log has the prefix property (a natural assumption). It is interesting to reflect on the inclusion of FIFO-linearisations in the language of the I-net (see Corollary 2 and Corollary 4.(1)) and the role of the channels. The exchange of unrelated occurrences of actions suggests a relationship to the well-known Mazurkiewicz traces (equivalence classes of words, see, eg., [25]) and their dependence graphs (defining their causal structure in the form of a labelled partial order, see [17]). There is however an important difference: independence in Mazurkiewicz' theory is between actions rather than their occurrences. The independence between occurrences considered here is determined by the history leading to these occurrences and hence to a theory of context dependent or local traces (see, eg., [11,19]). The I/O-Petri nets of [15] use communication channels modelled by places and channel properties are investigated in terms of asynchronous I/O-transition systems rather than languages. Note that, as can be seen from our results, choosing FIFO channels or "normal" places (in which the order of arrival of tokens is not taken into account) does not change the language of the resulting I-net.

Process mining is an active research area, that has resulted in many process discovery algorithms (see, eg., [6] for an overview). Typically, these algorithms are used for the discovery of local processes in isolation, i.e., interaction between processes is not taken into account. In [5] this state of affairs is identified as an omission that should be addressed. This motivated us to investigate to what extent existing algorithms for the discovery of single (isolated) process models could be used for the synthesis of composed systems. In [5], two challenges are identified. The first one is "context dependency" which refers to the observation that composition of services might restrict their behaviour. Therefore, event logs generated by collaborating services might not show every possible local behaviour. As a consequence, the process models discovered, can be underfitting. We provide a precise specification of the conditions that determine the extent to which such underfitting can occur. The second challenge is "instance correlation" which concerns the problem of the use of different case identifiers for the same case by different services. This complicates the identification of global behaviour associated with a single case from local behaviours associated with that case. In this paper, this issue is not addressed as here event logs are seen as consisting of executed actions without explicit reference to cases. Currently we are investigating how to deal with case information associated with event sequences. Then the problem of instance correlation, mentioned above, could eg., reappear as the problem of relating observations of local behaviour to observations (as projections) of global behaviour.

In [2,4], the problem of process mining from large event logs is addressed and various options to distribute the mining problem over sublogs (with overlapping activities) are considered. In [10], similar to our approach, the event logs of Multi Agent Systems are projected onto individual agents in order to discover component models in terms of workflow nets using existing process discovery algorithms. By means of α-morphisms an abstraction of each component model is derived and the goal is to show that if the composition of these abstract models is sound, the composition of the original component models is sound.

As the focus of this paper has been on the collaboration between different parties, we did not deal with the question which algorithms from the set of available algorithms (see eg., [8]) is most suitable to serve as a precursor for the discovery of E-nets, and how an implementation of an algorithm for the discovery of E-nets can be derived from it. Since we are in particular concerned with the discovery of models of communicating behaviour this might also involve reconsidering performance criteria like fitness and precision, to accommodate this concern, for instance by making a distinction between performance with respect to internal and external behaviour. An interesting and practically relevant research question concerns the exchange of messages between processes (abstracting from their internal actions). One could adapt the approach presented here using projections on communicating actions only. The message exchanges generated from these communicating actions, actually arise in the course of doing business between enterprises. For example, a significant volume of messages is exchanged on a daily basis, between the business processes of financial institutions connected by the computer network (SWIFTnet) that is maintained and monitored by the SWIFT organization[4]. Extending our model to include such indirect observations of communicating behaviour would open up the possibility to use these observations to support future, more empirical, research in this direction.

Acknowledgement. The authors are grateful to the anonymous reviewers for their constructive suggestions which have led to an improvement of the presentation of the results of this paper.

References

1. van der Aalst, W.M.P., Mooij, A.J., Stahl, C., Wolf, K.: Service interaction: patterns, formalization, and analysis. In: Bernardo, M., Padovani, L., Zavattaro, G. (eds.) SFM 2009. LNCS, vol. 5569, pp. 42–88. Springer, Heidelberg (2009). https://doi.org/10.1007/978-3-642-01918-0_2

2. Aalst, W.M.P.: Distributed process discovery and conformance checking. In: de Lara, J., Zisman, A. (eds.) FASE 2012. LNCS, vol. 7212, pp. 1–25. Springer, Heidelberg (2012). https://doi.org/10.1007/978-3-642-28872-2_1

3. van der Aalst, W.M.P., Weske, M.: Reflections on a decade of interorganizational workflow research. In: Seminal Contributions to Information Systems Engineering, pp. 307–313. Springer, Heidelberg (2013). https://doi.org/10.1007/978-3-642-36926-1_24

4. van der Aalst, W.M.P.: Decomposing petri nets for process mining: a generic approach. Distr. Parallel Databases **31**(4), 471–507 (2013)

5. van der Aalst, W.M.P.: Service mining: using process mining to discover, check, and improve service behavior. IEEE Trans. Serv. Comput. **6**(4), 525–535 (2013)

6. van der Aalst, W.M.P.: Process Mining - Data Science in Action, 2nd edn. Springer, Heidelberg (2019). https://doi.org/10.1007/978-3-662-49851-4

7. van der Aalst, W.M.P., Stahl, C.: Modeling Business Processes - A Petri Net-Oriented Approach. MIT Press, Cambridge (2011)

8. Augusto, A., et al.: Automated discovery of process models from event logs: review and benchmark. IEEE Trans. Knowl. Data Eng. **31**(4), 686–705 (2019)

9. Baldan, P., Corradini, A., Ehrig, H., Heckel, R.: Compositional modeling of reactive systems using open nets. In: Larsen, K.G., Nielsen, M. (eds.) CONCUR 2001. LNCS, vol. 2154, pp. 502–518. Springer, Heidelberg (2001). https://doi.org/10.1007/3-540-44685-0_34

10. Bernardinello, L., Lomazova, I.A., Nesterov, R., Pomello, L.: Compositional discovery of workflow nets from event logs using morphisms. In: ATAED 2018. CEUR Workshop Proceedings, vol. 2115, pp. 39–55 (2018)

11. Biermann, I., Rozoy, B.: Reliable generalized and context dependent commutation relations. In: Bidoit, M., Dauchet, M. (eds.) CAAP 1997. LNCS, vol. 1214, pp. 165–176. Springer, Heidelberg (1997). https://doi.org/10.1007/BFb0030594

---

[4] In March 2021 this volume was in the order of 21 Mln. FIN messages per day. Source: https://www.swift.com/about-us/swift-fin-traffic-figures.

12. Carmona, J., van Dongen, B.F., Solti, A., Weidlich, M.: Conformance Checking - Relating Processes and Models. Springer, Switzerland (2018). https://doi.org/10.1007/978-3-319-99414-7
13. EDSN: Marktfacilitering. [In Dutch] (2018).https://www.edsn.nl/
14. Gomes, L., Paulo Barros, J.: Structuring and composability issues in petri nets modeling. IEEE Trans. Indus. Inform. 1(2), 112–123 (2005)
15. Haddad, S., Hennicker, R., Møller, M.H.: Channel properties of asynchronously composed petri nets. In: Colom, J.-M., Desel, J. (eds.) PETRI NETS 2013. LNCS, vol. 7927, pp. 369–388. Springer, Heidelberg (2013). https://doi.org/10.1007/978-3-642-38697-8_20
16. Heckel, R.: Open petri nets as semantic model for workflow integration. In: Ehrig, H., Reisig, W., Rozenberg, G., Weber, H. (eds.) Petri Net Technology for Communication-Based Systems. LNCS, vol. 2472, pp. 281–294. Springer, Heidelberg (2003). https://doi.org/10.1007/978-3-540-40022-6_14
17. Hoogeboom, H.J., Rozenberg, G.: Dependence graphs. In: Diekert, V., Rozenberg, G. (eds.) The Book of Traces, pp. 43–67. World Scientific, Singapore (1995)
18. HL7: Health Level Seven International (2015). http://www.hl7.org/
19. Hoogers, P.W., Kleijn, H.C.M., Thiagarajan, P.S.: A trace semantics for petri nets. Inf. Comput. 117(1), 98–114 (1995)
20. Kwantes, P.M., Kleijn, J.: On discovering distributed process models - the case of asynchronous communication. In: ATAED 2020. CEUR Workshop Proceedings, vol. 2625, pp. 49–65 (2020)
21. Kwantes, P.M., Kleijn, J.: On the synthesis of industry level process models from enterprise level process models. In: ATAED 2018 CEUR Workshop Proceedings, vol. 2115, pp. 6–22 (2018)
22. Leemans, S.J.J., Fahland, D., van der Aalst, W.M.P.: Discovering block-structured process models from event logs - a constructive approach. In: Colom, J.-M., Desel, J. (eds.) PETRI NETS 2013. LNCS, vol. 7927, pp. 311–329. Springer, Heidelberg (2013). https://doi.org/10.1007/978-3-642-38697-8_17
23. Massuthe, P., Reisig, W., Schmidt, K.: An Operating Guideline Approach to the SOA. Humboldt-Universitat zu Berlin, Mathematisch-Naturwissenschaftliche Fakultat II, Institut fur Informatik (2005)
24. S.W.I.F.T: ISO20022 Universal financial industry message scheme (2015). http://www.iso20022.org
25. Mazurkiewicz, A.: Trace theory. In: Brauer, W., Reisig, W., Rozenberg, G. (eds.) ACPN 1986. LNCS, vol. 255, pp. 278–324. Springer, Heidelberg (1987). https://doi.org/10.1007/3-540-17906-2_30
26. Reisig, W.: Towards a conceptual foundation of service composition. Comput. Sci. Res. Dev. 33(3–4), 281–289 (2018)
27. Reisig, W.: Associative composition of components with double-sided interfaces. Acta Inf. 56(3), 229–253 (2019)
28. GS1US: RosettaNet (2018). http://www.rosettanet.org/
29. Wolf, K.: Does my service have partners? Trans. Petri Nets Other Model. Concurr. 2, 152–171 (2009)
30. Zaitsev, D., Sleptsov, A.: State equations and equivalent transformations for timed petri nets. Cybern. Syst. Anal. 33, 659–672 (1997)
31. Zaitsev, D.: Decomposition of petri nets. Cybern. Syst. Anal. 4, 131–140 (2004)

Using Approximation for the Verification of Token-Scaling Models

Torsten Liebke and Karsten Wolf[(⊠)]

Institut für Informatik, Universität Rostock, Rostock, Germany
{torsten.liebke,karsten.wolf}@uni-rostock.de

Abstract. In the model checking domain, the state explosion problem is the core issue. The cause is usually the sheer size of the model or the cardinality of tokens in the initial state. For the latter, which we call *token-scaling models*, we propose an *under-approximation* for reachable states. The idea is to freeze tokens in the initial state (i.e. they are not used for firing transitions) and thus reducing the state space. If in the reduced state space a witness path is found, then the witness path can also be executed in the original state space. This method preserves existential temporal properties (ECTL*) using a *simulation relation* between the reduced and the original state space. Since the cardinality of the initial marking varies from only a few tokens to multi-digit numbers of tokens, we apply heuristics to compute the number of tokens that should be frozen. We implemented the new method in the explicit model checker LoLA 2. The experiments, done on the model checking contest benchmark, show that this method can speed up the model checking process and verify additional queries.

Keywords: Model Checking · Under-Approximation · Witness Path

1 Introduction

Model checking is subject to the state explosion problem [4]. If the system is a place/transition net (P/T net for short), one possible cause for this problem is the size of the model. Another reason is the cardinality of the initial marking, i.e., the number of tokens on the places of the P/T net in the initial state. Here, we focus on P/T nets that have a large number of initial tokens. In many models, a scaling parameter describes how many tokens are in the initial marking. We call such P/T nets *token-scaling models*. Token-scaling models are widespread in several fields. For example, in biochemistry [6,9] the tokens represent chemical or biological entities, such as molecules, and their initial number is subject to a model parameter. In scheduling problems [10], tokens stand for available resources which are variables, too. Another example is an election protocol where tokens represent voters.

To tackle the state explosion problem on token-scaling models, we introduce an under-approximation for the verification of existentially quantified temporal properties (ECTL*). The idea is to simply freeze some tokens in the initial

© Springer-Verlag GmbH Germany, part of Springer Nature 2022
M. Koutny et al. (Eds.): ToPNoC XVI, LNCS 13220, pp. 73–90, 2022.
https://doi.org/10.1007/978-3-662-65303-6_4

marking, on places which have more than one token on them. Freezing means that we do not consider these tokens for firing transitions while we still use them for evaluating propositions. Freezing tokens will essentially reduce the state space. The question is how this affects the result of model checking. If we find a witness path for the property under investigation in the reduced state space, then this property also holds in the original state space. Otherwise, the result is indefinite.

Formally, a simulation relation [12] between the original and the reduced transition system needs to be established. Since propositions are evaluated in the same manner in both systems, the simulation relation preserves their validity. Consequently, ECTL* formulas are preserved. The introduced method works with all specifications, where a single path, either a witness path or a counterexample, is enough to verify the specification. This means next to ECTL* formulas with a witness path, we can refute ACTL* formulas (universal temporal properties) that have a counterexample path, and LTL formulas (linear time temporal logic). The proposed token-scaling verification only provides answers if a witness path or a counterexample exists and is therefore only a sufficient respectively a necessary condition. After reducing the initial marking, the method uses normal model checking algorithms. This means, this method can be combined with other reduction techniques like symmetries [16] or partial order reduction [7,14,17].

We implemented the introduced method in our award winning model checker LoLA 2 [19] and tested the performance on the model checking contest (MCC) benchmark. We run the token-scaling verification in parallel to several well-developed model checking algorithms such as the state space search with powerful stubborn sets [17] and the CEGAR approach for reachability [18]. The experiments show that the proposed token-scaling method can produce results faster and verify additional queries, which could not be verified before due to the large state space.

The remainder of this paper is organized as follows. Section 2 starts with a motivational example. In Sect. 3, we present basic definitions of P/T nets and temporal logic. In Sect. 4, we introduce the theory behind this method. Section 5 describes heuristics to reduce the initial marking, followed by some implementation remarks in Sect. 6. Sect. 7 carries out experimental validation which is discussed and concluded in Sect. 8. We also give directions for future research.

2   Motivational Example

An example token-scaling model of a biochemical process is *Angiogenesis* [6]. The model describes the formation of new vessels from existing ones. It consists of 39 places, 64 transitions, and 185 arcs. If the scaling parameter is set to 25, meaning that every initially marked place has 25 tokens on it, the state space contains more than $4.3 \cdot 10^{19}$ reachable markings.

The *RobotManipulation* model [10] as seen in Fig. 1 is an example for a scheduling problem. The model has several instances due to a scaling parameter

$n = 1..10000$, which defines the number of tokens on several initially marked places. In fact, the three marked places *p_i1*, *access* and *r_stopped* get the following number of tokens depending on n: $p\_i1 = 2 \cdot n + 1$ and $access = r\_stopped = 2 \cdot n$.

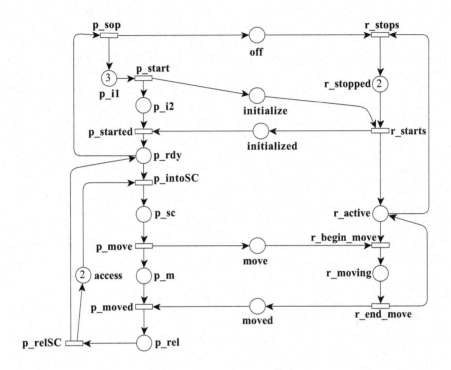

Fig. 1. RobotManipulation model [10] with $n = 1$.

The model consists of 15 places, 11 transitions, and 34 arcs. Despite its simple structure, the size of the state space for $n = 10000$ is rather large with $2.8 \cdot 10^{33}$ reachable markings. This happens by the large number of tokens in the model which end up on places in a huge number of combinations. This demonstrates that verification of token-scaling models can become extremely complex.

However, some properties are not really dependent on the actual number of tokens. An example for this is checking whether there is a reachable marking where the number of tokens on a certain place is more or less than the number of tokens on some another place or a given constant.

So, instead of using the actual number of initial tokens, the idea is to reduce their number on places with more than one token. This results in a smaller state space. Afterwards, the usual model checking techniques to verify the property can be applied. If a witness path or a counterexample for the property under investigation is found in the reduced state space, then the property also holds in the original setting. If not, we simply do not know.

For the RobotManipulation model with $n = 5000$, consider specification φ which compares the token cardinality of some places:

$$\varphi = \mathbf{EF}\,(p\_rel > p\_m \wedge p\_m > p\_rdy).$$

In other words, φ asks if there is an execution where finally p_rel has more tokens then p_m and where p_m has more tokens than p_rdy. With $n = 5000$ the places *access* and *r_stopped* would have 10000 tokens each, and p_i1 another 10001 tokens. With other optimizations switched off, our verification tool LoLA [19], could not verify this property, even after evaluating over 1 billion states. With partial order reduction [7,14,17] enabled a witness path consisting of 195006 transitions was found, while the overall number of computed reachable markings was 250010. Using the proposed idea from this article, we reduced the number of tokens to 5 on *access*, *r_stopped* and p_i1. With this, LoLA found a witness path of only 112 transitions, evaluating only 159 markings in total. Hence, the under-approximation approach resulted in a significant speed up.

3   Terminology

Definition 1 (Place/transition net). *A* place/transition net *(P/T net for short)* $N = (P, T, F, W, m_0)$ *consists of*

- *A finite set of* places *P;*
- *A finite set of* transitions *T such that $P \cap T = \emptyset$;*
- *A set of* arcs *$F \subseteq (P \times T) \cup (T \times P)$;*
- *A* weight function *$W : (P \times T) \cup (T \times P) \to \mathbb{N}$ such that $W(x, y) = 0$ if and only if $(x, y) \notin F$;*
- *An* initial marking *$m_0 : P \to \mathbb{N}$.*

A marking m *is a mapping $m : P \to \mathbb{N}$.*

The behaviour of a P/T net is defined by the transition rule.

Definition 2 (Transition rule of a P/T net). *Let $N = (P, T, F, W, m_0)$ be a P/T net. Transition $t \in T$ is* enabled *in marking m if, for all $p \in P$, $W(p, t) \leq m(p)$. If t is enabled in m, t can* fire, *producing a new marking m' where, for all $p \in P$, $m'(p) = m(p) - W(p, t) + W(t, p)$. This firing relation is denoted as $m \xrightarrow{t} m'$. It can be extended to a* marking sequence *by the following inductive scheme: $m \xrightarrow{\varepsilon} m$ (for the empty sequence ε), and $m \xrightarrow{\omega} m' \wedge m' \xrightarrow{t} m'' \implies m \xrightarrow{\omega t} m''$ (for a sequence $\omega \in T^*$ and a transition $t \in T$).*

Using the transition rule, a P/T net induces a transition system, which is also called the *reachability graph* or the *state space* of the P/T net.

Definition 3 (Labeled Transition System). *A* labeled transition system *(LTS for short) $TS = (S, L, \to, s_0)$ consists of:*

- *A finite set S of* states;
- *A finite label set L of* transitions;
- *A labeled transition relation* $\rightarrow \subseteq S \times L \times S$;
- *An* initial state $s_0 \in S$.

Definition 4 (Reachability graph). *The* reachability graph *of a P/T net* $N = (P, T, F, W, m_0)$ *is a transition system, where the set of markings, transitively reachable from the initial marking m_0 using the transition rule of the P/T net, is the set of states, and the transition rule defines the set of vertices. m_0 serves as initial state. A marking m' is* reachable *from a marking m in a P/T net if there is a marking sequence $\omega \in T^*$ with $m \xrightarrow{\omega} m'$.*

A Petri net may have infinitely many reachable markings. Throughout the whole paper, however, we restrict our considerations to Petri nets with finitely many reachable markings. In this case, the reachability graph forms a labelled transition system. We continue with the introduction of the syntax and semantics of the temporal logic CTL^*. We start with the presentation of atomic propositions.

Definition 5 (Atomic propositions). *Let $N = (P, T, F, W, m_0)$ be a P/T net. An* atomic proposition *is one of the constants* TRUE, FALSE, FIREABLE(t) *(for $t \in T$),* DEADLOCK, *or an expression of the shape $k_1 p_1 + \cdots + k_n p_n \leq k$, for some $n \in \mathbb{N}$, $k_1, \ldots, k_n, k \in \mathbb{Z}$, and $p_1, \ldots, p_n \in P$. For a marking m of N, m satisfies proposition $k_1 p_1 + \cdots + k_n p_n \leq k$ if and only if the term $\sum_{i=1}^{n} k_i m(p_i)$ actually evaluates to a number less or equal to k. The fact that m satisfies atomic proposition φ is denoted by $m \models \varphi$.*

Definition 6 (Syntax of CTL*). *For a given set of atomic proposition AP, the temporal logic CTL^* is inductively defined as follows:*

- *Every $\varphi \in AP$ is a state formula;*
- *If φ and ψ are state formulas, then $\neg \varphi$, $(\varphi \wedge \psi)$, and $(\varphi \vee \psi)$ are state formulas;*
- *Every state formula is a path formula;*
- *If φ and ψ are path formulas, then $\neg \varphi$, $(\varphi \wedge \psi)$, $(\varphi \vee \psi)$, $\mathbf{X} \varphi$, $\mathbf{F} \varphi$, $\mathbf{G} \varphi$, $(\varphi \mathbf{U} \psi)$, and $(\varphi \mathbf{R} \psi)$ are path formulas;*
- *If φ is a path formula, then $\mathbf{A} \varphi$ and $\mathbf{E} \varphi$ are state formulas.*

The set of all state formulas generated by these rules form the CTL^* formulas.

For a marking m of a reachability graph TS of a P/T net N, $L(m)$ registers the set of atomic propositions that are valid in m. The semantics of CTL^* is defined with respect to some labeled transition system, which in our case is TS.

Definition 7 (Semantics of CTL*). *Let TS be a labeled transition system and α an atomic proposition. Let φ_1 and φ_2 be state formulas and ψ_1 and ψ_2 path formulas. Marking m satisfies CTL^* state formula φ_1, denoted as $m \models \varphi_1$, and infinite path $\pi = m_0 \xrightarrow{t_0} m_1 \xrightarrow{t_1} \ldots$ satisfies CTL^* path formula π, denoted as $\pi \models \psi_1$, if and only if*

State Formulas

1. $m \models \alpha \qquad \Longleftrightarrow \quad \alpha \in L(m);$
2. $m \models \varphi_1 \wedge \varphi_2 \quad \Longleftrightarrow \quad m \models \varphi_1 \text{ and } m \models \varphi_1;$
3. $m \models \neg\varphi_1 \qquad \Longleftrightarrow \quad m \not\models \neg\varphi_1;$
4. $m \models \mathbf{E}\,\psi_1 \qquad \Longleftrightarrow \quad \pi \models \psi_1 \text{ for some path } \pi \text{ starting in } m.$

Path Formulas

Let π^i be the suffix of π starting at m_i.

1. $\pi \models \varphi_1 \qquad \Longleftrightarrow \quad m_0 \models \varphi_1;$
2. $\pi \models \neg\psi_1 \qquad \Longleftrightarrow \quad \pi \not\models \psi_1;$
3. $\pi \models \psi_1 \wedge \psi_2 \quad \Longleftrightarrow \quad \pi \models \psi_1 \text{ and } \pi \models \psi_2;$
4. $\pi \models \mathbf{X}\,\psi_1 \qquad \Longleftrightarrow \quad \pi^1 \models \psi_1;$
5. $\pi \models \psi_1 \mathbf{U}\,\psi_2 \quad \Longleftrightarrow \quad \text{there exists a } k \geq 0 \text{ such that } \pi^k \models \psi_2$
   $\text{and for all } 0 \leq j < k, \pi^j \models \psi_1;$

The semantics of the remaining CTL* operators is defined using the following tautologies:

- $(\varphi_2 \vee \varphi_2) \iff \neg(\neg\varphi_1 \wedge \neg\varphi_2);$
- $\mathbf{A}\,\psi \iff \neg\mathbf{E}\,(\neg\psi);$
- $\mathbf{F}\,\psi \iff (\text{TRUE}\,\mathbf{U}\,\psi);$
- $\mathbf{G}\,\psi \iff \neg F \neg \psi;$
- $\psi_1 \mathbf{R}\,\psi_2 \iff \neg(\neg\psi_1 \mathbf{U}\,\neg\psi_2).$

TS satisfies a state formula if its initial marking does, which is denoted by $(TS, m) \models \varphi$, *and it satisfies a path formula if all paths starting in the initial marking do, which is denoted by* $(TS, \pi) \models \varphi$.

We generally disregard finite paths (i.e. executions ending in a deadlock) in this paper. In the context of our proposed method, we do not consider them to be valid witnesses or counterexamples.

If it is clear which LTS we are using, we only write $m \models \varphi$ respectively $\pi \models \varphi$.

To define some subclasses of CTL*, we need to push negations to the level of atomic propositions.

Definition 8 (Negation normal form). *A CTL* formula is in* negation normal form *(NNF for short) if every negation occurs directly in front of an atomic propositions.*

With this, negations do not appear in front of path quantifiers or temporal operators.

For CTL^*, several fragments are frequently studied.

Definition 9 (Fragments of CTL^*). *If φ is CTL* formula, then φ is in*

- *ACTL* if φ does not contain $\mathbf{E}$ and is in NNF;*
- *ECTL* if φ does not contain $\mathbf{A}$ and is in NNF;*
- *CTL if every occurrence of $\mathbf{X}, \mathbf{F}, \mathbf{G}, \mathbf{R}, \mathbf{U}$ is immediately preceded by an occurrence of $\mathbf{A}$ or $\mathbf{E}$;*
- *LTL $\subset$ ACTL* if φ does neither contain $\mathbf{E}$ nor $\mathbf{A}$;*

4   The Theory of Under-Approximation

The under-approximation we are proposing is based on a so-called *simulation relation*. We recall the classical notion of simulation [12] in order to compare the behavior of two labeled transition systems, which, in our case, are given by two P/T nets. Intuitively, an LTS P is simulated by another LTS Q if P has less or equal behavior then Q. Technically, this is expressed by a simulation relation Σ between (the states of) P and (the states of) Q satisfying a certain semantic requirement. More precisely, every transition of P has to be somehow mimicked by an equally labeled transition of Q.

Definition 10 (Simulation [12]). *Let $P = (S, L, \rightarrow, s)$ and $Q = (S', L', \rightarrow', s'_0)$ be two labeled transition systems. A relation $\Sigma \subseteq S \times S'$ is called* simulation *relation where P is simulated by Q if and only if*

- *$(s_0, s'_0) \in \Sigma$;*
- *for each $(s_1, s'_1) \in \Sigma$, $t \in L$, and $s_2 \in S$ with $s_1 \xrightarrow{t} s_2$ in P, there exists a state s'_2, such that $s'_1 \xrightarrow{t} s'_2$ in Q and $(s_2, s'_2) \in \Sigma$.*

If there is a simulation relation Σ between P and Q, then we also say that Q *simulates P, Q is an* over-approximation *of P, or P is an* under-approximation *of Q.*

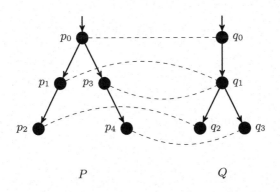

Fig. 2. LTS Q simulates LTS P

As an example for simulation consider Fig. 2. The figure shows two labeled transition systems P and Q. Q simulates P using the simulation relation $\Sigma = \{(p_0, q_0), (p_1, q_1), (p_3, q_1), (p_2, q_2), (p_4, q_3)\}$.

The simulation relation preserves certain temporal logic fragments.

Proposition 1 (Simulation preserves ACTL* [8]). *Let P and Q be two LTS with initial states s_0 and s'_0, respectively. If P simulates Q, then*

- *$(P, s_0) \models \varphi$ implies $(Q, s'_0) \models \varphi$, for any ACTL* formula φ;*

– $(Q, s_0') \models \varphi$ implies $(P, s_0) \models \varphi$, for any ECTL* formula φ.

Since negations only appear in front of atomic propositions, we cannot turn a universal path quantifier into an existential path quantifier or vice versa [3]. But, the negation of every ACTL* formula is an ECTL* formula and vice versa. The reason for this is that for all operators, we have opportunities to drive negations from the top of the formula to the bottom.

Simulation is used to show that some transformation of a labeled transition system preserves ACTL*. Using this, we can find a counterexample for ACTL* using an equivalent ECTL* formula.

Proposition 2 (Counterexample for ACTL* [3]). *For every ACTL* formula φ there exists an ECTL* formula ψ such that $\neg\varphi$ and ψ are equivalent CTL* formulas.*

We use this to propose our new idea for the verification of token scaling models. Places that contain more than a threshold of tokens in the initial marking are simply cut to a smaller number of tokens.

Definition 11 (Reduced net N_r). *Let $N = (P, T, F, W, m_0)$ be a P/T net, $n \leq |P|$ the number of initially marked places and $I = \{p_1, \ldots, p_n\} \subseteq P$ the set of initially marked places. For a given set of thresholds $\{\lambda_1, \ldots, \lambda_n\}$, a P/T net $N^r = (P, T, F, W, m_0^r)$ is called the reduced net, where the initial marking m_0 is substituted by the reduced initial marking m_0^r with*

$$m_0^r(p_i) = max\{1, min\{m_0(p_i), \lambda_i\}\}$$

for all $p_i \in I$ and $i \in \{1, \ldots, n\}$.

At least one token is kept in a place, if there were initially tokens in that place.

For keeping the evaluation of atomic propositions congruent between the reduced and the original net, we introduce the following method for evaluating propositions in the reduced net.

Definition 12 (Evaluation of propositions in the reduced net). *Let m^r be a marking reachable in the reduced net, m_0^r the initial marking of the reduced net, m_0 the initial marking of the original net, and φ an atomic proposition. Then, in the reduced net, the value of φ in m^r is defined as the value of φ in $(m^r + (m_0 - m_0^r))$, as defined for the initial net.*

Now we have all ingredients together to propose a new under-approximation for token-scaling models.

Theorem 1 (N simulates N^r). *If N is a P/T net, with LTS $P = (S, L, \rightarrow, s_0)$ and N^r is the corresponding reduced net, with LTS $Q = (S^r, L^r, \rightarrow^r, s_0^r)$, then P simulates Q with a property-preserving simulation relation, and $(Q, s_0^r) \models \varphi$ implies $(P, s_0) \models \varphi$, for all ECTL* formulas φ.*

Proof. The existence of a property-preserving simulation together with Proposition 1 preserves ECTL*. Since the reduced system Q is an under-approximation, it holds that the original LTS P is relative to the reduced system an over-approximation. Definition 12 guarantees that the removed tokens are still considered in the evaluation of the propositions, so the simulation relation that maps m^r to $mr + (m_0 - m_0^r)$ preserves the atomic propositions. For over-approximations, it is well known (Proposition 1) that the simulation preserves ACTL*. And with the inversion, which is the under-approximation, the simulation preserves ECTL*.

Proposition 3. *If an ECTL* formula φ is true in a reduced net N^r, then φ is also true in the original net N. If an ACTL* formula φ is false in the reduced net N^r, then φ is also false in N.*

Proof. Follows directly from Corollary 1.

Corollary 1. *Since LTL is a subset of ACTL*, the proposition for ACTL* is also true for very LTL formula.*

For model checking, we can use this approach with standard model checking algorithms on the reachability graph and can combine it with other reduction techniques such as partial order reduction [7,14,17]. The method is sufficient for ECTL* and reachability, and it is necessary for ACTL* and LTL.

5   Heuristics

Finding the optimal threshold for the reduced initial marking of a P/T net is hard, as two objectives oppose each other. On the one hand, a small state space is desired and therefore initially marked places should have as few tokens as possible. On the other hand, fewer tokens also mean a smaller probability to still verify the property under investigation. It, thus, is an optimization problem to exactly find the fewest number of tokens, which are needed to produce the witness path or counterexample, respectively. Since the solution to this problem is as hard as the original issue, we propose four heuristics to get a good threshold.

In the sequel, let $N = (P, T, F, W, m_0)$ be a P/T net, $n \leq |P|$ the number of initially marked places and $I = \{p_1, \ldots, p_n\} \subseteq P$ the set of initially marked places. Further, let $N^r = (P, T, F, W, m_0^r)$ be the reduced net and $\Lambda = \{\lambda_1, \ldots, \lambda_n\}$ the set of thresholds.

The idea behind the first heuristic is to assign each initially marked place a constant.

Definition 13 (Simple threshold heuristic). *Let $x \in \mathbb{N}$ be a constant. If we set $\lambda_i = x$ with $\lambda_i \in \Lambda$ and $i \in \{1, \ldots, n\}$, then the initial marking is computed by the* simple threshold heuristic.

If a constant is used, then it is also obvious to use a percentage.

Definition 14 (Percentage heuristic). *Let $x \in \mathbb{N}$ be a multiplier. If we set $\lambda_i = m_0(p_i)/100 \cdot x$ with $\lambda_i \in \Lambda$ and $i \in \{1, \ldots, n\}$, then the initial marking is computed by the* percent heuristic. *Here, "/" is assumed to be integer division.*

The hypothesis for the third heuristic is that at least as many tokens are needed to satisfy the greatest "constant" of the P/T net and the formula, where constants of the net include arc weights, and/ constants of the formula include the values of the k_i and k in propositions $k_1 p_1 + \cdots + k_n p_n \leq k$.

Definition 15 (Largest constant heuristic). *Let φ be a formula and $x \in \mathbb{N}$ a multiplier. Further, let W^* be the* maximal arc weight *with $W^* = max\{W(f)|f \in F\}$ of N. In addition, if φ has the form $k_1 p_1 + \cdots + k_n p_n \leq k$, then K^* is the* maximal formula constant *with $K^* = max\{k_i \mid k_i$ occurs in $\varphi, i \in \{1, \ldots, n\}\}$. Otherwise, $K^* = 0$. If we set $\lambda_i = max\{W^*, K^*\} \cdot x$ with $\lambda_i \in \Lambda$ and $i \in \{1, \ldots, n\}$, then the initial marking is computed by the* largest constant heuristic.

The multiplier x is used as an additional buffer. The size of x is arbitrary and a suitable value must be determined by experiments.

Our last heuristics exploits the state equation [13]. The general idea is that we want to keep as many tokens as necessary for realizing a minimal solution of the state equation. Given a conjunction of atomic propositions, the state equation delivers a transition indexed vector x such that, if every transition t is fired $x[t]$ times, a state satisfying the conjunction of propositions is reached. It does not, however, guarantee that any such sequence of transitions is indeed enabled. Our goal here is to keep enough tokens to enabled some sequence of transitions that corresponds to the solution of the state equation.

Of course, we need to approximate this idea in order to obtain a heuristics in due time. For defining the heuristics, we introduce some concepts. First, we assume the set of transitions to be ordered in a way that transitions enabled in the initial marking appear first, post-transitions of their post-places next, and so on. The idea is that appearance in this order has a certain probability of being indeed the order of an actual firing sequence. Let $\underline{s}$ be a transition-indexed vector $\underline{s} : T \to \mathbb{Z}$. For any such $\underline{s}$, let seq($\underline{s}$) be the sequence of transitions where every transition t occurs $\underline{s}(t)$ times and the order of appearance is as discussed above. For each transition sequence w, there exists a unique minimal marking m_w where w is enabled.

Definition 16 (State equation heuristic). *Let $\phi = \bigwedge_{i=1}^{n} \phi_i$ be a formula where each ϕ_i is just a conjunction of simple comparisons. Let $y \in \mathbb{N}$ be a multiplier. For each transition t, let x_t be a variable, and $\underline{x}$ the vector of these x_t. For each ϕ_i, let $\underline{s}_i$ be a solution of the linear program*

$$Minimise \sum_{t \in T} x_t \text{ in } C \cdot \underline{x} = m - m_0, m \models \phi_i$$

where C is the incidence matrix of the net.

If we set $\lambda_i = y \cdot max\{m_{seq(\underline{s}_i)}(p_i)\}$ with $\lambda_i \in \Lambda$ and $i \in \{1, \ldots, n\}$, then the initial marking is computed by the state equation heuristic.

So for each subformula ϕ_i, the threshold is the number of tokens necessary for enabling the sequence seq($\underline{s}$), where $\underline{s}$ solves a linear program describing the reachability of ϕ_i.

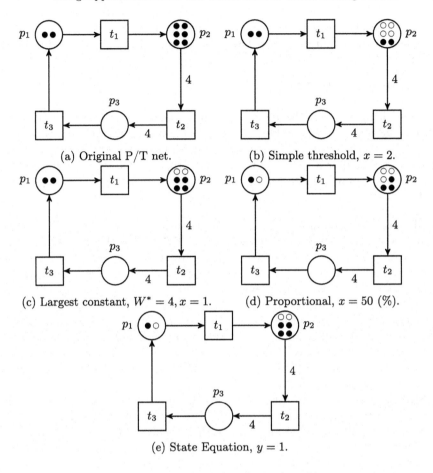

(a) Original P/T net.

(b) Simple threshold, $x = 2$.

(c) Largest constant, $W^* = 4, x = 1$.

(d) Proportional, $x = 50$ (%).

(e) State Equation, $y = 1$.

Fig. 3. Heuristics for reduced initial markings.

Figure 3 shows the different approaches to compute the reduced initial marking. The original P/T net can be seen in Fig. 3a. Places p_1 and p_2 have two respectively six tokens on them. Figure 3b shows the *simple threshold* approach with $x = 2$. The result is that the number of tokens on p_2 is reduced to two tokens. Place p_1 remains unchanged. The white tokens are the tokens that are frozen in the original initial marking. In Fig. 3c the *largest constant heuristic* is used. Since we do not use a formula in this example, the largest constant is based on the maximum arc weight, which is in this case four. Four is also the threshold, because the multiplier is one ($x = 1$). Only the number of tokens on p_2 is reduced to four. The *percentage heuristic*, with $x = 50$ (%), is shown in Fig. 3d. The token count is halved on all places. For the state equation heuristic, consider the formula **EF** $p_1 \geq 4$. The state equation, applied to the constraint $p_1 \geq 4$, would return the solution $x_{t_1} = 0$, $x_{t_2} = 1$, and $x_{t_3} = 2$. We would arrange this into the sequence $t_2 t_3 t_3$ and obtain $(0, 4, 0)$ as the minimal initial marking to enable that sequence. The resulting modification is shown in Fig. 3e.

6   Implementation

In the implementation of the under-approximation, we actually remove the frozen tokens and apply model checking procedures off the shelf. However, we need to reflect the frozen tokens in the atomic propositions of the property under investigation. This requires to adjust the atomic propositions, too. We differentiate between two approaches based on the type of atomic proposition we want to verify.

- **Monotonous method.** Consider a negation-free state predicate. If a certain atomic proposition is monotonic, meaning it compares the number of tokens to a marking in a way that we always state that we require the number of tokens to be greater or equal to a certain threshold, then we could use the original atomic proposition. Thus, the monotonous method is only applicable for positive comparisons, meaning that the places appear only with positive factors in the atomic proposition (whenever $k_i \cdot m(p_i)$ appears in an atomic proposition it holds that $k_i \geq 1$). This approach is basically valuable for FIREABLE(t) predicates which talk about the fireability of a transition t. Fireability is inherently the comparison of token counts to thresholds which are the weight of the arcs.
- **Shift method.** For all token count comparisons, we can use the shift approach. Here, we reflect the effect of the frozen tokens by a modification of the atomic proposition. Take for example the atomic proposition $2 \cdot p_1 + p_2 \leq 7$ which involves place p_1 with multiplier 2. Then, three frozen tokens mean that the threshold of the remaining tokens need to exceed only one, $2 \cdot p_1 + p_2 \leq 1$, in order for the original number of tokens to exceed seven. This approach is valuable for cardinality queries.

7   Experimental Validation

As a proof-of-concept, we implemented the under-approximation method in our explicit model checker LoLA [19]. For evaluating the method and its different heuristics, we used the benchmark provided by the MCC 2019 [5]. The benchmark consists of 94 models. Due to the scaling parameter this results in 1018 model instances. We only consider P/T nets that are not safe and where the initial marking has removable tokens. We also avoided one instance with more than 2^{32} tokens. Even though, this instance is well suited for the under-approximation method due to the enormous token count, we had to ignore it to avoid an overflow in LoLA.

As specifications, we used the reachability formulas provided in the MCC 2019, too. Although the introduced method works for ACTL*, ECTL*, and LTL formulas, we only present the experimental results for reachability queries, which have the form $\mathbf{AG}\,\varphi$ or $\mathbf{EF}\,\varphi$ and are part of ACTL* or ECTL*, respectively. The results for LTL and CTL are similar and so we simply skip them. For each instance, we have 32 reachability formulas: 16 of them are concerned with the cardinality of tokens on places, and the other 16 are concerned with the fireability of transitions. All in all, we consider 21 models resulting in 214 instances with 32 formulas for each instance. This results in a total of 6848 verification runs.

We executed the experiments on our machine Tajo, which has 96 physical cores running at 3.9 GHz max. and 1.5 TB RAM. The operation system running on Tajo is CentOS Linux 7 (Core).

We run our new method with partial order reduction in parallel to the entire reachability portfolio [20] of LoLA. The portfolio consists of the following techniques:

- Formula simplification [2,11] in the preprocessing;
- Net reduction [1] in the preprocessing;
- The actual state space search with partial order reduction [17];
- A structural method, namely a *counterexample guided abstraction refinement* (CEGAR) in combination with the state equation [18];
- A find path search [15] based on a guided random walk.

Table 1. Characteristics of benchmark. Preprocessing: the formula can be evaluated by just inspecting the initial marking; Unreachable: a true universally quantified or false existentially quantified formula; Reachable: a false universally quantified or true existentially quantified formula.

	All (6848)	
	#	%
Preprocessing	1252	18.3
Unreachable	2801	40.9
Reachable	2795	40.8

As Table 1 shows, 18.3% of all formulas are verified directly in the preprocessing. The remaining formulas can be separated into reachable or unreachable formulas. Reachable formulas have the form $\mathbf{EF}\,\varphi = \mathbf{true}$ or $\mathbf{AF}\,\varphi = \mathbf{false}$ and unreachable formulas have the opposite result. Table 1 shows also that 40.9% of the formulas are unreachable. Hence, our new method is applicable to 2795 (40.8%) formulas. We use this number as reference for the following experiments.

Table 2 shows that the entire portfolio run without our new method, is able to verify 6732 (98.3%) queries. The methods from the portfolio are available for many years, highly optimized, and already pushed to the limits. This means, the remaining 116 (1.7%) formulas are hard to verify.

We exhaustively tested the introduced method with its heuristics in several different settings for the parameters. We conducted experiments for the simple

Table 2. Percentage of formulas, separated by the winning technique in the portfolio.

Technique	All (6848)	
	#	%
Preprocessing	1252	18.3
Findpath	2248	32.8
State equation	268	3.9
Search	2964	43.3
All together	6732	98.3
Unknown	116	1.7

threshold, percentage, and largest constant heuristic with a variety of multipliers. The figures show the success rate (left y-axis) for different parameter settings (x-axis). The columns (right y-axis) indicate, how many formulas from the pile of 116 very hard formulas could be solved, where the whole portfolio with the standard setting of the parameters was not successful.

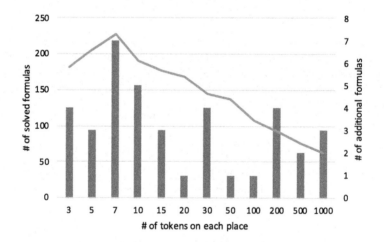

Fig. 4. Simple threshold heuristics.

The first experiments with the simple threshold show that if λ is set to 7, then 228 (8.2%) reachable formulas are verified by our new method. Even 7 (6%) additional formulas from the 116 hard-to-verify formulas could be solved. Figure 4 shows that a higher value for λ decreases the performance of our new method. However, in any case additional queries could be verified.

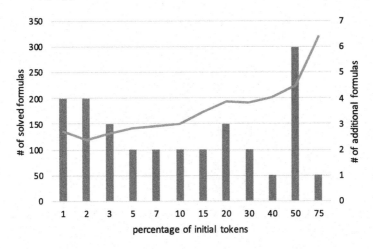

Fig. 5. Percentage heuristic.

As seen in Fig. 5, the experiments with the percentage heuristic show that with a higher percentage more queries could be verified, but the number of additional verified queries is decreasing. This behavior is also to be expected, since the higher the percentage, the more similar our new method is to the actual search. In all cases additional queries could be verified. The big outlier of additional verified formulas with λ set 50 is due to a single instance. We disregard this outlier as parameter over-fitting.

As seen in Fig. 6, the largest constant heuristic verifies less formulas than the other two heuristics. However, with a well chosen multiplier, five to six additional queries could be verified.

The state equation heuristic is only able to verify 30 (1.1%) of all queries and only one additional query is verified.

All in all, the experiments show that the under-approximation method is a valuable addition to a portfolio. The simple threshold and the percentage heuristic show the best overall performance. They are able to verify between 5% and 10% of all queries and they verify up to 5% or 6% of hard-to-solve formulas which no other technique could solve.

The implemented methods shall be available with the next release of LoLA 2.

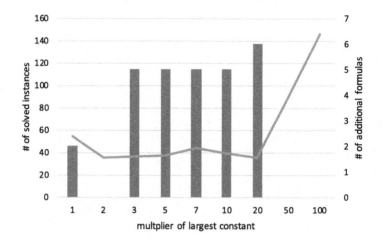

Fig. 6. Largest constant heuristic.

8   Conclusion

Token-scaling P/T nets tend to have large state spaces, since they have a large number of tokens on the initially marked places. They are used in several different fields and their applications are widespread, as for instance in biochemical reaction chains or in scheduling problems. Experiments showed that there are a lot of properties that can be verified using much fewer tokens in the initial marking.

We introduced an under-approximation for token-scaling P/T nets, as a lightweight addition to existing portfolios. It can be used as a sufficient, respectively necessary quick check, depending on the verified property. More precisely, the method can be applied to temporal logic formulas where a witness path or a counterexample path can be found, which happens to be all reachability problems, some ACTL* and ECTL* formulas, and all LTL formulas.

The method is compatible with other reduction techniques used in state space verification, such as partial order reduction, or symmetry [16]. Furthermore, the under-approximation method complements overapproximation approaches like the ones based on the state equation [18]. This is convenient since under-approximation gives a definite result in exactly the opposite cases then over-approximation.

The experiments show that running the under-approximation method in a portfolio with other model checking algorithms speeds up the verification process up to 10%, which, in reverse, gives more time to other aspects of verification. Furthermore, the new method is able to verify properties that no other technique could solve. But not only the runtime is reduced, but also the memory consumption. In addition to the smaller state space, fewer tokens are used in the markings, which means that storing a marking requires less memory.

The biggest open issue is to find the number of required tokens on the initially marked places, which results in the smallest possible state space that is still able to verify the property under investigation. To tackle this problem, we introduced four heuristics that were able to increase the performance. To find better heuristics using structural information of the P/T net and also information regarding the formula is left for future work. Another question is, whether it is possible to also prove unreachable queries with a reduced number of tokens in the initial marking. This would, for example, amount to analyzing, during the exploration of the reduced net, whether the frozen tokens would impact the choice of the stubborn sets used for state space reduction. A solution to this problem would make the method complete.

References

1. Berthelot, G., Terrat, R.: Petri nets theory for the correctness of protocols. In: Carl, A. Sunshine (ed.) Protocol Specification, Testing and Verification, Proceedings of the IFIP WG6.1 Second International Workshop on Protocol Specification, Testing and Verification, Idyllwild, CA, USA, 17–20 May, 1982, pp. 325–342. North-Holland (1982)
2. Bønneland, F., Dyhr, J., Jensen, P.G., Johannsen, M., Srba, J.: Simplification of CTL formulae for efficient model checking of petri nets. In: Khomenko, V., Roux, O.H. (eds.) PETRI NETS 2018. LNCS, vol. 10877, pp. 143–163. Springer, Cham (2018). https://doi.org/10.1007/978-3-319-91268-4_8
3. Clarke, E.M., Henzinger, T.A., Veith, H., Bloem, R.: Handbook of Model Checking. Springer, Cham (2018)
4. Clarke, E.M., Klieber, W., Nováček, M., Zuliani, P.: Model checking and the state explosion problem. In: Meyer, B., Nordio, M. (eds.) LASER 2011. LNCS, vol. 7682, pp. 1–30. Springer, Heidelberg (2012). https://doi.org/10.1007/978-3-642-35746-6_1
5. Amparore, E., et al.: Presentation of the 9th edition of the model checking contest. In: Beyer, D., Huisman, M., Kordon, F., Steffen, B. (eds.) TACAS 2019. LNCS, vol. 11429, pp. 50–68. Springer, Cham (2019). https://doi.org/10.1007/978-3-030-17502-3_4
6. Napione, L., et al.: On the use of stochastic petri nets in the analysis of signal transduction pathways for angiogenesis process. In: Degano, P., Gorrieri, R. (eds.) CMSB 2009. LNCS, vol. 5688, pp. 281–295. Springer, Heidelberg (2009). https://doi.org/10.1007/978-3-642-03845-7_19
7. Godefroid, P., Wolper, P.: A partial approach to model checking. Inf. Comput. **110**(2), 305–326 (1994)
8. Grumberg, O., Long, D.E.: Model checking and modular verification. In: Baeten, J.C.M., Groote, J.F. (eds.) CONCUR 1991. LNCS, vol. 527, pp. 250–265. Springer, Heidelberg (1991). https://doi.org/10.1007/3-540-54430-5_93
9. Heiner, M.: GPPP (2016). https://mcc.lip6.fr/pdf/GPPP-form.pdf. Accessed 15 Aug 2020
10. Kordon, F.: Robot Manipulation (2017). https://mcc.lip6.fr/pdf/RobotManipulation-form.pdf. Accessed 08 Dec 2020
11. Liebke, T., Wolf, K.: Taking some burden off an explicit CTL model checker. In: Donatelli, S., Haar, S. (eds.) PETRI NETS 2019. LNCS, vol. 11522, pp. 321–341. Springer, Cham (2019). https://doi.org/10.1007/978-3-030-21571-2_18

12. Milner, R.: Communication and Concurrency. Prentice Hall international series in computer science. Prentice Hall, New York (1989)
13. Murata, T.: Petri nets: properties, analysis and applications. Proc. IEEE **77**(4), 541–580 (1989)
14. Peled, D.: All from one, one for all: on model checking using representatives. In: Courcoubetis, C. (ed.) CAV 1993. LNCS, vol. 697, pp. 409–423. Springer, Heidelberg (1993). https://doi.org/10.1007/3-540-56922-7_34
15. Schmidt, K.: Lola wird pfadfinder. In: Desel, J., Oberweis, A., eds, 6. Workshop Algorithmen und Werkzeuge für Petrinetze (AWPN'99), Frankfurt, Germany, October 11–12, 1999, volume 26 of CEUR Workshop Proceedings. CEUR-WS.org (1999)
16. Schmidt, K.: How to calculate symmetries of petri nets. Acta Inf. **36**(7), 545–590 (2000)
17. Valmari, A.: Stubborn sets for reduced state space generation. In: Rozenberg, G. (ed.) ICATPN 1989. LNCS, vol. 483, pp. 491–515. Springer, Heidelberg (1991). https://doi.org/10.1007/3-540-53863-1_36
18. Wimmel, H., Wolf, K.: Applying CEGAR to the Petri net state equation. Logical Meth. Comput. Sci. **8**(3) (2012)
19. Wolf, K.: Petri net model checking with LoLA 2. In: Khomenko, V., Roux, O.H. (eds.) PETRI NETS 2018. LNCS, vol. 10877, pp. 351–362. Springer, Cham (2018). https://doi.org/10.1007/978-3-319-91268-4_18
20. Wolf, K.: Portfolio management in explicit model checking. In: Köhler-Bußmeier, M., Kindler, E., Rölke, H. (eds.) Proceedings of the International Workshop on Petri Nets and Software Engineering co-located with 41st International Conference on Application and Theory of Petri Nets and Concurrency (PETRI NETS 2020), Paris, France, June 24, 2020 (due to COVID-19: virtual conference), vol. 2651 of CEUR Workshop Proceedings, pp. 10–28. CEUR-WS.org (2020)

Portfolio Management in Explicit Model Checking

Karsten Wolf[(✉)]

Institut für Informatik, Universität Rostock, Rostock, Germany
karsten.wolf@uni.rostock.de

Abstract. Thanks to a rich Petri net theory, there exists a broad range of verification techniques for Petri nets. Most of them have a performance that highly depends on the particular combination of net and property. That is why several verification tools for Petri nets use portfolio approaches where various verification algorithms are run concurrently.

In this note, we sketch the architecture of a portfolio manager, using the tool LoLA 2.0 as a running example. The portfolio of a verification problem is organized as a task tree. The leafs of the task tree are actual verification algorithms while the inner nodes represent the logical structure of the portfolio. The portfolio manager schedules verification algorithms and assigns resources to them (processor cores, memory, and time). Moreover, it evaluates the consequences of returned results with regard to the original verification problem.

1 Introduction

There exist several approaches for verification, ranging from explicit model checking [4] via BDD based model checking [3] to SAT based model checking [24]. For Petri nets, the variety of methods is larger than elsewhere since we can also use unfoldings [6] and the whole bandwidth of Petri net structure theory.

The verification methods have in common that their performance on a particular model is almost unpredictable. Most methods have an unpleasant worst-case complexity ranging somewhere between NP-completeness and EXPSPACE-completeness [13]. Reduction techniques such as the stubborn set method [20] and the symmetry method [8,15] try to alleviate that complexity but their success again depends on the shape of the model and the property. For end users with limited expertise in Petri net theory, it is difficult to choose the most promising methods for their particular problem instance.

That is why several contemporary tools such as Tapaal [5], ITS-Tools [18], or LoLA [27] use portfolio approaches. That is, several promising algorithms are launched (sequentially or concurrently) until one of them delivers an answer to the original verification problem.

In this paper, we shall discuss the architecture of a portfolio manager, the component of a Petri net verification tool that takes care of organizing a portfolio

© Springer-Verlag GmbH Germany, part of Springer Nature 2022
M. Koutny et al. (Eds.): ToPNoC XVI, LNCS 13220, pp. 91–111, 2022.
https://doi.org/10.1007/978-3-662-65303-6_5

of verification algorithms. We use the portfolio manager of LoLA as a reference. However, we expect the central statements of the paper to be universal.

A portfolio manager has two main duties. First, it has to record the results of the launched verification algorithms and to trigger consequences for the remaining algorithms. Second, it has to schedule the resources (available processor cores and memory as well as available run time) to the running algorithms.

We shall first discuss typical ingredients of a portfolio (Sect. 2). We then encapsulate verification algorithms in *tasks*, the main object to be treated by the portfolio manager (Sect. 3). Section 4 reveals the lifecycle of a task. Subsequently, we introduce *task trees* for representing the logical dependencies between the portfolio members (Sect. 5). Finally, we discuss the scheduling of tasks (Sects. 7 and 8).

2 Constituents of a Portfolio

In this section, we give examples of verification algorithms that may serve as constituents of a verification portfolio.

Search Algorithms. Most verification problems can be solved by a traversal of the state space or the product of the state space and an automaton representing the verification problem. For reachability queries, a simple depth-first traversal of the state space is sufficient. For model checking CTL formulas [4,23] or LTL formulas [22], search needs to be combined with a detection of strongly connected components [17].

In all cases, search is subject to the state explosion problem. For concurrent systems, the main application domain of Petri nets, stubborn set methods are among the most important state space reduction methods. Stubborn set is a whole family of approaches (see [21] for a recent overview). The particular approach to be used depends on the property under verification. However, even for one and the same property, more than one stubborn set method may be available. In [10], several stubborn set methods for reachability and home properties are discussed. One of the reachability preserving methods performs particularly well if the given state predicate is indeed reachable. In this case, it tends to find a very short path to a target state. As soon as a target state is reached, search may be stopped. That is, when searching for reachable states, we typically produce only a tiny portion of the state space (a phenomenon that is referred to as on-the-fly verification). If that stubborn set, however, is applied to a state predicate that is unreachable, the whole reduced state space needs to be explored and is typically much larger than the reduced state space obtained using an alternative stubborn set method proposed in [10]. This asymmetric behavior with respect to the prospective outcome of verification can be observed in virtually all verification problems used in the yearly model checking contests (MCC, [9]). Needless to mention that it is not possible to select the right method in advance unless the answer to the problem is known anyway.

Consequently, a portfolio for reachability may already include two different search algorithms, one speculating on reachability of the predicate, the other speculating on unreachability of the predicate.

Similar pairs of stubborn set methods exist for other classes of properties as well.

Symbolic Methods. Symbolic methods include BDD based model checkers [3] or similar approaches [19], SAT based methods [24], and unfolding approaches [6]. As we have no particular experience with these methods, we cannot elaborate much on details of these methods.

Petri Net Structure Theory. In [25], a method for verifying reachability queries has been presented that is based on the Petri net state equation. It can give negative answers (state equation has no solution) as well as positive answers (state equation has a solution that can be turned into a fireable transition sequence). If the state equation has a solution that cannot be arranged to a fireable transition sequence, it searches for alternative solutions of the state equation. The method is not guaranteed to terminate. However, since solving a linear system of equations and inequations is "only" NP-complete and hence requires only polynomial space, memory consumption of the state equation approach is rather moderate.

Another purely structural approach is the invocation of the siphon/trap-property [7]. It establishes a sufficient criterion for non-reachability of a deadlock. The property can be verified as a SAT problem [14]. Hence, it requires only polynomial space but has a rather unpredictable (NP-complete) runtime. If the siphon/trap property does not hold, deadlocks may or may not be reachable.

Underapproximation. In some application domains (including biochemical reaction networks), Petri net models may have initial markings with a large number of tokens on some places. An extreme example is the GPPP benchmark [9] that is used in the MCC and has places with initially more than 2^{32} tokens. Consequently, moving these tokens just to the next place may include 2^{32} transition occurrences and induce more than 2^{32} states, too much for explicit model checking.

If a verification problem asks for the presence of just a few tokens on an initially empty place, it is unlikely that all of the 2^{32} tokens of an initially marked place are needed. Therefore, a portfolio for reachability and selected other problems may include a special search routine where most tokens on places with a large initial marking are "frozen". We obtain an underapproximation of the original state space which means that the property is indeed reachable in the original state space if it is reachable in the underapproximation while it may or may not be reachable in the original state space if it is unreachable in the underapproximation.

The dual approach, overapproximations, do not make sense in explicit verification since they require more space that the actual state space. For symbolic model checking, however, overapproximations are a valid tool for reducing the size of BDDs.

Skeleton Net. If the given net is a high-level net, we may consider the skeleton (the P/T net just obtained by ignoring colors). There is a net morphism between the high-level net and its skeleton, so some properties including reachability are preserved: if a marking is reachable in a high-level net, the corresponding marking is also reachable in the skeleton (the reverse is not true). Since it is very easy to obtain the skeleton from a high-level net, the approach may yield results for high-level nets that are too large to be unfolded to equivalent P/T nets. The MCC contains some high-level nets of this kind. For verifying the skeleton, we may again employ several algorithms such as search or the state equation.

If the original net is a P/T net, we may fold that into a high-level net for obtaining a skeleton, so the approach is applicable for both high-level and low-level input.

Strength Reduction. For some property ϕ, there may be a simpler property that implies ϕ or is implied by ϕ. Adding a verification algorithm for the simpler property may thus help for verifying ϕ. For instance, satisfaction of the CTL property $EF \psi$ is necessary for satisfaction of $E(\chi U \psi)$ while $AG \psi$ is sufficient for $EG \psi$. The pure reachability problems $EF \psi$ and $AG \psi$ are indeed simpler since they enable the use of additional verification algorithms such as the state equation approach mentioned above.

Random Walks. For properties where the witness or counterexample is just a single finite path, one can simply launch random walks through the state space. If such a walk hits a witness (counterexample), the property holds (does not holds) while otherwise the method does not terminate. The method is extremely memory-efficient since we do not need to store visited states. At the same time, it can fire transitions at an extremely high rate as we do not need to search nor store markings. Consequently, random walks are a poor verification method when applied standalone, but a very useful member of a portfolio. The likelihood of hitting a witness or counterexample path can be increased by applying suitable stubborn set methods in the selection of the next transition to be fired.

Boolean Combinations. If a formula to be verified is a Boolean combination, sub-formulas can be verified separately. That is, the verification algorithms for the individual sub-formulas establish separate portfolio members.

Conclusion. Portfolios may be large (with more than 10 constituents) and diverse. We have complete and incomplete methods (incomplete in the sense that they do not always terminate, or may terminate without a definite answer to the problem). Methods may answer to the original problem or only to a sub-problem. Methods have a broad range of expected memory and runtime consumption. It is therefore necessary to establish a structured approach to portfolios, the *portfolio manager.*

3   Tasks of a Portfolio

With the concept of a *task*, we design an object that encapsulates a particular verification algorithm and augments it with all necessary information to execute it as a portfolio member. These data include the necessary inputs, the status of the task in its lifecycle (see Sect. 4), results and statistics (for completed tasks), assigned resources (discussed in Sect. 8), and data that are relevant for execution and scheduling (also discussed there).

Input. Currently, LoLA is called with a single Petri net and a list of verification problems, given as CTL* formulas. This standard is established by the setup of the MCC. However, a verification tool needs to internally deal with more than one net and more than one formula, independent of the original input. Multiple formulas come into play since we may want to separately verify sub-formulas if the verification problem is a disjunction or conjunction. In addition, we may add distinct formulas using the strength reduction explained in Sect. 2. If we apply the skeleton approach explained in the same section, we have two distinct nets for every given verification problem. In addition, we may want to apply net reduction [1,16] to the net before running an actual verification algorithm. Since the applicability of reduction rules depends on the verification problem, we may end up with several different nets. We conclude that we need to assign an individual net and an individual formula to every verification task.

Results and Statistics. Since many portfolio members are only necessary or only sufficient, or do not terminate in all cases, it is reasonable to introduce a value *unknown* to the usual values *true* and *false*. In addition, we propose a fourth value *void* that is used if the verification algorithm has not yet run. The difference between *unknown* and *void* is that *unknown* may be propagated as final value to the original verification problem if no task in the portfolio delivers a *true* or *false*. In contrast, *void* is not propagated since a definite result may be found subsequently.

Beyond the plain yes/no answer to the verification problem approached by a task, results may include additional diagnostic information such as witness or counterexample paths as well as witness or counterexample states. If search algorithms use storage methods based on Bloom filtering, diagnostic information may include a likelihood of hash conflicts that may be used for judging about the risk that the state space is actually incomplete.

Statistical information includes the number of visited states, fired transitions, run time, consumed memory and other information that is useful for evaluating the performance of the algorithm or the difficulty of the problem instance with respect to the verification algorithm.

4   Lifecycle of a Task

Figure 1 depicts a state machine representing the lifecycle of a task. In the sequel, we shall describe its states and transitions.

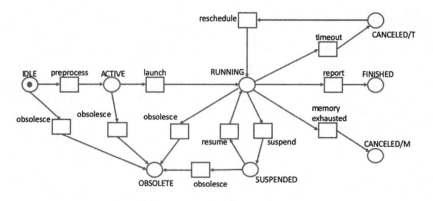

Fig. 1. The lifecycle of a task.

4.1   States of the Lifecycle

IDLE. This is the initial state of the lifecycle. The task is created as a result of the planning phase of the verification tool. The planning phase of a verification tool is run subsequent to parsing the net(s) and verification problem(s). For temporal logic formulas, rewriting is applied [2] since that may simplify the verification problem, or may identify it as tautology or contradiction. After rewriting, the formula is categorized. The planning phase then puts together the portfolio, based on the category of the problem and, if given, command line options of the verification tool. In state IDLE, the task is not ready for execution. In particular, the net assigned to the task may require preprocessing such as net reduction or the calculation of auxiliary data. For the latter, an interesting example is a pre-calculated set of conflicting transitions (the set $(\bullet t)\bullet$ for a given transition t). This information is needed in every marking of a search algorithm, especially for stubborn set calculations. Since a typical search visits hundreds of millions of markings, a pre-computed list of conflicting transitions saves a substantial amount of runtime. Its calculation may consume several seconds or even minutes. Although a task is not ready for execution in state IDLE, it is beneficial for the portfolio manager to know idle tasks since this information enables the portfolio manager to plan resources for their future execution.

ACTIVE. An active task is ready for execution, This means that all preprocessing of inputs is completed. The task is just lacking the assignment of resources for execution by the scheduler that is part of the portfolio manager.

RUNNING. A running task is executing the actual verification algorithm. During this phase, there are two kinds of interaction between the algorithm and the portfolio manager. First, the portfolio manager controls the use of resources assigned to the task. We discuss this issue in Sect. 7. Second, the portfolio manager collects status data of the algorithm (e.g. number of markings visited so far, number of fired transitions, etc.). Such status information is quite useful to give

```
                            FINISHED FORMULA: CATEGORY   VALUE  PRODUCED BY
SharedMemory-PT-000050-ReachabilityCardinality-00:  INITIAL    true   preprocessing
SharedMemory-PT-000050-ReachabilityCardinality-01:  AG         false  state space
SharedMemory-PT-000050-ReachabilityCardinality-02:  INITIAL    true   preprocessing
SharedMemory-PT-000050-ReachabilityCardinality-03:  AG         false  state space
SharedMemory-PT-000050-ReachabilityCardinality-05:  INITIAL    true   preprocessing
SharedMemory-PT-000050-ReachabilityCardinality-08:  AG         false  state equation
SharedMemory-PT-000050-ReachabilityCardinality-09:  AG         false  state equation
SharedMemory-PT-000050-ReachabilityCardinality-10:  EF         false  state equation
SharedMemory-PT-000050-ReachabilityCardinality-11:  EF         true   state equation
SharedMemory-PT-000050-ReachabilityCardinality-12:  EF         true   state equation
SharedMemory-PT-000050-ReachabilityCardinality-13:  AG         true   state equation

                            PENDING FORMULAS: CATEGORY  IDL  ACT  RUN  SUS  FIN  C/T  C/M  OBS
SharedMemory-PT-000050-ReachabilityCardinality-04:  EF    0    1    1    0    2    0    0    0
SharedMemory-PT-000050-ReachabilityCardinality-06:  AG    0    1    1    0    2    0    0    0
SharedMemory-PT-000050-ReachabilityCardinality-07:  EF    0    0    2    0    2    0    0    0
SharedMemory-PT-000050-ReachabilityCardinality-14:  AG    0    0    0    0    1    0    0    0
SharedMemory-PT-000050-ReachabilityCardinality-15:  EF    0    0    0    0    1    0    0    0

TASK CATEGORY  TYPE   TIME/TLIMIT  MEM PG/PGLIMIT  FORMULA                                            STATUS
  57    EF     STEQ   3/32000000   0/5             SharedMemory-PT-000050-ReachabilityCardinality-06  sara is running.
  60    EF     STEQ   3/32000000   0/5             SharedMemory-PT-000050-ReachabilityCardinality-07  sara is running.
  61    EF     EXCL   3/32000000   1/2048          SharedMemory-PT-000050-ReachabilityCardinality-07  152 m, 30 m/sec, 240 t fired, .
  63    EF     STEQ   3/32000000   0/5             SharedMemory-PT-000050-ReachabilityCardinality-04  sara is running.
```

Fig. 2. Displaying the status of tasks.

the user the impression that the tool is running properly. The status information needs to be aggregated for all running tasks in order to create a readable display.

Figure 2 shows an example of an aggregated status report in LoLA. The first block reports all verification problems (referred to by an identifier) which have already been solved, their category, their value, and the portfolio member that delivered the result for that problem. The second block displays, for every other formula, the number of portfolio members that are available for that problem, and the status of these tasks. The third block displays the running tasks with the type of underlying algorithm (in the example: three times state equation and one depth-first search), their assigned resources, and the algorithm-dependent status information collected by the portfolio manager.

FINISHED. A finished task has completed the execution of its verification algorithm and delivered its result.

OBSOLETE. A task is obsolete if its result is not needed anymore to determine the answer to an original verification problem. If, for instance, a verification problem is a disjunction of two subproblems, and one of the subproblems is found to be true, all tasks supporting the other subproblem become obsolete. The main factual difference between a finished and an obsolete task is that statistical information and results such as counterexamples or witnesses are present and meaningful only for finished, but not for obsolete tasks.

CANCELED/T, CANCELED/M. Tasks are canceled as soon as they exceed their assigned resources. We distinguish cancelation by exceeding the time limit from cancelation by exceeding the memory limit. This way, we may consider rescheduling the task if, later on, additional resources become available.

SUSPENDED. A task is suspended if assigned resources are not available. Consider, for example, memory resources. A task, for instance a search algorithm, does not need all its memory resources immediately. So we may optimistically assign more memory resources than actually available at a certain point in time, speculating that another task will meanwhile release its resources. Suspending a task permits a seamless continuation of an already running task as soon as required resources are indeed available. The difference between a suspended task and a canceled task is that a canceled task releases all assigned resources while a suspended task keeps its resources and may resume execution. Resuming a canceled task amounts to re-execution from the beginning.

4.2 Transitions of the Lifecycle

Preprocess (IDLE to ACTIVE). This transition is triggered by the completion of the preprocessing routines for the inputs to the task. In the LoLA implementation, we use the pthread condition mechanism to announce the completion of preprocessing routines.

The amount of necessary preprocessing depends on the verification algorithm. While search algorithms require intensive preprocessing (as already explained), the state equation approach just needs a simple net structure for deriving the incidence matrix. When skeleton nets are involved, we may skip net reduction since the resulting nets are already quite small. An individual transition from idle to active permits an early start of the actual verification. We may run tasks that require little preprocessing while other tasks are still in the preprocessing phase. If such early tasks deliver their result quickly, we may be able to skip some of the preprocessing thus saving resources for other verification problems.

Launch (ACTIVE to RUNNING). We launch a task by spawning a new thread for the actual verification algorithm of the task. The transition is triggered by the scheduler which is discussed in Sect. 8.

Report (RUNNING to FINISHED). When a verification algorithm terminates, it triggers the report activity. The results of the algorithm (value, witnesses or counterexamples, statistics) are recorded in the portfolio manager. Resources assigned to the task are released and a signal is sent to the portfolio manager that triggers the next scheduling activity (for launching another task).

Timeout (RUNNING to CANCELED/T), Memory Exhausted (RUNNING to CANCELED/M). These activities are triggered by the resource management of the portfolio manager. We discuss this issue separately in Sect. 7.

Suspend (RUNNING to SUSPENDED). This activity is triggered by the resource management of the portfolio manager. Suspension happens if a task is acquiring a granted resource tat is not immediately available. The thread executing the verification algorithm is frozen until the request can be satisfied.

Resume (SUSPENDED to RUNNING). When some task releases its resources (through cancelation or termination), the resource manager may trigger the resume transition and grant fresh resources to a suspended task.

Reschedule (CANCELED/T to RUNNING). The actual runtime of a verification algorithm is virtually unpredictable. It may this happen that a task needs much less runtime than originally scheduled. This way, additional runtime may become available. If, after having executed all tasks once, more runtime is available than originally scheduled for some canceled task, we may reschedule that task. Giving more runtime to it, we gain some opportunity to finish it successfully this time.

Obsolesce (Any to OBSOLETE). A task becomes obsolete if some other task for the same verification problem has answered the given problem. As soon as any task executes its report transition, all other tasks for the same verification problem are checked whether they can still contribute to the original problem. If not, they become obsolete. In case they are currently running or suspended, execution is stopped and resources are released. Obsolete tasks are detected by the evaluation of task trees to be introduced in Sect. 5.

Conclusion. Tasks have a complex life cycle. The transitions of the lifecycle are triggered by various components of the verification tool. Consequently, portfolio management requires a clean assignment of responsibilities to the various components. We have been experimenting with the portfolio manager of LoLA for several months before the structure of the lifecycle converged to the one just reported.

5   Task Trees

The leafs of the task tree are the tasks as discussed so far. Whenever tasks complete, the result value is propagated bottom-up in the tree. Whenever an inner node gets a final truth value, the remaining branches The inner nodes reflect the logical dependencies between the portfolio members. We identified several useful types of inner nodes and discuss them one by one.

Conjunction. This binary (or n-ary) node reflects the fact that the original problem is a conjunction of subproblems. The children of a conjunction node are the roots of the portfolios of the subproblems. The following table reflects the propagation of values of a conjunction node.

	true	false	unknown	void
true	true	false	unknown	void
false	false	false	false	false
unknown	unknown	false	unknown	void
void	void	false	void	void

Disjunction. This binary (or n-ary) node reflects the fact that the original problem is a disjunction of subproblems. The following table reflects the propagation of values.

	true	false	unknown	void
true	true	true	true	true
false	true	false	unknown	void
unknown	true	unknown	unknown	void
void	true	void	void	void

Aggregation. This binary (or n-ary) node represents a portfolio where two (or more) algorithms are available for exactly the same (sub-)problem. It propagation behavior can be reflected in the following table.

	true	false	unknown	void
true	true	(error)	true	true
false	(error)	false	false	false
unknown	true	false	unknown	void
void	true	false	void	void

There are two entries marked with *error*. If any of these situations would ever occur, one of the involved verification algorithms is wrong, or has an incorrect implementation.

Dual. This is a unary node in the task tree. It maps a verification problem to the corresponding dual problem. Using the dual node, we may have algorithms for reachability in a portfolio of an invariance problem, to name just one example. Whenever a dual node occurs, the verification problem of the child node refers to the negation of the verification problem for the current node. In the mentioned example, if we want to verify $AG\ \phi$, the child node is attached to formula $EF\ \neg\phi$. The behavior of this node is defined by the following table.

true	false	unknown	void
false	true	unknown	void

Sufficient. This unary node is used if the result of the child node only establishes a sufficient condition for the original verification problem. If, for instance, the original problem is $EG\ \phi$, a portfolio for $AG\ \phi$ can be wrapped with this node to reflect that, if the answer to $AG\ \phi$ is false, this does not means that $EG\ \phi$ is false, while a true answer to $AG\ \phi$ means that $EG\ \phi$ is indeed true. The following table can be used.

true	false	unknown	void
true	unknown	unknown	void

Necessary. This unary node is the dual counterpart of a *Sufficient* node for necessary conditions (such as $EF\ \psi$ for $E(\phi\ U\ \psi)$). Its table looks as follows.

true	false	unknown	void
unknown	false	unknown	void

Conclusion. With the help of the tables defining each inner node, every distribution of values for the actual tasks defines unique values for the inner nodes of a task tree. The value of the root node is the actual outcome of verification for the original verification problem. With the help of task trees, we obtain an easy criterion for obsolete tasks: Whenever a node has a value different from void, all void children are obsolete.

Figure 3 exhibits an example of a portfolio, organized as task tree. For every node, the corresponding net and formula are attached. N stands for the original net, $Skel(N)$ for the corresponding net obtained by the skeleton approach. In the figure, we abstract from potential differences between nets caused by net reduction.

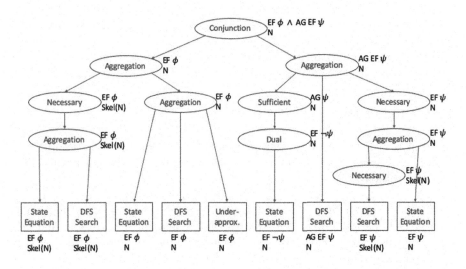

Fig. 3. An example of a task tree.

The original problem is the CTL formula $EF\ \phi \wedge AG\ EF\ \psi$, for any state predicates ϕ and ψ. This original problem forms the root of the task tree. The *conjunction* node signals that the two sub-formulas are verified separately. The first sub-formula, the reachability problem $EF\phi$, can be approached using the original net or the corresponding skeleton net (obtained by folding if N is a P/T net). These alternatives are modeled as an *aggregate* node. Reachability in the skeleton is only a necessary condition for reachability in the original net, so the results of the left branch are filtered by a *necessary* node. This way, despite possible true and false answers of the underlying algorithms, only a false result is propagated towards the root. The *aggregate* node below the *necessary* node reflects the fact that reachability in the skeleton can be investigated by two algorithms: evaluation of the state equation or depth-first search. For the original net, the task tree offers three alternative approaches: state equation, depth-first search, and an underapproximation that tries to freeze tokens in the initial marking. Reachability in the underapproximation is a sufficient condition for actual reachability. However, we do not need a *sufficient* node here since the algorithm itself would only answer yes or unknown.

For the sub-formula $AGEF\phi$, the task tree offers three alternative approaches. The one displayed in the middle is conventional depth-first search that, through investigation of strongly connected components, is able to answer the task. This search is flanked by a sufficient and a necessary condition that both have been obtained by strength reduction. Indeed, a net satisfying $AG\ \psi$ also satisfies $AG\ EF\ \psi$, and a net satisfying $AG\ EF\ \psi$ must also satisfy $EF\ \psi$. The verification of $AG\ \psi$ is traced back to the verification $EF\ \neg\psi$ using the tautology $AG\ \psi \iff \neg EF\ \neg\psi$. This way, actual verification algorithms only need to care about reachability and not about invariance. The *dual* node in the task tree is responsible for negating the result of the underlying algorithm. For checking the necessary criterion $EF\ \psi$, we employ the state equation and depth-first search in the skeleton.

The example shows the potential complexity of a portfolio and demonstrates the necessity of a systematic approach.

6   Creating the Task Tree

We propose a multi-tier approach for generating a task tree. We assume that we are given a net (P/T or CPN) and a formula. Multiple formulas would have separate task trees.

Tier 1: Boolean Combinations. As long as the top-level operator of the formula is a Boolean operator, we create a corresponding node in the task tree and proceed independently for each subformula. Only conjunction and disjunction need to be considered since we may assume the formula to be in negation free normal form, due to prior preprocessing. The same preprocessing can also force Boolean operators to appear as top-level operators in the formula. Some temporal modalities commute with Boolean operators, so we may prioritize rewriting such that Boolean operators are pushed up while temporal modalities are pushed down. This way, the verification problem is separated into several simpler independent problems.

Tier 2: Separation Between Original and Skeleton Net. Using an *Aggregation* node, we create two independent branches. In one of the branches, we collect all methods that use the given net, in the other branch, we proceed with all methods that concern the skeleton of the given net. This early separation is motivated by the unbalanced amount of preprocessing that is required for the skeleton and the given net.

If the net is given as a CPN, the skeleton may be immediately derived from the input. For the other branch, significant time is required for unfolding the CPN into its P/T equivalent. The set of benchmarks in the MCC contains a few CPN where unfolding would exceed space and/or time limits of the contest. Furthermore, setting up initial data structures for large nets requires a lot of care [11].

If the net is given as a P/T net, the skeleton is constructed by a folding procedure that may take a few seconds. In contrast, setting up initial data structures in the given net may require some time, as mentioned above.

In any case, tasks in the two branches may take a rather diverse time for being set up. Being able to schedule tasks in one of the branches early, may lead to results that arrive so quickly that preprocessing efforts in the other branch may be cancelled (thus freeing resources for other queries under investigation).

In the skeleton branch of the task tree, we immediately add a *Sufficient* (for ACTL* properties) or *Necessary* (for ECTL* properties) node. This reflects the fact that the preservation results for the skeleton abstraction are only simple implications. If an ACTL* property holds in the skeleton, it holds in the original net as well. If an ECTL* property holds in the original system, it holds in the skeleton as well. Then subsequent planning steps do not need to distinguish between the branches, with one exception. If the skeleton abstraction forms only a sufficient criterion for the property, we would not like to include a method into our portfolio that establishes only necessary condition, and vice versa.

There are cases where the skeleton approach is not applicable at all. This can be due to the fact that the formula is not preserved by skeleton abstraction. Another reason could be that, for a given P/T net, the resulting skeleton is not significantly smaller than the given net. In such cases, we add a previously unmentioned *Unknown Task* to the task tree. Such a task is executed immediately. Its only effect is to report *unknown* as result to its parent in the task tree.

Tier 3: Categorization According to Formula Type. The formula type is determined by an inspection of the formula. The more specific a formula type is, the more methods are available as portfolio members, and the more specific are the portfolio members for a given property. In LoLA, there are property specific search routines and property specific stubborn set methods for all classes of formulas containing just one temporal operator, many formula classes with two temporal operators, and even a few classes with three operators. Half of these formula classes can be traced back to the other half by negation. For instance, invariance ($AG\phi$) corresponds to reachability ($EF\phi$) through the tautology $AG\phi \iff \neg EF\neg\phi$. This relation is reflected by the *Negation* nodes in the task tree. Consequently, further construction of the task tree concerns only the remaining half of the formula types. In LoLA, we chose the formula classes with existential path quantifiers for further consideration, wherever possible.

The formula type also determines whether or not there are other formula types that establish strength reductions for the given formula. If so, construction of the task tree would recursively descend into these formulas.

Tier 4: Actual Verification Methods. This part has a separate implementation for each formula type. The formula type determines whether or not some method is available for its verification. This means that newly developed methods are integrated at this stage. The main purpose of this tier is, however, to evaluate the command line options that control whether or not a particular method is to be added to the portfolio. We have such an option for every portfolio member. This way, the user may tailor the portfolio according to domain specific assumption on the effectiveness and efficiency of available verification methods.

Conclusion. The planning processes brings together several aspects: net type (original/skeleton), formula type and its relation to other formula types, and command line options. Since parts of the construction may depend on expensive preprocessing routines, it is recommendable that tasks in one subtree are already scheduled for execution without waiting for other subtrees to finish construction.

7   Controlling Resources

Cores, memory, and runtime are the critical resources when running a portfolio. If the number of algorithms executed in parallel exceeds the number of available cores, the operating system is forced into frequent context switches, with negative impact on overall runtime and on caches. Since depth-first search is extremely space-consuming, we have to take care that algorithms running in parallel have a well-designed way of competing for memory. Last but not least, we need to make sure that all portfolio members get a fair portion of available runtime, if that is limited. The actual scheduling of resources is discussed in the next section. We can schedule resources only if we can control the access of tasks to these resources. That is why we included this section.

For controlling access to cores, we believe that it is sufficient to take care that we launch at most as many parallel threads (i.e. concurrent verification algorithms) as there are cores in the underlying machine. In case of LoLA, the user specifies that number using a command-line option. Runtime is controlled by an additional timer thread that is running as long as the portfolio manager is active. It is executing an infinite loop where, after sleeping for five seconds, it checks for tasks that have exceeded their time limit and, at the same time, collects status information from running tasks and displays them. According to our experience, the granularity of five seconds seems to be sufficient for controlling time limits of tasks. By sleeping a long time between activities, the timer thread does not severely interfere with the threads that execute the actual verification algorithms.

The most interesting resource with respect to resource control is memory. As a preliminary step, we discuss access to memory in general. Based on this discussion, we can then propose a strategy for controlling the amount of memory assigned to a task.

Depth first search, the main method for explicit verification, is an extremely memory-consuming task. Profiling with LoLA revealed that, during depth-first search, about 90% of the runtime is spent for checking whether or not the currently visited marking has been visited before, and to insert it into the data structure if it has not visited yet. To our own surprise, about 40% of that time is spent in *malloc*, the C routine for allocating memory on the heap of the main memory (including calls to the corresponding *new* operator in C++). The explanation of that large percentage has two aspects. First, it shows that the remaining parts of a depth-first search algorithm indeed have an extremely lightweight implementation. Second, it shows that allocating memory on the heap is a rather involved task. First, *malloc* needs to find a suitable portion of memory in the list of free memory segments, and to launch a call to the operating system if there is none. Second, it needs to take precautions for the eventual return of the memory to be allocated. And finally, malloc must be thread-safe, i.e. it must provide a mechanism for mutual exclusion between concurrent calls to the routine.

Based on this analysis, we conclude that depth-first search should include a tailored memory management. In LoLA, we allocate memory in large pages of, say, 100 MB. Then, our own memory manager allocates portions of such a page to individual requests of the search algorithm. We obtain the following runtime benefits:

- Since every concurrent depth first search uses its own memory management, we do not need to provide any mechanism for mutual exclusion during memory management;
- Since memory allocated for depth-first search is never returned before that search as such is finished, we do not need to provide any mechanism for returning memory to the list of free portions;
- Since memory is never returned, we have no fragmentation issues and memory management is mostly trivial;
- When depth-first search terminates, or is canceled, we only need to return the allocated pages instead of freeing hundreds of millions of individual data objects.

The first three items cause a speedup of 20% for our own memory allocation requests, compared to traditional calls to malloc. The last item reduces the time for terminating a depth-first search from several minutes to a fraction of a second. Hence, the page mechanism is a prerequisite for running nontrivial portfolios.

Once we have a page based memory management for depth-first search, we can gain complete control of the memory usage. We simply need to count (and limit) the number of pages that the memory manager of a depth-first search is allowed to allocate. A task is suspended by simply not answering to its request for memory. A task can be canceled by not answering to its memory request while releasing its resources (otherwise, canceling a pthread is a nontrivial endeavor).

Other verification algorithms involve depth-first search as well, like our under-approximation approach, or require only marginal memory resources, like random walks. For two classes of algorithms, we do not provide any control of their memory usage in LoLA: state equation and siphon/trap property. Here, we use off-the-shelf libraries for solving linear problems resp. SAT problems and so far we did not dare to intervene in their memory management. However, both problems are in NP and thus in PSPACE, so we hope that their memory requirements are less severe than that of depth-first search. With this sloppy way of controlling memory resources, we at least managed to stay within the harsh memory limit of 16 Gigabytes in recent issues of the MCC.

8   Scheduling Tasks

Scheduling refers to two kinds of decisions to be repeatedly taken in a running portfolio manager. First, we need to select the order in which we execute tasks. Second, we need to decide how many resources we assign to the selected tasks.

8.1   Selection Strategy

As long as we do not have a strict limit for runtime, the order of executing tasks is less important. That is why we discuss this issue under the assumption that there is in fact a time limit. Using such a strategy in a scenario without time limit, helps us to reduce the overall run time in many cases but has no severe impact if it fails.

So, assuming a strict time limit, our duty is to get as many as possible firm results (true or false) for the given verification problems. In [26], we observed that problems can be divided into simple, challenging, and impossible. Simple means that virtually all methods are able to solve the problem in little time. Impossible means that all known methods fail. Only for the challenging problems, selection and configuration of verification algorithms matter. Most problems in the MCC are either simple or impossible. This is, of course, an a posteriori classification. However, the size and shape of the net and the structure of a temporal logic formula may give us valuable a priori hints for guessing the category a problem.

Concerning the net, large nets tend to be more challenging than small nets. Nets with large conflict clusters tend to be more challenging than nets with small conflict clusters (more concurrency means better applicability of stubborn sets).

Regarding a temporal logic formula, the number of occurring temporal operators seems to be a good basis for judging its difficulty. The simplest case are without doubt formulas without temporal operators. They correspond to constants true or false, or to a state predicate that can be evaluated by just inspecting the initial marking. Such formulas frequently appear in the MCC as the result of linear programming approaches to the atomic propositions and application of temporal logic tautologies [2]. Of course, a portfolio manager will launch tasks for such formulas with highest priority since they do not require any measurable resources.

Of the remaining formulas, the ones with one or two temporal operators are the simplest. Most of these formulas are supported by specialized algorithms [12].

Their presence increases the success rate. In addition, also pointed out in [12], they occur more frequently than other formulas. For differentiating between formulas with one or two temporal operators, we employ the past issues of the MCC. Based on these data, we can calculate the success rate of LoLA for the various types of formulas. This success rate is an excellent measure for difficulty.

Formulas with more than two temporal operators occur less frequently in practice. That is why the number of occurring operators appears to be a sufficient criterion for judging their complexity. Alternatively, LTL formulas could be judged according to the number of states of the Büchi automata that represent the formulas and which are used in LTL model checking [22].

For formulas with the same temporal structure, the number of places mentioned in the formula is another criterion for differentiating the difficulty. A large number of mentioned places leads to a large number of visible transitions.

The overall difficulty of a problem would be some Pareto style aggregation of the difficulty of the formula and the difficulty of the net. In LoLA, we currently consider only the difficulty of the formula.

For search algorithms, we schedule the easiest problems first. If any of the problems is solvable then the easiest ones have the greatest likelihood to do so. For algorithms that require only few resources, such as random walks, we schedule the most difficult problems first. If a problem is indeed difficult, it appears to be easier to land a lucky punch with an unusual algorithm than with a state space exploration. In any case, we schedule tasks in a way that, if possible, tasks running in parallel concern different problems. In the case where some problems indeed turn out to be simple, we solve them without running too many algorithms in parallel on them, so more time remains for the challenging problems.

8.2 Assigning Resources

Cores. For sequential algorithms, a single core is assigned. This is the case for the whole LoLA portfolio manager. For parallel algorithms, it could be reasonable to assign more than one core. Here we have a conflict between assigning cores to that algorithm versus assigning cores to other portfolio members. To date, most parallel algorithms have a saturating behavior with respect to the number of cores. That is, there is a number of cores where additional cores do not lead to an improvement of runtime. If that number is known (by experimental evidence), it would be reasonable to assign not more than that number of cores to the parallel algorithm, and cores might be left for other portfolio members.

Memory. The memory-critical tasks are those that execute depth-first search. We pointed out above that, depending on the stubborn sets used, they are optimized for true (e.g. reachable) or false (e.g. unreachable) cases. One of the cases (reachable) benefits from the on-the-fly effect while in the other case the whole reduced state space needs to be computed. For memory assignment, we may derive two conclusions. First, if the task is set up for the case where we benefit from the on-the-fly effect, the task either delivers its result after having consumed only few memory pages, or it is unlikely to deliver a result at all. Second, if the task is setup for the case where the whole reduced state space needs to be computed, we either assign sufficient resources for finishing the search, or any assigned resource is wasted. In consequence, taking reachability as an example, we assign only few pages for tasks where search is optimized for reachability and we assign a lot of memory to tasks that are designed for unreachability. In the portfolio manager, we distinguish *search* (optimized for reachability) from *exclusive memory* (optimized for unreachability) tasks. The scheduler takes care that, at all times, only one exclusive memory task is running. All the other tasks get a fixed small number of memory pages assigned, and the single exclusive memory task basically is permitted to use all remaining memory.

Runtime. For runtime, we identified two major scenarios: limited versus unlimited availability. For the use of verification in practice, we expect that an unlimited amount of runtime is available. For search tasks, the monotonic request for memory establishes some bound for runtime anyway. For constant-memory tasks such as random walks, a scenario with unlimited runtime should implement some criterion for interrupting the method (number of tries or an algorithm-specific local time limit). Otherwise, we can schedule tasks as soon as cores and memory are available.

Use cases with a strict time limit include the MCC conditions as well as practical situations where we have a firm deadline for reporting results. Taking into consideration that we can schedule at most one *exclusive memory* task at a time, we propose the following strategy. First we separately schedule all remaining *exclusive memory* tasks. We compute the available time as the difference of deadline and current time. If an exclusive memory task is currently running, we replace the current time with the start time of the running task. This amount of time is divided by the number of remaining (and running) exclusive memory tasks. Every task is given that amount of time. The end time of the running task is replaced accordingly.

For all other tasks, we can use all available cores if no exclusive memory task is present, and we can use all but one core if there are remaining exclusive memory tasks. Depending on that number of tasks, we compute the largest number n of seconds such that all nonexclusive tasks can be scheduled for n seconds before the deadline expires. This is a bit tricky since we need to take care about already running tasks, and we need to reflect the fact that the runtime for a single algorithm cannot be parallelized. That is why the calculation requires more efforts than just dividing the available time by the number of remaining tasks.

We compute the remaining time per core which is the difference between the deadline and the start time of an already running task (there should be as many such tasks as we have available cores). If less tasks are running, we use the current time instead. Let k be the number of available cores, and n be the number of remaining nonexclusive tasks. Then we schedule n *div* k tasks for every core. The remaining n *mod* k tasks are schedule for the cores with largest remaining time. Then we can compute, for every core, the remaining time on that core and distribute it equally for the tasks planned for this core. That is, tasks do not necessarily get exactly the same time, but processing resources are used exhaustively.

We repeat the scheduling procedure every time a new task is checked in, or a running task finishes. This way, we continuously adapt our scheduling to the current situation.

Example. Suppose that we have four cores, and initially two exclusive memory tasks and ten other tasks. Let 1000 s be available. Then we would launch one exclusive memory task with a time limit of 500 s. For the remaining cores, we would assume a distribution of four versus three versus three tasks, so we would launch one task with 250 s, and two tasks with 333 s time limit. If, after 100 s, a non-exclusive task returns a result, we have nine remaining tasks (including the running tasks). Two cores have an available run-time of 1000 s (since the two running tasks have been launched initially) and the third core has 900 s remaining time. We have a distribution three versus three versus three, so we would launch a new task with a time limit of 300 s. If, after 200 s (counted from beginning), the exclusive memory task returns, we launch the remaining exclusive memory task with a time limit of 800 s. If it returns after 250 s (again counted from beginning) an additional core becomes available for the non-exclusive tasks. The individual available time is 1000 versus 1000 versus 900 versus 750 s and there are nine remaining tasks. So we would distribute them by the pattern three versus two versus two versus two. In effect, one of the running tasks would keep its time limit of 333 $(= 1000/3)$ s. The second task that was started in the very beginning would get a new time limit of 500 $(= 1000/2)$ s. The task started after 100 s would get a new time limit of 450 $(= 900/2)$ s, and we would launch a fresh task with a time limit of 375 $(= 750/2)$ s.

Using this scheduling policy, we benefit from low hanging fruits earned early in the scheduling sequence. If tasks finish early, remaining tasks immediately get more run-time assigned.

Sometimes it may happen that remaining tasks do not exhaust the scheduled time. In this case we check whether we have tasks that were canceled before due to lack of time. If they consumed less time than still available in the end, we reschedule such a task with a more generous time limit.

9 Conclusion

We have discussed the main design decisions to be made for the implementation of a portfolio manager for Petri net based verification. Due to the size and diversity of verification portfolios, a systematic approach is necessary. We also discussed possible deviations from the decision that we made in the LoLA tool. Since the first implementation of the task manager, we added several new verification algorithms to the portfolio and found that the design of the portfolio manager was robust with respect to the changes. This way, the integration of the new methods validated our major design decisions.

Our next step for improving the manager will be a prognostic feature for memory consumption. We observed that search algorithms request new memory at a roughly constant rate. We can use the past rate of memory requests for estimating the future memory requirement of an exclusive memory task. This way, we may be able to assign additional memory to nonexclusive tasks.

References

1. Berthelot, G.: Transformations and decompositions of nets. In: Brauer, W., Reisig, W., Rozenberg, G. (eds.) ACPN 1986. LNCS, vol. 254, pp. 359–376. Springer, Heidelberg (1987). https://doi.org/10.1007/978-3-540-47919-2_13
2. Bønneland, F., Dyhr, J., Jensen, P.G., Johannsen, M., Srba, J.: Simplification of CTL formulae for efficient model checking of Petri nets. In: Khomenko, V., Roux, O.H. (eds.) PETRI NETS 2018. LNCS, vol. 10877, pp. 143–163. Springer, Cham (2018). https://doi.org/10.1007/978-3-319-91268-4_8
3. Burch, J.R., Clarke, E.M., McMillan, K.L., Dill, D.L., Hwang, L.J.: Symbolic model checking: 10^{20} states and beyond. Inf. Comput. **98**(2), 142–170 (1992)
4. Clarke, E.M., Emerson, E.A., Sistla, A.P.: Automatic verification of finite-state concurrent systems using temporal logic specifications. ACM Trans. Program. Lang. Syst. **8**(2), 244–263 (1986)
5. David, A., Jacobsen, L., Jacobsen, M., Jørgensen, K.Y., Møller, M.H., Srba, J.: TAPAAL 2.0: integrated development environment for timed-arc Petri nets. In: Flanagan, C., König, B. (eds.) TACAS 2012. LNCS, vol. 7214, pp. 492–497. Springer, Heidelberg (2012). https://doi.org/10.1007/978-3-642-28756-5_36
6. Esparza, J., Heljanko, K.: Unfoldings - A Partial-Order Approach to Model Checking. Monographs in Theoretical Computer Science An EATCS Series, Springer, Heidelberg (2008). https://doi.org/10.1007/978-3-540-77426-6
7. Hack, M.H.T.: Analysis of production schemata by Petri nets. Master's thesis, MIT, Department of Electrical Engineering, Cambridge, Massachusetts (1972)
8. Jensen, K.: Condensed state spaces for symmetrical coloured Petri nets. Formal Methods Syst. Des. **9**(1/2), 7–40 (1996). https://doi.org/10.1007/BF00625967
9. Kordon, F., et al.: Complete Results for the 2019 Edition of the Model Checking Contest, April 2019. http://mcc.lip6.fr/2019/results.php
10. Kristensen, L.M., Schmidt, K., Valmari, A.: Question-guided stubborn set methods for state properties. Formal Methods Syst. Des. **29**(3), 215–251 (2006). https://doi.org/10.1007/s10703-006-0006-1
11. Liebke, T., Rosenke, C.: Faster enabledness-updates for the reachability graph computation. In: Proceedings of PNSE 2020, pp. 108–117 (2020)
12. Liebke, T., Wolf, K.: Taking some burden off an explicit CTL model checker. In: Donatelli, S., Haar, S. (eds.) PETRI NETS 2019. LNCS, vol. 11522, pp. 321–341. Springer, Cham (2019). https://doi.org/10.1007/978-3-030-21571-2_18
13. Lipton, R.: The reachability problem requires exponential space. Technical report 62, Yale University (1976)
14. Oanea, O., Wimmel, H., Wolf, K.: New algorithms for deciding the siphon-trap property. In: Lilius, J., Penczek, W. (eds.) PETRI NETS 2010. LNCS, vol. 6128, pp. 267–286. Springer, Heidelberg (2010). https://doi.org/10.1007/978-3-642-13675-7_16
15. Schmidt, K.: How to calculate symmetries of Petri nets. Acta Informatica **36**(7), 545–590 (2000). https://doi.org/10.1007/s002360050002

16. Shatz, S.M., Tu, S., Murata, T., Duri, S.: An application of Petri net reduction for Ada tasking deadlock analysis. IEEE Trans. Parallel Distrib. Syst. **7**(12), 1307–1322 (1996)

17. Tarjan, R.E.: Depth-first search and linear graph algorithms. SIAM J. Comput. **1**(2), 146–160 (1972)

18. Thierry-Mieg, Y.: Symbolic model-checking using ITS-tools. In: Baier, C., Tinelli, C. (eds.) TACAS 2015. LNCS, vol. 9035, pp. 231–237. Springer, Heidelberg (2015). https://doi.org/10.1007/978-3-662-46681-0_20

19. Tovchigrechko, A.A.: Efficient symbolic analysis of bounded Petri nets using interval decision diagrams. Ph.D. thesis, Brandenburg University of Technology, Cottbus - Senftenberg, Germany (2008)

20. Valmari, A.: Stubborn sets for reduced state space generation. In: Rozenberg, G. (ed.) ICATPN 1989. LNCS, vol. 483, pp. 491–515. Springer, Heidelberg (1991). https://doi.org/10.1007/3-540-53863-1_36

21. Valmari, A., Hansen, H.: Stubborn set intuition explained. In: Koutny, M., Kleijn, J., Penczek, W. (eds.) Transactions on Petri Nets and Other Models of Concurrency XII. LNCS, vol. 10470, pp. 140–165. Springer, Heidelberg (2017). https://doi.org/10.1007/978-3-662-55862-1_7

22. Vardi, M.Y., Wolper, P.: An automata-theoretic approach to automatic program verification (preliminary report). In: Proceedings of the Symposium on Logic in Computer Science. LICS, IEEE, pp. 332–344 (1986)

23. Vergauwen, B., Lewi, J.: A linear local model checking algorithm for CTL. In: Best, E. (ed.) CONCUR 1993. LNCS, vol. 715, pp. 447–461. Springer, Heidelberg (1993). https://doi.org/10.1007/3-540-57208-2_31

24. Williams, P.F., Biere, A., Clarke, E.M., Gupta, A.: Combining decision diagrams and SAT procedures for efficient symbolic model checking. In: Emerson, E.A., Sistla, A.P. (eds.) CAV 2000. LNCS, vol. 1855, pp. 124–138. Springer, Heidelberg (2000). https://doi.org/10.1007/10722167_13

25. Wimmel, H., Wolf, K.: Applying CEGAR to the Petri net state equation. Log. Methods Comput. Sci. **8**(3), 1–15 (2012)

26. Wolf, K.: Running LoLA 2.0 in a model checking competition. In: Koutny, M., Desel, J., Kleijn, J. (eds.) Transactions on Petri Nets and Other Models of Concurrency XI. LNCS, vol. 9930, pp. 274–285. Springer, Heidelberg (2016). https://doi.org/10.1007/978-3-662-53401-4_13

27. Wolf, K.: Petri net model checking with LoLA 2. In: Khomenko, V., Roux, O.H. (eds.) PETRI NETS 2018. LNCS, vol. 10877, pp. 351–362. Springer, Cham (2018). https://doi.org/10.1007/978-3-319-91268-4_18

Practical Distributed Implementation
of Very Large Scale Petri Net Simulations

Ashur Rafiev[1]([✉])[iD], Jordan Morris[1][iD], Fei Xia[1][iD], Alex Yakovlev[1][iD],
Matthew Naylor[2][iD], Simon Moore[2][iD], David Thomas[3], Graeme Bragg[4][iD],
Mark Vousden[4][iD], and Andrew Brown[4]

[1] School of Engineering, Newcastle University, Newcastle upon Tyne, UK
{ashur.rafiev,jordan.morris,fei.xia,alex.yakovlev}@ncl.ac.uk
[2] Computer Architecture Group, Cambridge University, Cambridge, UK
{matthew.naylor,simon.moore}@cl.cam.ac.uk
[3] Department of Electrical and Electronic Engineering, Imperial College London,
London, UK
d.thomas1@imperial.ac.uk
[4] Electronics and Computer Science, University of Southampton, Southampton, UK
{gmb,m.vousden,adb}@soton.ac.uk

Abstract. With the continued increase of size and complexity of contemporary digital systems, there is a growing need for models of large
size and high complexity, as well as methods of analyzing such models. This paper presents a method for simulating large-scale concurrent Petri net models using parallel distributed hardware platforms. By
using POETS architecture, our method allows the mapping of concurrent
Petri net executions onto 49,152 parallel processing hardware threads to
achieve orders of magnitude (45 to 220 times) improvements of simulation speed, compared to conventional simulation methods using single
processor systems. The presented method employs techniques including
Petri net model partitioning, the use of max-step and locally-interleaving
semantics, and the fair firing of transitions.

Keywords: Distributed simulation · Petri nets · event-based · Global
synchronization

1 Introduction

With the advance of digital computing, there has been a growing demand for
modeling very large and complex systems. The research areas of circuit design [1],
developmental biology [2], and modeling machine-learning automata [3,4] study
systems with millions of interacting elements. At this scale, the models are no
longer hand-crafted but automatically synthesized from libraries of components.
While the constituent components are small enough to be formally verifiable,
the statistical quantitative properties as well as the emergent behavior of the
system as a whole call for different kinds of exploration techniques, such as
simulation [5].

© Springer-Verlag GmbH Germany, part of Springer Nature 2022
M. Koutny et al. (Eds.): ToPNoC XVI, LNCS 13220, pp. 112–139, 2022.
https://doi.org/10.1007/978-3-662-65303-6_6

Petri nets (PNs) is the formalism that underpins the design and analysis of these examples [1–3]. This demonstrates the usefulness of PNs as an *interpreted graph model* [6,7] for exploring current and future very large concurrent systems. Such explorations include large-scale simulations of PN models, which have many uses, including, for instance, providing visualizations and improving the interpretability and explainability of complex system designs [4].

At the component level, rigorous qualitative analysis using PNs for properties such as deadlock freeness and output persistency is provided by verification tools including PN unfoldings (e.g., PUNF [8]) or SAT solvers (e.g., MPSAT [8]); reachability analysis can be achieved by synthesis tools (e.g., Petrify [9]). These tools are capable of handling models consisting of up to several thousand places, as shown in Fig. 1; however, the detailed system-level models can reach millions of places.

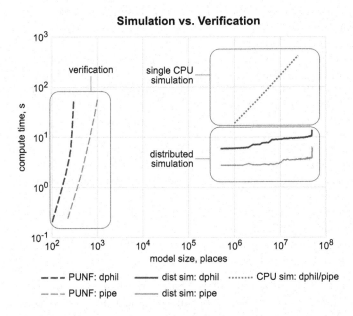

Fig. 1. PN unfolding computation time (PUNF) puts into perspective the sizes of PNs suitable for formal verification in comparison with those suitable for single-core (CPU sim) and distributed (dist sim) simulations. The *pipe* and *dphil* examples are described in Sect. 5.

Component-level analysis, as well as single cycle analytics, may be insufficient for certain applications. For instance, machine learning typically evolves over large datasets and huge numbers of epochs [4]. For full-system model explorations, therefore, the simulation approach is more practical. But even then, millions of places and transitions in a PN present a significant time cost for each simulation run (Fig. 1, single-core simulation examples). With modern technology giving rise to the cloud computing and many-core platforms, a natural way to speed up the simulation is to make a parallel distributed implementation (Fig. 1, distributed simulation examples).

Even though PNs are well suited for describing concurrency, simulating them does not immediately lend itself well to parallelism, as shown in [10], in which Janicki et al. explore different execution semantics for PNs with respect to their level of concurrency. They also suggest a view of any simulation as a composition of an execution platform model and a simulated PN, where the execution policy (or semantics) acts as a mediator. Bergenthum in [11] investigates transition firing policies using partial orders, which has the potential to discover and exploit internal concurrency within the net.

Distributed discrete event (DDE) [12] simulation technique has a long history of development. It has been applied to PN simulations, first, using a centralized event scheduler and then followed by a fully asynchronous decentralized solution based on complex multi-phase communication protocols [13]. In addition to execution concurrency, PN partitioning across multiple execution devices also poses a challenge as it has a substantial impact on the amount of inter-device communication [14].

In this paper, we employ and extend the ideas from [10,11,13] to create a practical implementation of a PN simulator on an event-based massively parallel platform called POETS [15]. The platform consists of a large number of execution devices (49,152 hardware threads) supported by a communication fabric.

Specifically, we make the following **contributions**:

- A new algorithm for distributed PN simulation in highly concurrent event-based hardware;
- A partitioning approach that enables purely forwards communication to resolve choices;
- A concrete implementation of this approach in a highly-concurrent hardware platform called POETS;
- Experimental results showing that an 8-box POETS cluster is 45 to 220 times faster than a single-core simulator.

This paper is organized as follows: Sect. 2 discusses non-distributed PN simulation, including basic elements of our simulation method. Section 3 provides a high-level description of the POETS programming model. Section 4 presents our distributed PN simulation method. Section 5 presents the experimental validation of our simulation method on the POETS hardware platform. Finally, conclusions are drawn in Sect. 6.

2   Non-distributed Petri Net Simulation

A *Petri net* is a quadruple $\mathcal{N} := \langle P, T, F, m_0 \rangle$, where P is a finite non-empty set of places, T is a finite non-empty set of transitions, $F \subseteq (T \times P) \cup (P \times T)$ is the flow relation between places and transitions and m_0 is the initial marking. A pair $(p, t) \in F$ is called an arc. The multiplicity of an arc (p, t) denoted as $|p, t|$ is the number of occurrences of (p, t) in the multiset F.

The set of places $\bullet t = \{p \in P \mid (p,t) \in F\}$ is called the preset of a transition $t \in T$, and $t\bullet = \{p \in P \mid (t,p) \in F\}$ is called the postset of t.

A PN marking is a function $m : P \to \mathbb{Z}_+$, where $m(p)$ is called the number of tokens in place $p \in P$ at the marking m. Safe PNs allow no more than one token per place, i.e., $m : P \to \{0,1\}$ and also $|p,t| \leq 1$.

A transition $t \in T$ is enabled at marking m if $\forall p \in \bullet t, m(p) > 0$. A transition $t \in T$ enabled at marking m can fire, producing a new marking m', such that

$$m'(p) = m(p) - |p,t| + |t,p| \tag{1}$$

for each $p \in P$, thus achieving the flow of information within the net. A deadlock happens when a PN has no enabled transitions.

A pair of transitions $\{t_1, t_2\} \in T$ is called conflicting if $\bullet t_1 \cap \bullet t_2 \neq \emptyset$. A place $p \in (\bullet t_1 \cap \bullet t_2)$ is called a place with a choice. A PN that does not contain any conflicting transitions is called a choice-free PN.

2.1   Fairness and Execution Semantics

The transition firing rule (1) defines what happens when an enabled transition fires. However, what happens when multiple transitions are enabled in a single marking must be properly defined to complete the execution semantics (policy). Traditionally, the *interleaving semantics* is followed, which says that only one of the enabled transitions may fire; the choice of which transition to fire is resolved non-deterministically.

The downside of the interleaving semantics is that it is inherently non-parallelizable because it assumes no more than one transition may fire at any marking, based on a narrow interpretation of (1). An alternative is the step semantics, which allows the firing of more than one transition per simulation "step", so long as they are non-conflicting and enabled at a marking [10]. When multiple transitions fire in a step, the new marking is the collective result of firing these transitions together:

$$m'(p) = m(p) - \sum_{t \in T_f} |p,t| + \sum_{t \in T_f} |t,p|, \tag{2}$$

where $T_f \subseteq T$ is the set of enabled transitions selected to fire at this step. Firing as many transitions as possible in a step (*max-step semantics*) is favorable for parallelism; however, always choosing the largest number of transitions to fire may lead to the biased execution of choices. Choice-free PN behavior is deterministic for the max-step semantics.

Although simulations cannot replace qualitative verification with absolute confidence, we still want to explore as much of the state space as possible. Monte Carlo search [16] is an example of using randomized non-deterministic simulations for state exploration. Additionally, system designers may benefit from simulation for the quantitative analysis of system properties, which also requires simulation stochasticity.

The notion of *fairness* in the randomization procedure is important for both these uses of simulation. In a non-timed PN simulation, fairness is applied to the resolution of choices. For the fair interleaving semantics, all enabled transitions in a marking have an equal probability of firing. There is no generally accepted formal definition of fairness for the step semantics. For the purposes of code optimization in our version of PN simulation, we propose to select the step firing transitions in a way that attempts to preserve or mimic the firing ratios of the "fair" interleaving semantics described above. If we also consider a subnet with only $p \rightarrow t$ arcs and no $t \rightarrow p$ arcs (while calculating these ratios), it would give us maximum step execution with fairness.

Let's consider an example PN with choice as shown in Fig. 2. Transition t1 is mutually exclusive with transitions t2 and t3, so it cannot fire if any of those fires and vice versa. However, t2 and t3 are not mutually exclusive. The flow networks show all possible firing sequences: for the interleaving semantics, initially, any of the transitions could fire.

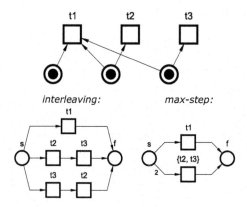

Fig. 2. Fairness example net 1 and corresponding flow networks for the interleaving and max-step semantics.

As a quantitative metric for comparing fairness between different types of semantics, we define the overall *firing ratio* of a transition t as the ratio between the number of times it fires during all possible executions and the number of times it is enabled:

$$f_t = \frac{k_{\text{fire}}}{k_{\text{enabled}}}. \tag{3}$$

In a choice-free PN, this number is always one for all transitions that can be enabled. This ratio is undefined for transitions that do not get enabled. (The firing ratio is not to be confused with the firing rate, which is the ratio of the number of times a transition fires to the duration of the simulation, i.e., the total number of simulation "steps").

The fairness of the interleaving semantics means that each flow "branch" has the same probability of being selected, therefore:

$$f_{t1} = \frac{1}{3}. \tag{4}$$

The overall firing ratios for t2 and t3 are different because when one fires the other remains enabled and will fire eventually:

$$f_{t2} = \underbrace{\frac{1}{3}}_{\text{t2 fires}} + \underbrace{\frac{1}{3} \cdot 1}_{\text{t2 will always fire if t3 fires}} = \frac{2}{3}, \tag{5}$$

$$f_{t3} = \underbrace{\frac{1}{3}}_{\text{t3 fires}} + \underbrace{\frac{1}{3} \cdot 1}_{\text{t3 will always fire if t2 fires}} = \frac{2}{3}. \tag{6}$$

Flow networks can be used to derive maximum step execution with these firing ratios. Non-branching sequences are collapsed into single transition steps, i.e. t2 followed by t3 becomes {t2, t3}. Equivalent branches are combined with their weights multiplied respectively: t3 followed by t2 also becomes {t2, t3}, so the branch {t2, t3} gets the weight of 2. This approach ensures that the max-step execution will be at least as fair as the equivalent interleaving semantics. A more formal way to represent this approach to deriving max-step semantics with fairness is by executing the so-called *preset subnets*. The preset subnet of $\mathcal{N}$ at marking m is defined as $\bullet\mathcal{N}(m) := \langle P, T, F \cap (P \times T), m \rangle$, where m acts as the initial marking, and the flow relation contains only the place-to-transition arcs of the original PN. If we keep executing this preset subnet using fair interleaving semantics until deadlock, the set of all fired transitions $T_s \subseteq T$ will represent a "fair" maximum execution step with the equivalent firing ratios. Subsequently in this paper, whenever the term max-step semantics is used, it implies this type of fairness.

For composing firing ratios from different initial markings, consider the example shown in Fig. 3; it has an additional place p1 that may have a token in the initial marking with a probability of 0.5, hence transition t3 may be enabled or not enabled depending on the initial marking and this would influence the respective flow network. If p1 has a token ({p1} case), all transitions are initially enabled as in Fig. 2 and the flow matches the previous example. If p1 is empty or not marked ({} case), the choice is only between t1 and t2 with equal probabilities.

Since {} and {p1} each has a probability of 0.5, the overall firing ratio is calculated as follows:

$$f_{t1} = \underbrace{\frac{1}{2} \cdot \frac{1}{2}}_{\{\}\text{case}} + \underbrace{\frac{1}{2} \cdot \frac{1}{3}}_{\{p1\}\text{case}} = 0.42, \tag{7}$$

$$f_{t2} = \underbrace{\frac{1}{2} \cdot \frac{1}{2}}_{\{\}\text{case}} + \underbrace{\frac{1}{2} \cdot \frac{2}{3}}_{\{p1\}\text{case}} = 0.58. \tag{8}$$

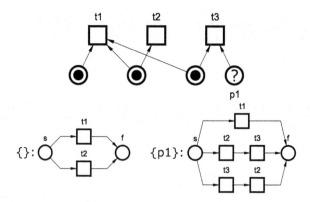

Fig. 3. Fairness example net 2. Place p1 has a 0.5 probability of having a token in the initial marking, which selects the respective flow network.

However, since t3 is not enabled at {}, we do not consider this case for calculating the overall firing, i.e. it is enabled in {p1} with the probability of one:

$$f_{t3} = \underbrace{1 \cdot \frac{2}{3}}_{\{p1\}\text{case only}} = 0.67. \tag{9}$$

We are interested in simulating PNs while ensuring the fairness property for both interleaving and max-step semantics as described in the presented definitions. These definitions are realized in the simulation algorithm in the next subsection.

2.2   Iterative Stepping Simulation

The Eq. (1) of firing a transition t can be split into two phases:

$$m'(p) = \underbrace{m(p) - |p, t|}_{\text{firing phase}} \underbrace{+ |t, p|}_{\text{update phase}} \tag{10}$$

The firing phase is equivalent to executing a preset subnet $\bullet\mathcal{N}(m)$. The update phase adds back the tokens removed during the firing phase to create a new valid marking m'.

The firing phase can be executed multiple times for different transitions before the update phase. In this case, removed tokens should be "remembered" in a temporary buffer m_+. Algorithm 1 shows the implementation of this approach for both interleaving semantics and max-step semantics with fairness: the difference is in lines 6 and 7 that break iterating over T as soon as a single transition fires. The choices are resolved by iteratively modifying (removing tokens from) m on line 5, which disables conflicting transitions in the subsequent enable checks in line 4. The fairness of the interleaving semantics is guaranteed by iterating through T in random order. The fairness of max-step semantics is derived from iteratively executing the preset subnet $\bullet\mathcal{N}(m)$ using a fair sequential execution over the firing phase of the algorithm.

Algorithm 1. Two-phase implementation of the iterative stepping simulation.

1: **function** STEP
                                                                            ▷ *Firing phase:*
2:     **for all** $t \in T$ in random order **do**
3:         **if** $\forall p \in \bullet t, m(p) > 0$ **then**   ▷ if t is enabled
4:             $\forall p \in \bullet t, m(p) \leftarrow m(p) - |p, t|$ ▷ remove tokens from the preset
5:             $\forall p \in t\bullet, m_+(p) \leftarrow |t, p|$ ▷ add tokens to the temporary buffer
6:             **if** interleaving semantics **then**
7:                 **break for**   ▷ only one transition firing per step
8:             **end if**
9:         **end if**
10:    **end for**

                                                                            ▷ *Update phase:*
11:    $\forall p \in P, m(p) \leftarrow m(p) + m_+(p)$ ▷ add tokens from the buffer
12: **end function**

So far, we have considered non-distributed simulation that runs on a single execution device, therefore the phases of the algorithm are naturally globally atomic. Distributed PN simulation is discussed in Sect. 4; however, first we need to define a distributed execution environment.

3   POETS Event-Triggered System

This section describes the abstract view of the parallel execution system used as a platform for the distributed PN simulation. The system consists of a number of logical execution devices connected via a communication fabric forming a *device graph*.

A device graph is a tuple $\langle V, E, s, E_s \rangle$, where V is the finite non-empty set of parallel compute devices (vertices), $E \subseteq V \times V$ is the set of edges defining inter-device communication, s is the centralized supervisor and $E_s = V \times \{s\}$ are the bi-directional communication edges from all vertices to the supervisor.

The system detects certain local conditions in the graph as *events* (e.g., receiving of a message over the communication fabric) and devices implement application functionality as reactions (*handlers*) to these events. The ordering and transitions between the events form a finite state machine (FSM) in each execution device.

Figure 4 shows the model of the device and its state transition diagram. Each vertex has access to an application-specific local state $\mathcal{S}$, a mailbox connected to the communication fabric (edges of the graph), and a *ready-to-send (rts)* Boolean flag indicating that the vertex wants to send a message. The *inc* control signal coming from the mailbox indicates the reception of an incoming message.

120   A. Rafiev et al.

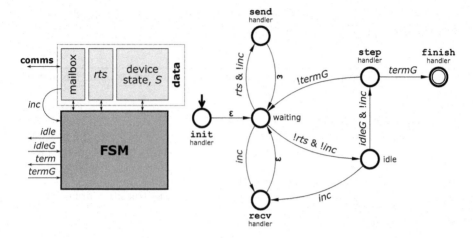

Fig. 4. Device (vertex) behavior model for the current version of POETS. Event handlers are uninterruptible (atomic), hence all state transition arcs have an implied condition of "handler code is not running".

A message can arrive at any time, therefore this signal is triggered by the vertex environment; *rts* flag can be set or reset only by the event handlers.

Event handlers are atomic; all state transitions in the FSM have an implicit condition for the handler code to be finished. Only the waiting state can be interrupted by an external signal (event) at any time.

Initialization handler. The init handler is invoked once for every vertex when the application starts, before any other events. Vertices should initialize *rts* in the init handler.

Receive handler. A message arriving at a vertex causes the recv handler of the vertex to be called. The access to the contents of the message is provided within the handler procedure.

Send handler. Any vertex indicating that it wishes to send will eventually have its send handler called. When called, the send handler is provided with a message buffer, to which the outgoing message should be written. It is an application's responsibility to clear the *rts* flag; otherwise, the system assumes the vertex wants to send more messages (the latter case is useful for implementing large multi-message protocols). Note that the send handler condition is $(rts \land \neg inc)$, which means the recv handler always triggers before send if *inc* is set. This prioritizes draining the network of messages before sending new ones.

Global idle and global termination detection are managed by a centralized control, communicating with vertices via *idle*, *idleG*, *term*, and *termG* signals over E_s edges. A vertex sends the *idle* signal when it enters a so-called "idle" state triggered by the $(\neg rts \land \neg inc)$ condition. This condition puts it in the lowest priority against the **send** and **recv** events. This state represents a *refutable* barrier primitive, which means that it can be canceled by a reception of a message (*inc* signal). If idle state is detected at every vertex and the network is devoid of in-flight messages, the *idleG* signal is sent to all vertices.

In order to provide support for the new termination-detection feature, the API is extended with the following events:

Step handler. The **step** handler is called when termination is detected, i.e. no vertex in the entire graph wishes to send, and there are no messages in-flight (*idleG* signal is set). The step handler may set the *term* signal to indicate whether it wishes to stop the execution. Typically, an asynchronous application will set *term*, while a synchronous one will do some compute, perhaps requesting to send again, and does not set *term* to start a new time step.

Finish handler. If the conditions for calling the **step** handler are met, but the previous call of the **step** handler returned *term* at every vertex, then the **finish** handler is called. This condition is detected globally at the supervisor and communicated back to the vertices via the *termG* flag. At this stage, each vertex may optionally post a message to the mailbox, which will then be sent directly to the supervisor (this is useful for collecting the results of the computation/simulation).

We use the described structure of the POETS system in the following implementation of the distributed PN simulation.

4   Distributed PN Simulation

We view a distributed simulation of PN as a number of execution devices simulating partitions of a large PN in parallel. The marking within such a partition creates a *local state* for a device. The entire graph of devices is organised so that the combination of all the device local states represents a global PN state (marking) that is consistent with a simulation of that PN.

For a given parallel execution device $v \in V$, a local partition of the PN $\mathcal{N} = \langle P, T, F, m_0 \rangle$ is denoted as $\mathcal{N}^{(v)} := \left\langle P^{(v)}, T^{(v)}, F^{(v)}, m_0^{(v)} \right\rangle$, where $P^{(v)} \subseteq P$ is the local set of places, $T^{(v)} \subseteq T$ is the local set of transitions, and $F^{(v)} \subseteq F$ is the local flow relation. Sets $P^{(v)}$, $T^{(v)}$, and relation $F^{(v)}$ are immutable and can be stored in a local instruction memory or cache. A mutable state represents the local marking $m^{(v)} : P^{(v)} \to \{0, 1\}$ for safe PNs.

For two different devices $v \in V$ and $w \in V$, we require $T^{(v)} \cap T^{(w)} = \emptyset$ and $P^{(v)} \cap P^{(w)} = \emptyset$ so there is no transition or place duplication. Also, the union of all local partitions must fully represent the original PN: $T = \bigcup_{v \in V} T^{(v)}$ and $P = \bigcup_{v \in V} P^{(v)}$, and $F = \bigcup_{v \in V} F^{(v)}$. The union of all local markings uniquely represents the global marking: $m = \bigcup_{v \in V} m^{(v)}$.

According to the two-phase algorithm described in Sect. 2.2, the firing and update phases must be atomic. If the preset and postset places are located in separate parallel device states, this atomicity is not guaranteed unless synchronization protocols are enforced. The distributed platform used in this work, presented in Sect. 3, provides the means for global synchronization. The simulation of a PN $\mathcal{N}$ is, therefore, the product of a composition of the execution platform model (Fig. 4) and $\mathcal{N}$.

Enable-condition consistency requires all preset places of a transition to be put in the same local state with the transition. Atomic choices follow from local state partitioning: since preset places must occupy the same device, if a place has a choice, all transitions in the choice have to be on the same device as well. In other words, choices cannot be distributed across multiple devices.

Let the *local preset* $\bullet T^{(v)}$ be defined as the union of presets for all local transitions:

$$\bullet T^{(v)} = \bigcup_{t \in T^{(v)}} \bullet t, \tag{11}$$

and the *local postset* $T\bullet^{(v)}$ be defined as the union of postsets for all local transitions:

$$T\bullet^{(v)} = \bigcup_{t \in T^{(v)}} t\bullet. \tag{12}$$

The following definition of the *local flow relation* $F^{(v)}$ encompasses the rule of PN partitioning:

$$F^{(v)} \subseteq \left(T^{(v)} \times P \right) \cup \left(P^{(v)} \times T^{(v)} \right). \tag{13}$$

Note the global set P. According to the partitioning rule outlined above, $\bullet T^{(v)} \subseteq P^{(v)}$ is required; however, the local postset $T\bullet^{(v)}$ may contain places from other devices, in which case inter-device communication is needed to correctly update the global state of the PN. Therefore, the outgoing communication edges for a given device $v \in V$ are defined as $\left\{ (v, w) \mid T\bullet^{(v)} \cap P^{(w)} \neq \emptyset \right\} \subseteq E$. We also denote external output places as $P_{\text{out}}^{(v)}$ so that $T\bullet^{(v)} = P^{(v)} \cup P_{\text{out}}^{(v)}$.

Algorithm 2 shows the event-based implementation for a device $v \in V$. The device references a local partition of the PN as a constant data structure $\mathcal{C} := \left\langle P^{(v)}, P_{\text{out}}^{(v)}, T^{(v)}, F^{(v)}, m_0^{(v)} \right\rangle$ described above. A dynamic state of the device $\mathcal{S}$ is defined as $\left\langle m^{(v)}, m_+^{(v)} \right\rangle$, where $m^{(v)}$ represents current local marking and $m_+ : P \to \mathbb{Z}_+$ is a temporary buffer used for two-phase simulation protocol as described in Sect. 2.2. Communication is done via messages of the type $\mathcal{M} := \langle p, m_+ (p) \rangle$, i.e., each message sends information about a place $\mathcal{M}.p$ that should receive tokens and the number of tokens to add $\mathcal{M}.m_+ (p)$. We only need to send information about positively marked places as the place markings are returned to zero by local transitions on the receiving side. Therefore, for safe PNs, the $\mathcal{M}.m_+ (p)$ component is redundant (always one) and can be removed.

Algorithm 2. Event-based implementation of a distributed PN simulation; the code runs concurrently on every device $v \in V$

1: $\mathcal{C} := \left\langle P^{(v)}, P_{\text{out}}^{(v)}, T^{(v)}, F^{(v)}, m_0^{(v)} \right\rangle$ ▷ constant data

2: $\mathcal{S} := \left\langle m^{(v)}, m_+^{(v)} \right\rangle$ ▷ device state

3: $\mathcal{M} := \langle p, m_+(p) \rangle$ ▷ message type

4: **procedure** INIT   ▷ initialisation phase

5:      $\forall p \in P^{(v)}, m^{(v)}(p) \leftarrow m_0^{(v)}(p)$ ▷ reset to initial marking

6:      $\forall p \in T\bullet^{(v)}, m_+^{(v)}(p) \leftarrow 0$ ▷ reset temporary buffer

7:      $rts \leftarrow$ false   ▷ nothing to send

8: **end procedure**

9: **function** STEP   ▷ on detecting idle network, start firing phase

            ▷ *Firing phase for* $\forall t \in T^{(v)}$:

10:     (see lines 2–10 in Algorithm 1)

            ▷ *Update phase (local)*:

11:     $\forall p \in P^{(v)}, m^{(v)}(p) \leftarrow m^{(v)}(p) + m_+^{(v)}(p)$ ▷ add tokens from the buffer

12:     $rts \leftarrow$ true   ▷ trigger global update via SEND

13: **end function**

14: **procedure** SEND(out $\mathcal{M}$)   ▷ on sending a message

15:     **if** $\exists p \in P_{\text{out}}^{(v)} \mid m_+^{(v)}(p) > 0$ **then**   ▷ get a place from the buffer

16:        $\mathcal{M}.p \leftarrow p$ ▷ create message: pass the place

17:        $\mathcal{M}.m_+(p) \leftarrow m_+^{(v)}(p)$ ▷ pass the number of tokens to add

18:        $m_+^{(v)}(p) \leftarrow 0$ ▷ remove p from the buffer

19:     **else**

20:        $rts \leftarrow$ false   ▷ clear SEND trigger

21:     **end if**

22: **end procedure**

23: **procedure** RECV($\mathcal{M}$)   ▷ on receiving a message $\mathcal{M}$

24:     **if** $\mathcal{M}.p \in P^{(v)}$ **then**

25:        $m(\mathcal{M}.p) \leftarrow m(\mathcal{M}.p) + \mathcal{M}.m_+(p)$ ▷ add tokens to $m(\mathcal{M}.p)$

26:     **end if**

27: **end procedure**

The simulation starts with the initialization (`init`), which resets the local marking $m^{(v)}$ to the initial state and clears the buffer $m_+^{(v)}$. Initially, there is nothing to send between the devices, so the system immediately triggers the first firing phase with the `step` handler. The firing of the local transitions $T^{(v)}$ is implemented in the same way as in the non-distributed simulator (line 11 of Algorithm 2 refers to lines 2–11 in Algorithm 1), the difference is in the update phase. Since the buffer $m_+^{(v)}$ serves the entire postset $T\bullet^{(v)}$, some of the updates refer to the local marking and some to the external marking that needs to be communicated to other devices. The local marking $m^{(v)}(p) \mid p \in T\bullet^{(v)} \cap P^{(v)}$ is updated normally before leaving the step handler. The communication phase is triggered by setting the *rts* flag to true.

When *rts* is set, the device will eventually enter the send handler, where it picks an output place $p \in P_{\text{out}}^{(v)}$ with a positive value in the local $m_+^{(v)}$ buffer, i.e. for which there are tokens to transfer. The place p and the number of tokens form a new message $\mathcal{M}$. The message is put into the mailbox and sent when the communication fabric is ready. The function also clears the local value $m_+^{(v)}(p)$ to denote that this place has been processed. The *rts* flag is left set until there are no more output places matching the criteria so that the device keeps visiting the send handler to service all enabled places. Once *rts* is cleared, the device is ready to move to the next firing phase (step). Meanwhile, incoming messages from other devices trigger the recv handler, which simply adds the number of tokens to the local place $\mathcal{M}.p \in P^{(v)}$ as specified in the received message, thus completing the communication protocol.

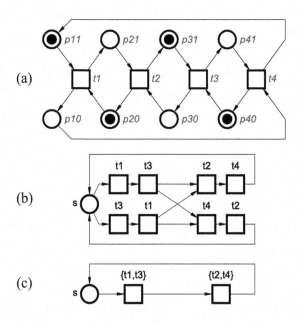

Fig. 5. PN example (a) and corresponding flow networks for (b) interleaving semantics and (c) max-step semantics.

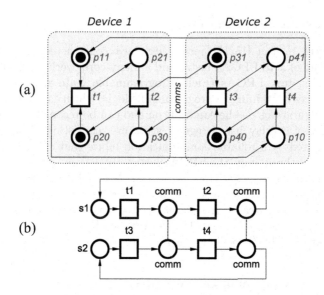

Fig. 6. (a) PN example distributed over two execution devices and (b) corresponding flow networks synchronized at *comm* states.

Figure 5 shows an example of a PN and its execution on a single device. Figure 6 distributes this PN over two parallel devices. The simulation consists of two alternating phases: the communication phase and the transition firing phase. The devices are synchronized at the communication phase shown as *comm* states. The union of the device flow networks is equivalent to the non-distributed max-step semantics shown in Fig. 5(c). With max-step semantics, the synchronization does not reduce the parallelism (although the synchronization itself may have performance overheads – see the results in Sect. 5). Interleaving semantics is not effective with globally synchronized simulation steps as it would imply only one transition firing during one simulation step, which defeats the parallelism in the simulation. Instead, we propose a so-called *locally-interleaving semantics* (loc-int), whereby one concurrent firing event occurs in each device within one simulation step (between synchronization barriers). In our experiments, the performance of loc-inc and max-step semantics are analysed and compared separately.

5   Experimental Observations and Results

This section presents the experimental study of the performance capabilities and scalability of the described PN simulation approach on the POETS hardware. From the algorithmic description of the PN simulations, we expect linear or close-to-linear complexities in all aspects of both distributed and centralized implementations, therefore we are interested in speedup coefficients. Optimizing random ordering yields up to an order of magnitude performance improvement, while parallel execution improves to several orders of magnitude.

5.1   POETS Hardware Platform

On the POETS project [15,17], researchers have constructed a prototype platform consisting of a 48-FPGA cluster and a many-core overlay called Tinsel [18]
programmed on top. FPGAs (Field Programmable Gate Arrays) are flexible
hardware devices containing re-programmable logic, which can implement different logic configurations on the same silicon and can be reconfigured for different
uses. The Tinsel overlay has a regular structure, consisting of a scalable grid
of *tiles* connected by a reliable communication fabric that extends both within
each FPGA and throughout the FPGA cluster. By default, a tile consists of four
RISC-V multithreaded cores [19], clocked at 240 MHz, sharing an FPU, 128
KB thread-partitioned data cache, and a *mailbox*. Each core supports 16 barrel-
scheduled hardware threads. A separate network is used to connect caches in
tiles to off-chip memories. A single-FPGA view of the overlay is depicted in
Fig. 7(b), and a single tile is shown in Fig. 7(c).

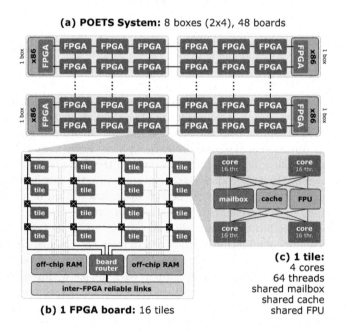

Fig. 7. Current version of the POETS cluster architecture (a) with zooming in on a
single FPGA board (b) and a tile (c).

Each POETS mailbox serves four cores and contains a memory-mapped
scratchpad storing up to 64KB of incoming and outgoing messages, which can
also be used as a small general-purpose local memory. Messages are variable-
length, containing up to four flits, with each flit holding 128 bits of payload. The
mailbox allows threads to trigger the transmission of outgoing messages, allocate

space for incoming messages, and to consume those messages when they arrive, all via custom RISC-V CSRs (control/status registers).

The FPGA cluster comprises a grid of 48 DE5-Net boards (8 server boxes, 6 boards per box) connected together using 10G reliable links, as shown in Fig. 7(a). Each box also contains an x86 host with an additional bridge FPGA board that connects to the Tinsel mesh. The overlay distributes naturally over this cluster to yield a 3,072 core system (49,152 hardware threads), where any thread can send messages to any other thread.

A high-level API is introduced to accommodate the event-based programming model described in Sect. 3 by creating a relation between logical devices (graph nodes) and hardware threads, and by routing arbitrary application-level edges on top of the regular Tinsel communication mesh.

Originally the POETS platform only supported message passing, but an additional feature that has been added in [20] is hardware termination detection, which can also be used as a global synchronization barrier. In order to achieve greater scalability, we implement the hierarchical termination-detection in hardware with Safra's algorithm working at the granularity of FPGAs rather than threads and synchronous pipelined trees at the intra-FPGA level, as illustrated in Fig. 8. Safra's algorithm, as presented by Dijkstra [21], is a classic solution to the problem of detecting termination in distributed systems. It considers a set of *machines*, each of which is either *passive*, if it has indicated that it has no further messages to send, or *active*, otherwise. A machine in the passive state automatically transitions to the active state upon receiving a message. The algorithm detects the case in which all machines are passive and there are no undelivered messages.

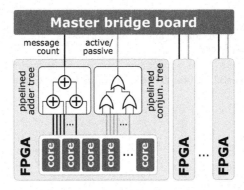

Fig. 8. Hierarchical structure of the dedicated termination detection hardware.

5.2 A Note on Random Shuffle Implementations

The PN simulation algorithm (Algorithm 1) requires iterating through transitions in random order. This serves two purposes: 1) for interleaving and locally-interleaving semantics, which ensures non-deterministic transition firing as we randomly search for an enabled transition; 2) non-deterministically resolving choices according to Sect. 2 definition of fairness. We use Knuth's *linear congruential generator* (LCG) [22], which provides 64-bit pseudo-random numbers using the following code:

```
next_seed = seed * 6364136223846793005L + 1442695040888963407L;
```

Even though the LCG is 64-bit, it is preferred to use only the higher 48-bits for random values as the lower bits may contain periodic patterns.

The straightforward solution to randomizing the order of iteration is the **direct shuffle** approach listed in Algorithm 3. It generates a new random number every cycle and also requires an additional buffer for caching the order of items (as indices or references). It is slow because of multiple memory accesses to the buffer in each cycle. These accesses are random by definition, which puts an additional strain on the memory caches. This is especially bad for a single-core implementation, where all transitions are stored in a large list. In a distributed implementation, we need to do shuffle locally, so the number of transitions to iterate through is relatively small.

Algorithm 3. Direct shuffle (slow).

```
uint64_t seed;
uint32_t sh[transitions]; // ordering cache

// in init():
for(uint32_t ti = 0; ti<num_transitions; ti++)
  sh[ti] = ti; // default order

// in step():
for(uint32_t ti = 0; ti<num_transitions; ti++) {
  seed = lcg64(seed);
  // get random number between 0 and (num_transitions-ti-1):
  uint32_t x = (uint32_t)(seed>>16L) % (num_transitions-ti);
  // swap order:
  t_index = sh[ti+x];
  sh[ti+x] = sh[ti];
  sh[ti] = t_index;

  // ... process transition t_index
}
```

The global **XOR shuffle** approach is based on bit flipping: we generate a random mask **sh** once per simulation step and then XOR this mask with the loop iterator, i.e., t_index = ti^sh. Performance-wise, it is practically just as fast as no shuffling since it has minimal per-cycle overheads. The problem is that this approach is not truly random, as shown in Fig. 9. This is because when choosing multiple transitions to fire based on a single XOR mask, the choices are non-independent. On the other hand, it can still be used if exactly one choice is performed per bit-mask: there is nothing for a single choice to be non-independent with. Although a PN may have more than one choice, in locally-interleaving execution, only one transition is fired in one step, therefore only one choice is resolved in one step. An additional out-of-range check is required if the number of transitions is not a power of two.

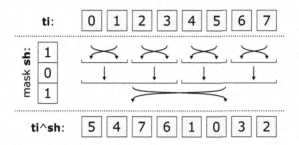

Fig. 9. An example of an XOR-shuffle over eight elements using a 3-bit random mask **sh**. Note that the swapping of elements with the same bit significance in binary representation is not mutually independent. Therefore, the same mask cannot be used to resolve multiple choices in one simulation step as it would create a deterministic dependency between them.

The **block-XOR shuffle** similarly works only if there is exactly one choice per random mask, but it creates multiple "blocks" of iteration and applies different random masks within each block, i.e., the ordering within each block is shuffled but the blocks are executed in order. Blocks are organized so that transitions needing to be independent with one another (in the same step) are put into a block, but blocks do not need to be independent with other blocks, thus saving the number of randomizations and especially randomized memory accesses. The technique is shown in Algorithm 4. For an x bit-mask, the block size is 2^x, and it is preferred that the total number of transitions is divisible by 2^x to avoid additional out-of-range checks.

No shuffle can also be used for choice-free PN max-step semantics. Here, t_index equals to ti.

A performance comparison of different shuffle techniques is shown in Table 1. In our experiments (both POETS and CPU), we use global XOR shuffle for locally-interleaving semantics, block-XOR shuffle for max-step with choices, and no shuffle for choice-free max-step simulations.

5.3   Performance Results

Figure 10 shows a Muller pipeline ring example (referred to as *pipe* in this paper). Benchmarks used in our experiments are set up in such a way that they can be

Algorithm 4. Block-XOR shuffle; block size is (1<<RANDOM_BITS).

```
#define RANDOM_BITS 2
#define BLOCK_SIZE (1<<RANDOM_BITS)
#define RANDOM_MASK (BLOCK_SIZE-1)

uint64_t seed;

// in step():
uint64_t rand = 0; // random bit cache
uint8_t sh = 0; // XOR mask
// enforce multiple of block size:
uint32_t ti_max = (num_transitions+RANDOM_MASK)&(~RANDOM_MASK);
for(uint32_t ti = 0; ti<ti_max; ti++) {
  if(!(ti&RANDOM_MASK)) { // start of a block
    if(!rand) { // if random bits are depleted
       seed = lcg64(seed);
       rand = seed>>16; // get 48 random bits
    }
    // use lower bits as the next XOR mask:
    sh = (uint8_t)(rand&RANDOM_MASK);
    rand >>= RANDOM_BITS;
  }
  t_index = ti^sh; // apply XOR mask
  // range check if num_transitions is not divisible by the block size:
  if(t_index>=num_transitions)
    continue;

  // ... process transition t_index
}
```

scaled to any PN size by repeating subgraph patterns. For instance, the place next_p0 in Fig. 10 can be the place p0 of the next tile in the ring, the same is true of next_p2 and p2 places. Places prev_p1 and prev_p3 make a reverse connection to a tile on the opposite side. Splitting tiles is always done at places, not transitions.

Figure 11 shows the dining philosophers (*dphil*) example which demonstrates a PN with choices. The deadlock-free solution means that there are added ordering places that ensure the priority of choosing the left fork over the right fork or vice versa. In fact, the ring of philosophers only works if there are alternating left-to-right and right-to-left philosophers, which means that one tile of this PN has to contain both. However, an important requirement outlined in Sect. 4 is that we cannot split the choice between execution devices, which means that both left and right fork places and the transitions connected from them have to be on the same tile. Because of this constraint, the *dphil* tile must contain one whole philosopher net, part of the philosopher to their right and part of the philosopher to their left. To form a tile, we "cut" the two-philosopher net

Table 1. Performance of random shuffle implementations: speedup is calculated with reference to the direct shuffle on the same platform.

implementation	speedup	
	CPU	POETS
direct shuffle	1	1
block-XOR shuffle	5.95	3.39
global XOR	10.52	3.43
no shuffle	10.52	3.43

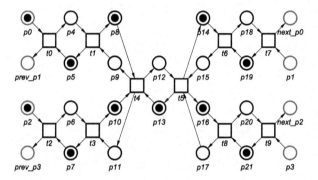

Fig. 10. A piece of Muller pipeline model (*pipe*). The net can be tiled to make a choice-free PN benchmark of arbitrary size.

at the places: ordering, before put_left_fork transition, and after take_left_fork transition of the left-to-right ordered philosopher labeled as "south" in Fig. 11.

Table 2. Benchmark-specific properties and results

property	*dphil*	*pipe*
net "tiles" per device	50	46
places per device	1000	1012
transitions per device	600	460
transitions fired per step, per device: max-step	49.028	230
transitions fired per step, per device: loc-int	0.794	1

For the performance evaluation experiments, we simulate up to 50 million places PNs for 10,000 simulation steps. The number of transition firings per step depends on execution semantics. We slice the models to have approximately 1,000 places per logical device. Locally-interleaving semantics fires one transition per step, per device unless there are no enabled transitions in a local partition of the net. The number of firings for max-step semantics is model-specific and is listed in Table 2.

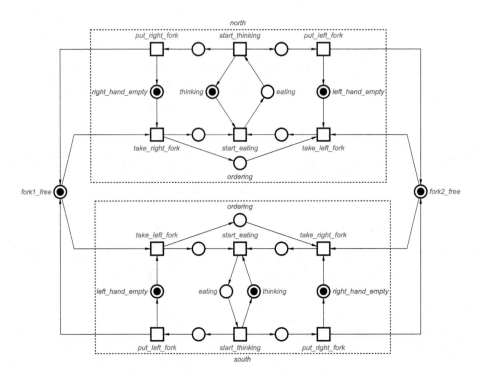

Fig. 11. Use case example of a PN with choices: deadlock-free solution to the dining philosophers problem (*dphil*).

Figure 12 shows the performance and scaling of the simulation for both use cases in different execution semantics running on just one POETS box, which provides 6144 parallel hardware threads. For larger net sizes, we put more than one logical device on each hardware thread. The effect is visible on the graphs as "bumps". Figures 13 and 14 provide the experimental evidence for scaling to multiple POETS boxes. Single-core CPU performance results (obtained from 3.50 GHz Intel Core i7-7800X) are given as a reference. Locally-interleaving execution may seem faster, however, the total number of transitions fired is smaller than for max-step semantics. The latter represents much further evolution of the PN within the same number of simulation steps – millions or billions of transition firings.

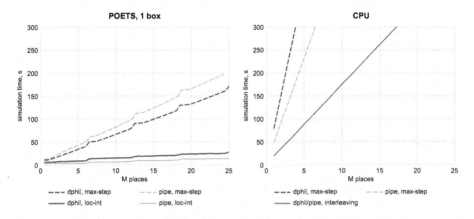

Fig. 12. Performance results for pipeline and dining philosophers benchmarks in different execution semantics on a single POETS box (up to 6144 parallel hardware threads) compared to a single thread CPU simulation.

Performance impacting factors are identified as global synchronization, communications, and computation. Global synchronization depends on the number of simulation steps and the size of the hardware, it does not depend on the number of places or transitions. Compute has $O(N)$ cost in the number of transitions and by extension also to the number of places as the proportion of places to transitions remains the same with the increase in net size. As can be seen from the figures for max-step, the simulation is mostly dominated by the compute with only small horizontal "notches" corresponding to underfull hardware threads. Locally-interleaving semantics is dominated by communications, therefore the performance pattern is harder to predict, but the observed scaling generally follows a linear trend that is much shallower than max-step, as expected.

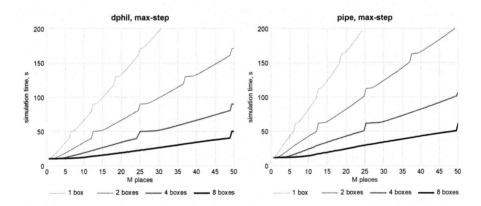

Fig. 13. Max-step semantics performance results for multiple POETS boxes: Muller pipeline benchmark (left), dining philosophers benchmark (right).

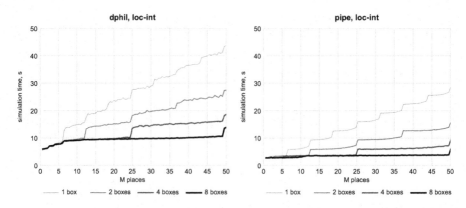

Fig. 14. Locally-interleaving semantics performance results for multiple POETS boxes: Muller pipeline benchmark (left), dining philosophers benchmark (right)

Calculation of the per-transition performance costs can be achieved by solving the following equations:

$$t_{\text{max-step}}/n_{\text{sim}} = \alpha \, |T| + \beta \, |T_{\text{fired}}| + \varepsilon, \tag{14}$$

$$t_{\text{loc-int}}/n_{\text{sim}} = \alpha \, |T| + \beta + \varepsilon, \tag{15}$$

where n_{sim} is the number of simulation steps; $t_{\text{max-step}}$ and $t_{\text{loc-int}}$ are the measured time to complete the simulation for the max-step and locally-interleaving execution semantics respectively; $|T_{\text{fired}}|$ is the number of transitions fired during the simulation (the simulation tracks the number of firings); $|T|$ is the total number of transitions. Assuming negligible constant offset $\varepsilon \approx 0$ (this should be true for sufficiently large simulations), coefficients α and β can be calculated from the experimental results using (14) and (15) as shown in Table 3. Coefficient β represents the performance cost of firing one million transitions; α represents the performance cost per million transitions caused by enabled condition checking and, in the case of *dphil*, random shuffling.

Table 3. Calculated coefficients for the performance cost estimation (14) and (15)

cost factor	POETS		CPU	
	dphil	*pipe*	*dphil*	*pipe*
α, ms per step per M trans.	0.241	0.132	2.903	3.832
β, ms per step per M trans. fired	0.105	0.033	1.215	0.127

Comparing these coefficients for one-box POETS system with a single-core CPU implementation: *dphil* is 11.7 times faster on POETS; *pipe* max-step is overall 5.7 times faster with performance costs distributed as 3.8 times faster transition firing and 28.9 faster for the total number of transitions, the latter also corresponds to the locally-interleaving speedup factor for *pipe*. For the full 8-box POETS cluster, the speedup numbers go up almost perfectly by a factor of 7.9 for the max-step semantics, as listed in Table 4. Locally-interleaving semantics does not scale as efficiently giving 3.87 and 6.83 speedup on eight POETS boxes. Compared to the CPU, an overall achieved speedup is 45 to 220. This indicates that the POETS hardware scales very efficiently for PN simulations.

Table 4. Multi-box POETS speedup against a single POETS box

	max-step		loc-int	
	dphil	*pipe*	*dphil*	*pipe*
2 boxes	1.9900	1.9993	1.6581	1.9340
4 boxes	3.9767	3.9815	2.5687	3.6535
8 boxes	7.9007	7.9196	3.8710	6.8324

5.4   Quantitative Analysis

In this section, we study the behavior of a hybrid 2-phase-4-phase pipeline (called *hype*). This use case is chosen to demonstrate the capabilities of our method and link to the real-world application area of asynchronous circuit design [1]. Figure 15 shows one hybrid "tile". In the 4-phase part of the pipeline, the places form pairs (p0a, p1a), (p2a, p3a), etc. The first (upper) place corresponds to no data, the second (lower) place corresponds to a data packet in the pipeline. The 4-phase protocol is implemented using Muller C-elements. We can formally verify one tile of this hybrid pipeline using the MPSAT tool [8] to confirm that it does not have any deadlocks or non-persistency.

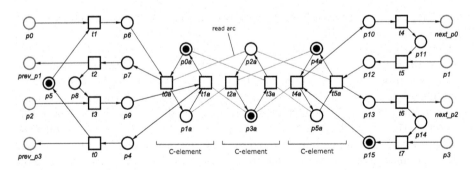

Fig. 15. A piece of hybrid 2-phase-4-phase pipeline model (*hype*).

As with most circuit Perti nets [1], the model heavily relies on using *read arcs* (denoted as lines without arrows). A read arc is a shorthand for two arcs going in opposite directions. Read arcs do not remove tokens or, to be exact, remove and immediately place them back. For example, read arcs from p0a and p5a to the transition t3a in Fig. 15 serve as guards, so the transition is enabled only when both places (and also p3a) have tokens. When the transition fires, the token is moved from p3a to p2a, while p0a and p5a are not affected. The current version of our simulator does not consider read arcs as a special case and replaces them with two directed arcs. This does not violate the correctness of the simulation but enforces locally-interleaving semantics as these loops of arcs create choice structures.

Simulating the pipeline consisting of only *hype* tiles is not particularly interesting as it just confirms that the pipeline works. We introduce a "faulty" tile, shown in Fig. 16, that has an AND gate replacing one of the C-elements. This implementation is hazard-prone and potentially leads to the loss of data packets in the modelled pipeline.

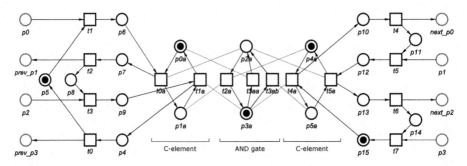

Fig. 16. Alternative hazard-prone implementation of the hybrid pipeline that uses an AND gate in place of one Muller C-element. Only some stages of the pipeline are replaced with this implementation to form a heterogeneous hybrid pipeline (*h-hype*).

Comparing the two versions of the tile at the marking shown in the preceding figures, transition t3a in Fig. 15 is not enabled while transition t3aa in Fig. 16, which is one of the counterparts of t3a, is enabled because of the OR-causality. Firing t3aa at this marking will cause a data packet loss. However, since this firing is non-deterministic, there is a chance that transition t4a fires before t3aa, in which case there will be no data packet loss. Eventually, the faulty pipeline can lose all data and the system will stop. Formal verification tools are able to detect this in small examples as a deadlock condition. However, in full-scale examples, it is not immediately apparent how the interactions would scale: will the time until deadlock reduce due to increased numbers of faulty tiles or grow if there are more data packets initially available?

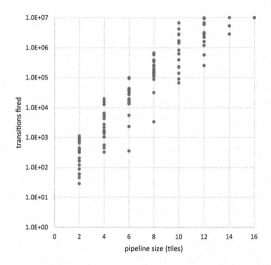

Fig. 17. Relation between the pipeline size and the time to deadlock for hybrid pipelines with alternating *hype* and *h-hype* tiles.

Figure 17 presents simulation results from multiple sizes of hybrid pipelines with alternating *hype* and *h-hype* tiles. The number of transition firings until the system deadlocks not only grows with the size of the pipeline but grows exponentially. The results demonstrate that such a system can appear functional for a long time while gradually losing data, therefore a deadlock is not a good indicator for erroneous behavior in the system. A better solution is to monitor output persistency. Counting persistency violations shows that transitions t1a, t3aa, t3ab, and t4a in an *h-hype* tile violate persistency about 10% of the time on average. This number is consistent throughout all pipeline sizes, therefore can be detected from a relatively small and constant number of simulation steps (in the order of thousands) regardless of the model size.

6   Conclusions

In this paper, we present a method of using powerful distributed computing platforms to perform distributed simulations of PN models of concurrent systems. This is in recognition of the need to improve simulation methods for complex event systems, beyond what can be accomplished by conventional computers.

With simulations, systems of much greater sizes can be analysed realistically than that possible with rigorous forms of analysis such as model checking. Our method further stretches this system size increase, and can be used to study the behavior and properties of PNs with tens of millions of places and transitions within reasonable amounts of time. The method is shown to achieve 45–220 times better simulation performance than with a single CPU. This speedup mainly comes from mapping the event-based execution onto 49,152 parallel hardware threads. The nearly-perfect performance scaling results suggest that the method can take advantage of platforms of greater sizes.

We have shown that the POETS architecture, with its distributed massively parallel hardware and support for event-based programming, is capable of reducing the time taken to simulate large and highly concurrent Petri net models. Instead of relying on a centralized event scheduler, our implementation of the simulator uses global synchronization to ensure state consistency without resorting to complex communication protocols. POETS provides an efficient hardware-implemented termination detection feature, which can be used as a self-timed and refutable synchronization barrier.

Although this work demonstrates the advantages of using POETS, many of the constituent techniques and the principles behind the method are platform-independent. For instance, the PN partitioning rule which stipulates that all preset places of a transition must be mapped to the same device is true for the vast majority of parallel distributed hardware. In other words, our mapping method of concurrent PN to distributed processing hardware has very wide applicability.

By implementing the notion of fair transition firing, our simulation method makes it possible to expose the quantitative properties of system behavior, which are generally not the target of qualitative model analysis. With this, these types of full-system PN model simulations can be used in conjunction with component-level rigorous analysis by designers of complex systems during different stages of system design.

Acknowledgment. This work is supported by EPSRC/UK as a part of the POETS project EP/N031768/1.

References

1. Poliakov, I., Mokhov, A., Rafiev, A., Sokolov, D., Yakovlev, A.: Automated verification of asynchronous circuits using circuit petri nets. In: 14th IEEE International Symposium on Asynchronous Circuits and Systems, ASYNC 2008, Newcastle upon Tyne, UK, 7–10 April 2008, pp. 161–170. IEEE Computer Society (2008). https://doi.org/10.1109/ASYNC.2008.18
2. Bertens, L.M.F., Kleijn, J., Koutny, M., Verbeek, F.J.: Modelling gradients using petri nets. In: Proceedings of the Workshops of PETRI NETS 2010 and ACSD 2010, Braga, Portugal, June 2010, vol. 827, pp. 39–53 (2010). http://ceur-ws.org/Vol-827/4_LauraBertens_article.pdf
3. Wheeldon, A., Yakovlev, A., Shafik, R.: Self-timed reinforcement learning using tsetlin machine. In: 27th IEEE International Symposium on Asynchronous Circuits and Systems, ASYNC, 7–10 September 2021, pp. 40–47. IEEE Computer Society (2021). https://arxiv.org/abs/2109.00846
4. Shafik, R., Wheeldon, A., Yakovlev, A.: Explainability and dependability analysis of learning automata based AI hardware. In: 2020 IEEE 26th International Symposium on On-Line Testing and Robust System Design (IOLTS) (2020)
5. Mitrani, I.: Simulation Techniques for Discrete Event Systems. Cambridge University Press, Cambridge (2009)

6. Poliakov, I.: Interpreted graph models. School of Electrical, Electronic and Computer Engineering, Ph.D. thesis (2011). https://theses.ncl.ac.uk/jspui/bitstream/10443/1183/1/Poliakov11.pdf

7. Poliakov, I., Khomenko, V., Yakovlev, A.: WORKCRAFT – a framework for interpreted graph models. In: Franceschinis, G., Wolf, K. (eds.) PETRI NETS 2009. LNCS, vol. 5606, pp. 333–342. Springer, Heidelberg (2009). https://doi.org/10.1007/978-3-642-02424-5_21. http://workcraft.org

8. Khomenko, V.: Model checking based on prefixes of Petri Net unfoldings. School of Computing Science, Newcastle University, Ph.D. thesis (2003). https://theses.ncl.ac.uk/jspui/handle/10443/743

9. Cortadella, J., Kishinevsky, M., Kondratyev, A., Lavagno, L., Yakovlev, A.: Petrify: a tool for manipulating concurrent specifications and synthesis of asynchronous controllers. IEICE Trans. Inf. Syst. **E80–D**(3), 315–325 (1997)

10. Janicki, R., Lauer, P.E., Koutny, M., Devillers, R.R.: Concurrent and maximally concurrent evolution of nonsequential systems. Theor. Comput. Sci. **43**, 213–238 (1986). https://doi.org/10.1016/0304-3975(86)90177-5

11. Bergenthum, R.: Firing partial orders in a petri net. In: Buchs, D., Carmona, J. (eds.) PETRI NETS 2021. LNCS, vol. 12734, pp. 399–419. Springer, Cham (2021). https://doi.org/10.1007/978-3-030-76983-3_20

12. Misra, J.: Distributed discrete-event simulation. ACM Comput. Surv. **18**(1), 39–65 (1986). https://doi.org/10.1145/6462.6485

13. Ferscha, A.: Parallel and distributed simulation of Petri Nets (tutorial). In: Performance Tools 1995, September 1995. https://www.researchgate.net/publication/2532088

14. Fernandes, J.: Elastic bundles: modelling and architecting asynchronous circuits with granular rigidity. EEE, School of Engineering, Newcastle University, Ph.D. thesis NCL-EEE-MICRO-TR-2017-206 (2017). http://async.org.uk/tech-reports/NCL-EEE-MICRO-TR-2017-206.pdf

15. POETS project website. https://poets-project.org

16. Kroese, D.P., Brereton, T., Taimre, T., Botev, Z.I.: Why the Monte Carlo method is so important today. WIREs Comput. Stat. **6**(6), 386–392 (2014)

17. Brown, A., et al.: Distributed event-based computing (2018). https://gow.epsrc.ukri.org/NGBOViewGrant.aspx?GrantRef=EP/N031768/1

18. Naylor, M., Moore, S.W., Thomas, D.: Tinsel: a manythread overlay for FPGA clusters. In: Proceedings to FPL (2019)

19. RISC-V: The free and open RISC instruction set architecture. https://riscv.org

20. Naylor, M., et al.: Termination detection for fine-grained message-passing architectures. In: Proceedings to ASAP. IEEE (2020)

21. Dijkstra, E.W.: Shmuel Safra's version of termination detection. https://www.cs.utexas.edu/users/EWD/ewd09xx/EWD998.PDF

22. Knuth, D.E.: The Art of Computer Programming, Volume 2: Seminumerical Algorithms, 3rd edn. Addison-Wesley, Boston (1997)

Author Index

Printed in the United States
by Baker & Taylor Publisher Services